Keepers of the Green

Keepers of the Green

A History of Golf Course Management

BOB LABBANCE | GORDON WITTEVEEN

ANN ARBOR PRESS AND
GOLF COURSE SUPERINTENDENTS ASSOCIATION OF AMERICA

Ann Arbor Press
310 North Main Street
P.O. Box 20
Chelsea, MI 48118
www.sleepingbearpress.com
Ann Arbor Press is an imprint of Sleeping Bear Press

Printed and bound in Canada.
10 9 8 7 6 5 4 3 2 1

Library of Congress Cataloging-in-Publication Data

Labbance, Bob.
Keepers of the green / By Bob Labbance and Gordon Witteveen.
p. cm.
ISBN 1-57504-164-2
1. Golf courses—Maintenance—History. 2. Greenkeepers
(Golf)—History. 3. Golf—History. I. Witteveen, Gordon. II. Title.
GV975.5 .L33 2002
796.352'06'80922—dc21
2001006349

To the young men and women who will manage golf courses in years
to come with the same degree of diligence that Old Tom exhibited.

Foreword

I have frequently been asked to identify the one aspect of golf that distinguishes it from any other sport. While golf shares many of the same characteristics of most other athletic endeavors, I believe the true essence of the game can be narrowed down to a single word—respect.

My father, who for nearly 50 years was the greenkeeper and golf professional at Latrobe CC, introduced me to the game at the tender age of three. While he put my hands on a cut-down club and showed me the grip that I have basically had ever since, the most important advice he gave me was a healthy dose of respect for the game, my opponents and the grounds on which golf is played. I was taught to play by the rules, be considerate of my fellow competitors and leave the golf course in the same or better shape than I found it.

Keepers of the Green touches upon a subject that is near and dear to me: the golf course. For it was at the golf course where I learned many of life's great lessons. It has been the scene of great competition, the cultivation of friendships and the strengthening of values. The attraction of the golf course has been so strong that other members of my family have pursued careers that involve them directly with golf's playing field. There is an almost indescribable feeling associated with being on the golf course. The crisp morning air with dew blanketing the grass, the grace and beauty of wildlife and the serenity of a setting sun create an irresistible allure that has never waned for me in my 70 some years around the game.

I have the utmost admiration for the men and women who maintain and manage the grounds upon which millions derive such great pleasure. The task of providing fair, challenging and consistent conditions against the obstacles presented by Mother Nature and human nature is great. We as golfers also owe our gratitude to these professionals who have pushed themselves to higher standards of education, training and performance that have resulted in making golf a more enjoyable game. Those who derive income, either as a competitor or as a businessman, are equally indebted to the superintendents for their contributions. This has a particular meaning to me as the head of a major golf course design company. Together with my architects, I work closely with and rely on the superintendents and their workers as the courses are created from the raw land. I entrust the finished products to them to insure that they mature and flourish after we have completed our efforts.

If you have a passion for the game of golf, then you understand the unconquerable call of the golf course. *Keepers of the Green* will truly heighten your respect for the game. If you have only a passing interest, then I assure you that this book will whet your appetite for this game that has given us so much for more than 500 years.

Arnold Palmer

Contents

Chapter One

Greenkeeping, Born of Necessity

1400-1873

By Bob Labbance

Jeu de mail was one of many early games played with ball and stick on cultivated surfaces.

Man has always sought an improvement in his surroundings. Primitive peoples may have demonstrated it unconsciously as they searched for better caves, but as tribes were formed and societal structure infiltrated, the desire to improve was driven also by ego, jealousy, and pride. "Why should his cave floor be smooth and soft, while mine is rocky and hard," the Neanderthal doubtlessly wondered. Such observations were quickly translated into action: "Mine shall be better than his." So began the drive to refine and cultivate the environment by manipulating the elements that compose one's habitat.

It was these same early peoples who discovered the joys of game playing. What started as the simple act of hitting a rock with a stick grew into the desire to hit the rock farther than everyone else and eventually matured into one person or one group demonstrating his greater skills to another. The skills of running and jumping, the qualities of endurance and courage and the desire for muscular strength and coordination were developed in game playing. Early people found that applying these talents to competition was a more peaceful pursuit than using them to wage war.

At first, participants moved the location of the game to find a better environment, but eventually they sought to improve the field they had selected rather than relocate their play. So began the cultivation of sporting grounds that has ultimately led to the immaculate surfaces we enjoy today.

The debate over which ball-and-stick game gave birth to golf is one that still engages historians. Some believe the origin reverts all the way back to the Romans and their games of *paganica* and *cambuca*—two games played with leather-cased balls filled with feathers that were propelled by crooked wooden sticks. When they invaded Scotland 2,000 years ago, the Romans may have brought this game with them. Others believe the games of *colf, jeu de mail*, *chole* or *kolf* gave birth to the game we know today. This debate will never be settled.

What can be determined is that of all these games, it is colf—played in Holland as early as the 1300s—that reveals the first written documentation of the desire to cultivate and improve the playing field. Colf was played in a contained area, often with wooden balls, where the goal was to strike a post. In the city of Haarlem, Aelbrecht, Count of Holland, granted a charter to formalize the residents' right to play colf. He identified a common sporting ground as containing "the course." He acknowledged that the green area was used for many purposes and was generally referred to as "a playing field," but he specifically singled out, "the course that lies without the Forest Gate towards the forest, as big and as small as it lies there in these days." This reference suggests that improvements to the course were made often enough that it was impossible to chart its exact location, though by the mid-1400s the course had grown to approximately 320 meters long. According to the town charters the residents were granted colf playing rights "for eternal days," though multiple usages of the grounds were still sanctioned by the governors.

Providing a Surface

Throughout the 1400s the city's archery companies were charged with the upkeep of the space, but on December 12, 1483, when Aelbrecht granted scything rights to the "Masters of the Hours" of the parish church we have our first written reference to the maintenance of a grass surface for a golf-like game. Though the church's interest in maintaining the green was born from a desire to harvest and sell the hay, the side effect was that the colf course was now being prioritized above *archery*, *kaatsen*, *futeball* and other athletic pursuits. In 1497, Philip the Fair confirmed the ordinance of 14 years previous, and Haarlem went on to establish and maintain a second course just outside the city gates.

The Book of Days, *circa 1510,*
portrayed one of the earliest known
drawings of a golf-like game being
played on a lawn area.

 At the turn of the sixteenth century, few tools were available to greenkeepers. Animals could graze the field, but their ability to keep the grass short was more than offset by the damage of their hooves and the uncontrolled spreading of fertilizer they left behind. With the most primitive mowing machine still more than two centuries in the future, keepers of the green turned to the scythe.

 This ancient tool, produced in many different forms since the days of the Romans, was already the main device responsible for harvesting hay and grain. Originally made with a short blade and short handle, the multitude of uses had given rise to many variations of the tool, and the long-bladed model that allowed upright use by the laborer proved effective for maintaining grass. The user could now stand erect in a relaxed position and develop a rhythm, which, while trimming the grass, also served to exercise and strengthen the body. Coincidentally, the pendulum motion was not that unlike the stroke of the golfer.

 Facing forward, the swinging of the scythe results from a full twist of the torso, leaving the chest pointing left, while the arms scribe merely enough arc to keep the blade parallel to the ground at the same height as where the swing commenced. The last bit of energy left at the culmination of the swing begins a recoil that returns the blade to its starting point, while the chest now points to the right. The greenkeeper takes a small step forward with both feet and continues to cut a crescent-shaped path, casting the cut grass to the left. The precision obtained by an experienced operator could rival most machines that would succeed it, and many of the great lawns of the European elite were maintained to a standard nearly comparable to today.

Many Games Become One

At the same time colf was popular in the Netherlands, *mail* and *chole* were being played elsewhere. The most popular ball-and-stick game in France was known as *jeu de mail*—a game that was eventually brought to Perth in 1502. Originally played along the grand avenues and promenades of the Tuileres and at Versailles, *mail* used a croquet-like mallet along a playing surface of packed clay and loam topped with crushed seashells, bordered by carefully tended Parisian gardens.

But similar sites in London and Edinburgh did not afford the same comfort and the game moved to the town linksland, a perfect stage for a more expansive version of the pursuit. Although the cleared area between the heather was merely the width of two roadways, once freed from the confines of the city buildings a freer swinging style of play developed and with it the average length of players' drives nearly doubled.

Chole took advantage of this increased length of play, being a team game played across miles of links terrain with balls and clubs the most similar to today's standards. The goal was to strike a target, with one player or team making three chole strokes before the opposition was allowed a de-choling, or backwards stroke that put the ball farther from the agreed upon destination. Both *chole* and *mail* were played in the 1300s, and some believe golf followed shortly thereafter.

In Scotland, evidence of when golf was first played revolves around the various decrees issued by Parliament banning sports in favor of archery practice. In the first Act from 1424, King James I forbids football, but fails to mention golf. This is corrected when the playing of the "gouff" is included in the 1457 decree, causing

Scything the greens at St. Andrews.

some historians to conclude golf began between these two dates. "This is nonsense," concludes Reverend John Kerr in *The Golf Book of East Lothian*. "The game could not in such a very short time have taken such a strong hold of the people as to require to be put down by Parliament. Its omission at first was more likely to be a mere accident."

More likely, the evolution to golf was gradual. Cross-country golfing, team games, golf played to fixed targets and, in the city, many versions of *mail* continued to be played throughout the sixteenth and seventeenth centuries. But slowly, playing to a series of holes in the ground became the dominant game. And although accounts of the play from that era suggest a cultivated course for the competition, no references to keepers of the green come to light during these formative years in Scotland.

As early as the 1620s however, the Fraserburgh GC in northern Scotland had golf holes that consisted of "permanent granite cups sunk into the links at different places," according to its club history. By 1650 there were golfing grounds at Leith, St. Andrews, Carnoustie, Montrose, Aberdeen, Banff, and Dornoch—and at each site a local ball or club maker kept the greens. Though the job had few of today's stresses it was not without its own set of problems.

The slow growing dwarf grasses of the linksland, constantly

TOP: *Sheep provided maintenance services at many golf courses long before a human superintendent was hired.*

BOTTOM: *Brushing the ground around the hole was the first job golf clubs paid a worker to perform.*

grazed and fertilized by rabbits, needed little tending. On inland courses, when the grasses grew too tall in the summer, play was simply suspended until fall. Until the advent of the lawn mower, golf was generally played inland from October to May—the town council on the Leith Links, for example, formally banned play from June 1 to September 30. In many cases, the hay crop that was given priority was essential to the well-being of the town.

Out on the linksland, golf continued nearly year-round. Human traffic that resulted from the multiple-use nature of the links, a perpetual sanding of the course by wind-blown silt, the grazing of sheep or rabbits and the poor soils combined to keep the turf in check. A greenkeeper's role was primarily to cut the hole and sweep for ten paces around the hole in anticipation of the monthly meetings, but slowly through the march of decades, men began to be paid to perform this task on a more regular basis.

The first written record of payment for greenkeeping services is in 1744 when the Royal Burgess Golfing Society engaged a boy as "our cady," or "greenkeeper" with a remuneration of six shillings per quarter year, together with a suit of clothes. Another half century would pass before recorded history would remember the names of such laborers.

The Rabbits of St. Andrews

Men paid as hole-cutters were the first real greenkeepers, and although they remained anonymous until the mid-1700s, it is clear an assortment of artisans were given this charge from the early years of the century onward. As early as 1764, notations in the St. Andrews record show a payment of one guinea a year for cutting new holes, filling old ones and repairing the rabbit scrapes. The first named greenkeeper who performed these services was George Mill—serving from the 1760s to the 1780s. Peter Robertson, grandfather of Allan Robertson, the man many recognize as the world's first golf professional, followed him.

Licenses to breed rabbits on the linksland had been issued for decades before a problem arose at the end of the 18th century involving St. Andrews merchants Charles Dempster and Son that rose the ire of the golfing populace. Generally, golfers felt the pasturing of animals had gotten out of hand and their rights for the protection of the golf links had been violated. Specifically, in a complaint dated February 8, 1805, the golfers brought the matter before the Court, arguing that the immense population of rabbits was doing permanent damage to the golfing grounds.

When the Court scheduled hearings for September 3-7, 1805, the names of the greenkeepers installed as witnesses were entered into the public record for the first time. "Charles Robertson testified that he was a ballmaker and caddie aged fifty-two years who had been employed by the golfers to take charge of the Links for twenty-five years," notes Alastair Johnston in his book *The Chronicles of Golf*. "His duties included making new holes prior to each monthly meeting. However the job had become so troublesome on account of the rabbits that he retired in 1801."

Charles Robertson was followed by Thomas Robertson, who was dismissed for incompetence before a year was up, and then by Robert Morris, age 49. Morris was paid £4 to £5 per year, and was part of a continually changing group of links supervisors.

Eventually the Court decided in the golfers' favor, and on February 19, 1806, issued an edict allowing citizens to take and kill rabbits as they had done in times past. The decision was appealed to the House of Lords and the controversy would continue for sev-

Allan Robertson has long been recognized as the first golf professional, but his father Charles Robertson was one of the first greenkeepers at St. Andrews, serving from approximately 1776 to 1801.

eral more years, giving the greenkeeper the first of many headaches resulting from the destruction of the links by outside forces—and a political battle over the matter to boot. When finding someone to take the job became difficult, St. Andrews raised the rate of pay, and instituted a fee of five shillings a year per member for upkeep of the links.

The Profession Grows

St. Andrews was not the only golfing enclave that found the need to employ a greenkeeper in the early years of the nineteenth century. At Bruntsfield, clubmaker David Denholm of Royal Burgess was given the added title of keeper of the green from 1809 to 1820. In Montrose, a keeper was employed in 1828, but was terminated a year later after numerous complaints from the golfers. David Marshall was named as his replacement in 1829, but despite a doubling of the salary, he was sacked within a year as well. From these early records one may assume that job security was a problem for greenkeepers ever since the profession developed.

At Royal Blackheath, clubmakers were paid an additional fee when they also cut the holes, and the tradition began with a Mr. Donaldson in the 1780s. Ballantyne, Cockburn, Poke, and Corporal Archibald Sharpe followed, until 1822 when the two positions were separated and Old Alick was employed as the regular hole cutter.

Old Alick is the first greenkeeper whose story still survives. Old Alick was born Alick Brotherston in 1756. After a journey to sea from his hometown of Leith at age 13, he returned to serve the Blackheath club for many years as a caddie before ascending to the role of greenkeeper.

Alick was an innovator. He used a net for recovering golf balls from ponds and ditches and may have pioneered the use of flags to mark the holes. He cut holes with a knife—as was the early custom —a difficult task in the gravel and stone of Blackheath. He also had the first staff, employing uniformed men from the Greenwich Royal Naval Hospital to attend to the flags. According to the Club history: "Payments were made to the Greenwich men of 1 shilling on Medal Days; each man was assigned a hole to look after—so there were seven in all on the Hazard Course—his job being to look after the 'green' (meaning the entire hole) and the flag. These men were solely concerned with the course and were additional to the caddies and forecaddies which all players would have."

Old Alick was the first greenkeeper of notoriety, and a progressive turf manager who advanced the technology and skills of the profession as much as anyone in the nineteenth century.

Alick was held in high regard at Blackheath and Robert Samuel Ennis Gallon, a London painter and lithographer who exhibited at the Royal Academy between 1830 and 1868, painted his portrait. Despite his status as a laborer, Alick was portrayed in white top hat and tails; similar to the garb the players of high social position would don to appear on the links. This elegant portrait still hangs at Royal Blackheath, in addition to a second painting that also honors one of the world's first greenkeepers.

Improving the Hole

It is at Royal Musselburgh where a major advance in greenkeeping occurred. The first employee of Musselburgh was Officer Brook, appointed in 1784 at a salary of one shilling and sixpence for each of the nine meetings held on the second Friday of every month— with the exception of July, August and September, when play was suspended. Brook collected fees and delivered notices, perhaps also cutting the cups by hand in addition to his organizational duties.

Although there were no standards for ball or cup size in the late 1700s, a device that was manufactured in Musselburgh set a mark that has scarcely been deviated from in the nearly 300 years since. According to the club minutes of March 13, 1829, the Honorable Secretary was authorized to pay Mr. R. Gay "for the instrument for forming the holes the sum of £1." The sturdy tool that the club purchased was comprised of a wooden handle, iron shaft and an open-ended metal barrel at the end, and it scribed a circle of four-and-a-half inches in diameter—approximately the official size of the hole adopted by the Royal and Ancient nearly 65 years later. "The hole shall be 4¼ inches (108 mm) in diameter and at least 4 inches (100 mm) deep," states the present day Rules of Golf. Although it is not known if St. Andrews took its cue from this device when it standardized the measurement, it is uncanny how similar the standards are. The instrument was clearly an advancement in the art of hole cutting.

The object, which disappeared for a century, was later donated to Royal Musselburgh by Harry B. Wood of Manchester, England, who wrote this account in his 1911 book, *Golfing Curios and the Like*: "A friend, knowing of my 'craze' for the acquisition of golfing relics, some time ago presented me with the original hole-cutter. Upon its evidently ancient cross-handle there was a brass-plate attached by metal pins, presumably before the introduction of the

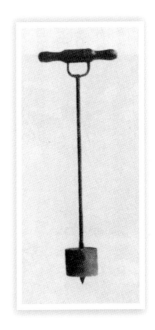

Hole cutter from Musselburgh.

comparatively modern screw about 1850, and inscribed in old-fashioned incised characters — 'Musselburgh Golf Club A.D. 1774.' My friend had himself forgotten the existence of the relic until my hobby recurred to him, nor was he very clear as to how the hole-cutter actually came into his possession; his impression was, however, that some 25 years previously, when in the throes of an acute attack of 'golf fever,' he had instructed his gardener to make some holes in the grounds for putting practice, and noticing how beautifully symmetrical and 'clean' they were, my friend enquired how they were made and was shown the instrument by the gardener, after which it reached the 'lumber room,' only to be recovered after many years and restored to the Royal Musselburgh GC, in whose care it now reposes for all time."

Wood goes on to note that initially the clubs that utilized the Musselburgh golfing grounds shared the device. "I understand that this particular hole cutter was the 'Key to the Situation' at that time, being used for making the holes as required by the several clubs playing over the course at Musselburgh. No wonder the members of the Royal Musselburgh Club esteem this fine old relic as one of their most valuable and interesting possessions (and they have many) relating to the past history of the society."

ABOVE: *Horses needed hoof booties to prevent damage to the areas being mowed.*

RIGHT: *Many other companies marketed mowers in the latter half of the nineteenth century.*

Though the device may be considered a "fine old relic" today, when it was handed over to Sargent Scott, officer of the club in 1829, it was state-of-the-art. The minutes made it clear that "Sgt. Scott is to pay more attention to the forming of the holes," and when new playing regulations were instituted five years later, "the Club Officer was to see that no damage was done to the holes, no new ones dug or old ones redug without authority." Names of the offending hole diggers were to be forwarded to the club officers for punishment. Minutes show that members were satisfied with the new holes and Scott continued in his position until 1838. At that time, two men were employed to manage the green: William Doleman served as Stand Attendant to look after the club boxes at a salary of £3 a year, and Thomas Alexander was engaged as hole cutter for £2.

A Key Tool—The Mower

At about the same time, in another part of the British Empire, a second piece of equipment—one that would eventually cast a larger shadow than the hole cutter in the world of greenkeeping— was being developed. In 1828, Edwin Beard Budding, a carpenter and engineer of Stroud, England, was employed at a carpet mill in Gloucestershire. Carpets of the day were made from raw wool and in the initial manufacture of the rug, the nap was left rough and uneven. The final trimming involved rotating blades that passed over the surface of the carpet and evened out the cut, producing a smooth texture.

Budding observed the process, and being an inventor at heart he mulled over other possible uses for this rotating blade arrangement. When he considered the possibility of trimming grass he

TOP: *Edwin Beard Budding patented the first lawn mower in 1830. It was produced by Budding and partner James Ferrabee at their Phoenix Foundry in Stroud, England.*

BOTTOM: *J.R. & A. Ransome of Ipswich was the first company to mass-market the mower.*

LEFT: *Early horse-drawn mower.*

LEFT: *Eventually mowers were powered —first by steam, later by gasoline.*

RIGHT: *Specialized mowers grew ever larger with the advent of twentieth century technology.*

was enthused. He adapted the concept of sharp blades rotating on a turning cylinder to clip uneven grass to a uniform height. Downsizing the scale of the machine, Budding developed a portable unit that could be rolled on wheels, and he tinkered with the details until he had it right. He then took on James Ferrabee— a partner with the resources to turn his prototype into production—and in 1828 established the Phoenix Foundry.

His patent application identified the machine as "a new combination and application of machinery for the purpose of cropping or shearing the vegetable surfaces of lawns, grass-plats and pleasure grounds, constituting a machine which may be used with advantage instead of a scythe for that purpose." He even went so far as to equate the work-saving product with recreation. "Country gentlemen may find in using my machine themselves an amusing, useful and healthy exercise." The patent was granted on August 31, 1830, and the company was off and running.

When the partners demonstrated their idea at Regent's Park in 1831, the grounds superintendent remarked that the machine did the work of eight men with scythes—and did it better. The Phoenix Foundry was successful and Budding worked to improve the efficiency of the mower. Though the first models were pushed by hand, other companies sought to power them by having them dragged by horses, ponies and donkeys, before eventually adapting steam-powered engines to their design. J.R. & A. Ransome of Ipswich, England, was the first company to obtain a license to produce its own version of the machine. A similar device was not produced in the United States until the Chadborn & Coldwell Company of Newburgh, New York, marketed a model in 1868. Gang mower patents did not surface on either continent until 1891.

Though there have been many improvements in the 170 years since its introduction, the original mower used the same principles found in hand-powered reel mowers today. The wheels turned the drum, which in turn rotated the blades that clipped the grass and discarded the residue. The movements were made smoother, the job became easier and the public more interested. Home lawns became a status symbol at first, a necessity shortly thereafter, and it is no coincidence that beautiful lawns became known as carpets of grass.

The implications for golf courses were enormous. Greens could be manicured to new standards and inland courses were able to play a longer season. Even the cutting of fairways was made possible with the advent of horse-drawn mowers. Maintenance of the course was about to take a major step forward and St. Andrews would once again lead the way.

The Old Tom Era

Tom Morris was born at the west end of North Street in the town of St. Andrews to John and Jean Bruce Morris on June 16, 1821. His father was a letter carrier, weaver, carpenter and, at times, a professional caddie. Not surprisingly, he started Tom in the playing of golf at the tender age of six. Although the elder Morris expected his son to follow him into the professions of either weaving or carpentry, Tom had other notions after a discussion with caddie Alexander Herd, grandfather to future British Open winner Sandy Herd. The venerable golfer asked if Morris—who was attending Madra College at the time—would consider an apprenticeship to Allan Robertson, and the idea of a career in golf blossomed in the young man's head. In 1839, Robertson agreed to take him on as a feather ball maker and the two became good friends.

At the time, Robertson was 24 and already regarded as one of the finest golfers in the world; Morris was 18 and sharpening his skills both as a player and professional. Their partnership in ball making was a busy and profitable enterprise, and their business records show that they made and sold nearly 2,500 balls in the year 1844 alone. Robertson had been given the charge of improving the links by Sir Hugh Playfair, provost of St. Andrews and one-time captain of the R&A, and in 1848, with Morris's labor, set out to widen fairways and create the huge double greens that still characterize St. Andrews today. "I don't know, I am sure, if the people

Even the earliest mowers produced a smooth grass surface unlike anything before.

nowadays realize how much they are indebted to the late Provost Sir Hugh Playfair for the great and successful efforts he made for the betterment of our links," Morris noted in retrospect.

In 1848, the gutta percha ball was beginning to gain in popularity, and Robertson and Morris made an agreement to never play the new ball, for fear it would be the end of their business. But in 1851, a bitter dispute over the new guttie ball developed between the two. Tom was playing a round with Master Campbell when he ran out of featheries and accepted a guttie from his playing partner to complete his round. Robertson happened to pass by the group at the time and Campbell made note of the ball in use, teasing Robertson with his partner's actions. The resulting argument broke apart the partnership and sent Morris to Prestwick, where he was employed as pro/greenkeeper for the next 13 years. Robertson passed away prematurely in 1859, just one year after becoming the first person to break 80 on the Old Course and one year before the inaugural British Open. Morris continued to refine his game and claimed three Open titles before returning to St. Andrews for good in 1864.

Morris benefited both from his time with Robertson and his time away from him, later stating, "I must say that Allan had a great deal to do with the making of me, both as a golfer and otherwise." Learning all he could from the man, and then having the opportunity to experiment, question and alter what he had gleaned allowed him to develop a theory of course maintenance and a program to practice. He left Prestwick with a stand of excellent turf and a reputation as the finest 12-hole course in Great Britain. When Morris returned to St. Andrews, the next era of course upkeep began.

After struggling with various greenkeepers in part-time positions, the R&A had decided to appoint "a custodian at a salary considerably larger than that hitherto given," and that "the entire charge of the course should be entrusted to him." For this they were willing to pay £50 a year, with an additional £20 for expenses incurred in maintaining the course. According to the R&A minutes book, Morris was hired on January 9, 1865, to "make the holes, look after the flags and mend the turf," and allowed him "one man for two days a week when heavy work such as carting was to be done, plus barrow, spade and shovel." But Morris longed to accomplish much more. At the time, holes were changed every Monday or before monthly meetings and Sunday was a day of rest for the course. A deeply religious man who read the Bible daily and later became an elder in his church, Morris believed that even if the

Old Tom Morris set a new standard for greenkeeping when he assumed the head position at St. Andrews in 1864.

golfers refused to admit they needed a contemplative day on the Sabbath, there was still no playing of golf on Sundays. "The Links needed a rest, even if the golfers didn't," was his official position. The course was closed to play and open to the townspeople for strolling and socializing.

Under his care the course flourished, but like today, the changes he instituted were not advanced without opposition. Some argued the constant smoothing of surfaces was unnatural and that golf must be played without changing the natural habitat. Reverend McPherson complained "that one could simply skirt around the hazards now—the whole challenge of the course is gone." Members liked the variety of putting surfaces, defended the wild untended areas encroaching on the line of play and embraced the random nature of the hazards.

Still, Morris quietly went about creating the opposite. He widened the cultivated fairway surfaces expanding them from 40 to 100 yards in breadth, outlined and defined the bunkers, allowed the worms to remain on the greens and their holes to serve as aeration, raised and returfed the greens, used metal cups to line the holes, supported tabled areas with turf bricks and top-dressed to increase green speed and uniformity. "Mair saund, Honeyman," was a common call to his assistant James Honeyman, to pour on the fine sand, a practice Morris stumbled on quite by accident.

While working at Prestwick, Morris spilled a wheelbarrow full of sand on a putting surface he was having difficulty growing grass on. Rather than shoveling it back into his wheelbarrow, Morris spread the sand across the green. When he later found the grass restored and healthy, Morris recognized the improvement in the putting surface and brought attention to the value of topdressing. Horace Hutchinson wrote, "Tom Morris has discovered that there is nothing like sand for links grass. If he sees an iron cut, he at once has it filled up level with sand, which experiment has convinced him encourages a growth of young grass."

Morris capped off his first five years as steward of St. Andrews with the drilling of the first well for watering the greens. In 1870, a well was sunk adjacent to the sixth green and a plentiful supply of good-quality water was found. In the years to follow, additional wells were opened until, by 1887, every green had a water supply and the turf was provided for, even during the drought periods. This final "tool" allowed Morris to bring the Old Course to a new standard in the final 25 years of the nineteenth century. It drove Hutchinson to glow: "The High Priest of this hierarchy of professional golf is, beyond question, the custodian of the green for the Royal and Ancient Golf Club of St. Andrews—at the present time (and long may he continue to hold his office!) 'Old Tom' Morris. If not, possibly, the most lucrative, it is certainly the most distinguished position to which the golf professional proper can aspire."

Hutchinson went on to detail all the attributes of Old Tom—attributes that all topflight greenkeepers should aspire to, a manifesto that still applies in the twenty-first century. "He will need to have some knowledge of turf-cutting, and the technical knowledge generally necessary for keeping the turf on the putting-greens in fine order. He will need to be an observer of the growth of grasses…to look after the ground, arrange the tees, and read the Riot Act to small boys who play off the greens with their irons, and generally to act as custodian. He will also be the overseer of one or more horny-handed sons of toil who, under his directions, roll, sweep, and mow the greens and fill up iron-skelps and other wounds in the ground. He will need, in the first place, to be a man of not unpleasing manner, or strangers will naturally be disgusted at their reception; for it is him that they will probably first address themselves. He will need to have a certain power of organisation, and a moral influence over the forces—the caddies and professionals—who are more or less under his orders. And he will need to have a thorough knowledge of the theory and practice of the game of golf, so as to be able to tutor aright the young idea."

Morris possessed all these attributes, but it was his friendly accommodating manner that welcomed travelers and locals into the St. Andrews fold. He set a maintenance standard that was copied by the 30 clubs in existence when he began his tenure at St. Andrews and by the dozens more that were opened during his long career.

His improvements did not go unnoticed by his peers. Avid golfer and R&A Captain James Balfour commented, "The links are far more carefully kept than they used to be. Tom Morris superintends this with great assiduity. The putting greens, instead of being left in their natural state as formerly, are now carefully rolled with a heavy roller, mowed with a machine and watered in dry weather. The putting is made smoother and better, and much truer."

Morris also worked on the bunkers for, "the bunkers were doubly hazardous, in that for nearly whole seasons they stood feet deep in water. In order to prevent a recurrence of this, Tom Morris has raised the level of their foundations and they are not nearly so deep as they at one time were."

Morris also eliminated the long-standing practice of teeing off two clubs length from the previous hole, a procedure that did more damage to greens than any other. Balfour concluded, "A separate teeing ground has also been provided at each hole, which preserves the putting-greens from being broken by the tee strokes." By 1875, the new grooming practices, combined with the architectural work that Morris instituted, brought the Old Course to a standard that is not far from how the course plays today.

The improvements at St. Andrews were not lost on the golfing public who, through the expanded British railway system could now easily travel to distant greens. Every course was compared to St. Andrews, and the players who had been there were seldom satisfied elsewhere. Old Tom Morris had created a new standard and the other greenkeepers were increasingly being held to it. One unfortunate side effect may have been the formation of the first green committee. In March, 1878, the Royal Blackheath minutes show this entry: "The Putting Greens being in a very unsatisfactory state for a considerable time it was thought to form a Greens Committee."

Even the master himself fell prey to such oversight. After constructing a new eighteenth green and first hole in 1870, Morris suggested that the course could now be played clockwise or counterclockwise. As a result he filled in several old bunkers, while creating various new sand pits. This brought the admonition that Morris was "in future to submit proposals to a general meeting before proceeding to fill up any bunkers or otherwise materially to alter the course." Having already achieved most of his goals, Morris let the course design rest, while continuing to upgrade its maintenance in the final quarter of the nineteenth century.

Morris lived to the practically unheard-of age of 87 (in an era when the average life expectancy was 45), dying as the result of

Morris was the first to establish tees on a golf course. Previously, players teed off two club lengths from the hole just completed, destroying turf in close proximity to putting areas.

accidentally falling down the cellar stairs on May 24, 1908. He had remained greenkeeper and professional at St. Andrews until the autumn of 1903, when he stepped down so the R&A could appoint a younger and stronger man to take the strains of the job. "I've played gowf close on eighty years, and that's longer than most folk get living," Morris said at his retirement. "I began on the links doon there as soon as I could handle a club, and I have been doing little else ever since." The R&A voted to continue his salary in addition to a lifetime annuity of £100 per year. His legacy lives on today.

Early American Roots

While the origins of greenkeeping are difficult to fully document in the United Kingdom, they are nearly impossible to detail in North America, despite the fact that golfing records go back nearly as far. The earliest reference to a golf-like game being played in what would become the United States revolves around the Dutch in central New York State.

In 1609, Henry Hudson, an Englishman employed by the Dutch, sailed north up the waterway that would later bear his name, the Hudson River. An expedition that followed in 1614 established a fur-trading outpost on Castle Island, south of present-day Albany. When that settlement was destroyed by flood, another was built at Fort Orange in 1617 and populated by 30 families in 1624. Other colonies between Manhattan and what became known as New Netherland were established over the next three decades, and by 1650 permanent jurisdictions included homes and businesses in van Rensselaerswyck, as well as a court at Beverwyck.

Court records reveal the first known reference to *kolf* in the New World when, on December 13, 1650, Jacob Jansz Stol was convicted of striking "Gysbert Comelisz, tavern keeper, and Claes Andriesz, with a golf club at the house of Steven Jansz." Seven years later, the same court levied a fine against Messrs. Hendricksen, Hoogenboom, and Van Loenen for playing *kolf* during the day of prayer.

While *kolf* was originally played on the ice, and then moved to the city streets, an edict issued in 1659 forced the game to take to the fields. "The honorable commissary and Magistrates of Fort Orange and the village of Beverwyck, having heard divers complaints from the burghers of this place against the practice of playing golf along the streets, which causes great damage to the windows of the houses, and also exposes people to the danger of being injured and is contrary to the freedom of the public streets; Therefore their honours, wishing to prevent the same, hereby forbid all persons to play golf in the streets, under the penalty of forfeiture of 25 Florins for each person who shall be found doing so."

While the ordinance did nothing to curtail golf enthusiasm, it did force the game to move to open areas. Evidence suggests that the common green in New Amsterdam was the premier choice for players over the next half-century. Once installed, it is inevitable that someone was put in charge of the playing field and its upkeep, especially given the more than two-century history of playing golf-like games on cultivated grass surfaces that the Dutch brought from their homeland. Unfortunately, no other written record exists regarding the Dutch game playing, and our first North American greenkeeper from New Amsterdam remains anonymous.

Southern Outpost

Typical of the disparate factions playing ball-and-stick games in Europe, a band of Scottish golfers were at work elsewhere in North America. Strong ties to Scotland existed in the coastal settlements of South Carolina, and by 1729 a band of Scots had formed the St. Andrew's Society to help others make the transition to America and to educate their children about their heritage. It is not surprising that these Scottish settlers were responsible for the first documented shipment of golfing implements to the New World in the middle of the eighteenth century.

The freight listing aboard the ship Magdalen, leaving the port of Leith on May 10, 1743, included "eight dozen golf clubs and three gross golf balls," to be delivered to David Deas of Charleston upon safe passage. The Deas family, including Colonel Alston Deas and sons David and John, were known as the golfing pioneers of Charleston, though many other transplanted Scots joined them in their pursuits.

The Johnston brothers—John, Archibald, Thomas, and Andrew—also settled in Charleston in the 1730s and imported golf clubs from their home in Glasgow. Merchant Andrew listed 12 golf sticks and balls in his personal inventory when he died in 1764, and was known to sell golfing paraphernalia from his store on the Charleston waterfront.

With the port growing ever more active during and after the

Revolutionary War, Charleston became a trading outpost, connecting England, France, the West Indies, Canada and even the Far East with the American South. Rice, indigo, cotton, tobacco, flax, hemp and barley were exported; coal, spices, fabrics and luxuries from Europe were imported. When the remaining Caribbean pirates were driven away early in the eighteenth century and the Revolutionary War hostilities subsided, the waterfront developed into a thriving business center that rivaled any commercial port on the East Coast of the continent.

The city of Charleston possessed another attribute that was perfect for golf. The land resembled Scottish links—having been formed from the gradual recession of the oceanic tides. The sandy deposits that were left contained no rocks or stones and grew strong stands of slow-growing grasses. There was seldom a frost in the subtropical climate and the subsoil drained well when doused with the frequent late afternoon showers.

As the area attracted more and more ethnic groups, clubs of all varieties were formed to preserve the heritage of the homeland and offer social intercourse. There was an Agriculture Society, the Jockey Club, a Medical Society, the German Friendly Society, the French Patriotic Society and three British clubs: the Ugly Club, the Evening Club and the Amateur Society. It was not surprising that in September 1786, the South Carolina GC was established.

Although it has been suggested that this club was merely a social club existing to host lavish dinner parties it seems highly improbable that a group of Scots would get together over the course of 25 years on perfect links soil, in a delightful climate, at a town where golf clubs had been used for 50 years and not play golf.

An October 13, 1795 announcement stated that the club's anniversary would be celebrated "on Saturday next, at the Club House on Harleston's Green where the members are requested to attend at one o'clock."

At the time, according to historian Charles Fraser, the word green denoted "large, vacant spaces along the margin of the town," and "there was Bouquet's Green, immediately in front of the house lately occupied by John Hume, Esq., and extending to the west and south-west to tide water, Harleston's Green, extending north of it to a considerable distance." It was at Harleston's Green where the golf club was centered, with many of the meetings taking place at the Williams Coffee House.

The club paid a surtax for the use of the public land along the harbor, sharing it with spectators, horse and carriage, fishermen and sailors. There is no account of who maintained the space and the open acreage has long since been smothered by the expanding city. No financial records or club minutes have yet been found.

But Charleston was not the only southern golfing outpost where the green was maintained. One hundred miles south, a golf club was formed in Savannah, Georgia, sometime prior to 1796. Notices appeared in the paper as late as 1811, including one that read, "The members of the Savannah GC are requested to meet at Mr. Thomas Bribbin's hotel, on the Bay, this evening (Nov. 11), at 7 o'clock to draw for finders and enter into other arrangements for the season." Finders were forecaddies who ran ahead of the match and helped golfers locate the hole, and their employment would have been contingent upon the playing of the game, not merely the gathering for social occasion. Perhaps some also served as greenkeepers—unfortunately none of these early forays into the ancient sport would endure into the latter days of the nineteenth century.

While these southern courses went out of existence before their practices and employees could be firmly documented, there is no doubt that greenkeeping in North America began with both the Dutch and the Scots, many years before the clubs we know today were formed. For courses that would stand the test of time, golfers needed to wait nearly a century.

View of Charleston, South Carolina waterfront. Golf was most likely played on the green adjacent to the water.

Chapter Two

Golf in North America
1874-1918

By Gordon Witteveen

Organized golf came to North America in the latter part of the
nineteenth century, first to Canada in Montreal (1873) and Quebec
City (1874) and a few years later to New York at the St. Andrews
Golf Course in 1888. For convenience and necessity the game in
the beginning was played on large open spaces such as pasture
farms, parks, old battlefields, and often on the common on the
outskirts of the cities. In Montreal golf was played on Fletcher's
Field, a park on top of Mount Royal where golfers shared the
course with ladies pushing prams. In the case of Quebec City,
golfers chose the Plains of Abraham, a battlefield where General
Wolfe had defeated Montcalm for the dominance of Canada. In
New York, John Reid, who is considered the father of American
golf, laid out three holes in a pasture near his home. A few years
later they moved to an apple orchard and these first American
golfers became forever afterward known as the "Apple Tree Gang."

Other clubs and courses have laid claim to being the first golf
course in America but none have been able to substantiate their
claims with documented evidence. The members at Foxburg CC
north of Pittsburgh, Pennsylvania claim that their club and golf
course is at least one year older than St. Andrews but their claim is
based on the oral history of older members and they lack documentation of early meetings. Similarly, the Dorset Field Club in
Vermont claims to have been organized in 1886, fully two years
ahead of the St. Andrews GC in New York, but again they lack
written evidence of the events that were supposed to have taken
place many years ago. Interestingly, the Dorset Field Club claims
another first. It is their certain conviction that their greenkeeper,
Grant Matson (1904-1937), invented the first gang mower just
prior to World War I. This latter claim can easily be repudiated
since the Pennsylvania Lawn Mower Company had manufactured
gang mowers since 1900 and before.

The greens were quite rough in the early days. John Reid (foreground), father of American golf with the Apple Tree Gang on the St. Andrews Golf Course in Yonkers, NY, November 1888.

Andy Bell, who studied at Edinburgh University in Scotland in 1880, came back to his native Burlington, Iowa and promptly laid out three holes on which to play his favorite game in 1883. With Andy Bell as the golf professional, architect and greenkeeper, the course flourished and soon became a regular 9-hole course but in spite of this auspicious record, Andy Bell never has replaced John Reid as the father of American golf.

Perhaps the strongest claim for being the first golf course in America comes from the Oakhurst Links golf course near White Sulphur Springs, West Virginia. Golf was played at Oakhurst as early as 1881 and medal competitions took place beginning in 1888. The course was discontinued in the early 1900s. It was resurrected in 1994 and today golf is played at Oakhurst Links just as it was more than a century ago, with old style clubs and balls from small teeing grounds while sheep graze the fairways.

The Early Courses

The first golfers were often transplanted Scotsmen who had played the game in their native land and brought along their sticks and balls when they emigrated to North America. The first golf courses were often quite primitive and were laid out by the very same people who had imported the game. The first greens at St. Andrews in Yonkers measured just 15 foot across and were as rough and uneven as the adjacent fairways.

To improve the putting surface the greens were flattened with shovels and rakes and rolled with heavy wooden rollers sometimes fashioned from tree logs. When sprigs of grass raised their heads they were cut with a razor-sharp scythe or with a small lawn-mower, whichever was handiest. The early caretakers of these primitive golf courses were often in the employ as gardeners at the estates of the first golfers.

Older men who had been trained in the use of a scythe knew how to cut grass on lawns to perfection. They did the same on the early putting greens The best time to use the scythe was early in the morning while the grass was still wet with dew. At that time the grass is firm and the scythe will cut more easily and less physical effort is required to mow it. Of course the opposite is true in the case of the reel-type mower that always performs best when the turf is dry. To be able to use a scythe and to sharpen a scythe was a skill that took a long time to acquire. Mowing by scythe was

Horse-drawn mowers.

labor-intensive and at first, only the wealthy could afford the luxury of a fine lawn or closely mown greens and fairways.

After scything a green, it was necessary to remove the clippings by sweeping the turf with a birch broom or a *besum* as such implements were and are still known in Scotland. The birch broom helped break up the objectionable worm casts and made the grass stand up, thus reducing grain.

The first reel-type lawnmowers had been invented in England in the 1830s and were slowly becoming available to North Americans for use on lawns, parks, and even on the early golf courses. The establishment of golf courses increased the demands for walk-behind reel mowers in America and soon lawn mowers were mass-produced. The early models were very narrow and it took a long time to cut a green. Catchers for the mowers, to gather the clippings, came later.

The early courses were often laid out on areas that were already covered with pasture grasses, mainly bluegrasses, red top, timothy, and clover. The early greens were cut at near half an inch and it was only the persistent rolling that made smooth putting possible. Just the same, the early greens were somewhat rough and very slow by modern standards.

The fairways developed naturally from the same pasture grasses. There may have been other grasses and weeds in this mixture but they would gradually disappear under a constant regimen of cutting the grass short with a single-horse mower or with a flock of sheep or even cows. The Worthington Mower Company produced single gang units before the turn of the century, circa 1895. The first recorded purchase of a 30" reel-type mower took place at the Victoria GC on Vancouver Island in 1903. The Pennsylvania Lawn Mower Company manufactured the mower and the quoted price was $100. The drawbars for the horse and the sulky seat for the operator were an extra $25. We may assume that the Pennsylvania Lawn Mower Company did a booming business since by the year 1900 there were already more than 1,000 golf courses on the North American continent.

It is hard to imagine that a single reel-type mower was sufficient to cut all the fairways on a golf course, even a 9-hole course and, of course, it was not. We must remember that the fairways did not start until about 100 yards from the tee and they were quite narrow strips. The first courses were short with many par-3 holes and the wealthier clubs had of course more horses and more mowers. The Toronto GC, established in 1883, maintained a stable of a dozen horses which had to be fed and looked after every day of the week, thus necessitating greens staff to come in for weekend duty long before greens were cut on Sundays. Many of the early clubs did not permit golf to be played on the Day of the Lord. Besides drawing mowers, horses were also used to pull the water wagon for the greens and to haul sand, topdressing and compost.

The tees were small, square mounds, mostly void of grass. When golf was in its infancy, there was no need for an elaborate teeing surface. At first, golfers were required to tee off within two club lengths from where they had holed out. With time, the tees were moved farther away from the rough greens. Golfers themselves or their caddies fashioned a small mound of loose sand on which they placed their gutta percha ball and flailed away. Eventually the distance between tee and green increased to a safer distance but on some of the early courses such as the National on Long Island and the Victoria GC on Canada's west coast, tees are still in very close proximity of the greens.

Fred Hawkins, longtime greenkeeper at Toronto Lakeview GC, came to Canada from England in 1906. Shortly after his arrival, he spent a day helping to lay out a course. In the following paragraphs Hawkins tells in his own words of his first experience on a golf course in Canada:

"I would like to tell you of my first experience in seeing a golf course laid out. The club I am speaking of was a 9-hole course under the supervision of the professional, who had under him a head grounds man, as he was called in those days. This professional, who in later years was recognized as one of the leading golf architects, was about to lay out nine more holes and as he was trying to get me interested in golf, he invited me along.

"We started out with the grounds man carrying a bundle of stakes and a hammer until we came to a spot where they drove in four stakes 12 ft apart, which they called the 10th tee. After traveling further on, they drove in a stake, walked around it, then decided to take it a few yards further down into a hollow where they drove in four stakes 24 yards apart. This was the 10th green. I asked why they moved it from the first position and was told that the green would get more moisture down there. This was the procedure all around the course. The only difference being that they made one or two greens round instead of square.

"The bunkers were put in across the fairway, pits of about one foot deep, eight feet wide and twenty five feet long, with the soil thrown to the back about two feet high. Their methods of making greens was simply to cut and roll and topdress with some compost and a little bone meal and work them up out of the old sod that was there. In six weeks we were playing on them."

In the beginning there were no irrigation systems and grass depended on the water wagon for survival. Pipes and sprinklers came later.

Although the incident that Hawkins described occurred more than 20 years after golf became established, it can reasonably be surmised that the methodology had not changed significantly during that time period. If anything, it must have been even more primitive in the beginning when the players also laid out the first golf courses. They barely knew how to play the game, let alone organize the holes. At least the Scottish professionals, who came later and laid out many of the early courses, had a better understanding of the game.

From Grounds Man to Greenkeeper

The centennial booklet of the Brantford GC in Ontario (1880) records that the club hired a caretaker who "was paid 15 cents an hour to push a handmower over the greens and to keep the course in some sort of shape. He was helped by a herd of cattle which grazed on the course." The Royal Montreal GC, once it became established at Fletcher's Field in 1880, hired Mr. McNulty as a grounds man and paid him $20 "for his services in connection with caring for the Green." It must be explained that the "Green" is a very ancient term, meaning the whole course including the putting greens. The term "fairgreen" is also an old term for fairway. As it turned out, McNulty's efforts were felt to be inadequate and he missed an opportunity to become North America's first greenkeeper. That distinction belongs to William Davis who was hired in 1881 to be the pro/greenkeeper. Davis, a Scot, had been assistant professional at an English golf course before crossing the Atlantic Ocean and was in the vanguard of an invasion of British golf professionals and greenkeepers.

These were the instructions Davis received from the Club Captain at the time:

"If you take every afternoon a wheelbarrow and spade or the small lawnmower(!) and take the green from hole to hole, removing all objectionable obstacles and cutting all the grass that can be cut, you would soon have the green in a very different state from what it is."

There is no mention of a horse-drawn mower for the fairways, but in any case Davis would have none of it and he resigned on the spot and his services were terminated. Thereby he became the first professional and the first greenkeeper in North America whose record of employment was also one of the shortest. He returned to Britain but came back to Canada and the Royal

Montreal GC at a later date. This time he lasted five years but was then lured to New York, where he assisted with the establishment of the first 12 holes at the Shinnecock GC on Long Island. These holes were found to be inadequate and were redesigned by Willie Dunn Jr. in 1912.

With both greenkeeping and golf only just in its infancy in the United States, it is not surprising that the great English golfer, Harry Vardon, should find our courses lacking when he came for a tour to North America in 1900. Vardon played exhibition matches from coast to coast and in between he also won the U.S. Open by a nine-stroke margin. Vardon was a gracious winner but he spoke in harsh terms about the quality of our golf courses. Vardon played an exhibition match at Rosedale in Toronto, and although "a half dozen men and a team of horses had been out rolling and cutting the course by lantern the previous night," Vardon was not impressed. He criticized the roughness of the course and the lack of sand bunkers in no gentle terms. Nor did he change his opinions of other courses when he played more exhibitions. Since Vardon's tour of North America spanned the entire continent, his influence was substantial and many were forced to take another look at the maintenance of their courses. Something had to be done and something was done. The clubs turned to their Scottish professionals for help.

Golf Professionals as Greenkeepers

The first greenkeepers were also the professionals, not only in Scotland and England but also in Canada and the United States. According to Horace Hutchinson, the British golfer and writer, the high priest of golf and greenkeeping was Old Tom Morris. At the Old Course in St. Andrews, Old Tom trained many young men in his ways and many followed in his footsteps. A résumé that included time spent at St. Andrews under the guidance of Old Tom was a sure guarantee to a good livelihood on a golf course anywhere in the world. The opportunities for advancement in golf were most plentiful in North America.

One of the first to cross the ocean and make a success of himself was Willie Park, twice winner of the British Open, who came to Shinnecock GC in 1891 as pro/greenkeeper, and he redesigned the course. Ernest Way became pro/greenkeeper at the Detroit GC, a course laid out by his brother Jack. A third brother, Bert

Way, was also a successful pro/greenkeeper in Cleveland, Ohio. One of the Way brothers eventually became full-time superintendent in the Detroit area.

Robert White from St. Andrews, Scotland, a pro/greenkeeper at the Myopia Hunt Club in Massachusetts moved to the Ravisloe GC in Illinois. He studied agronomy and became a pioneer in scientific turfgrass management. In 1916 he became the founder of the PGA. Another Scot, Willie Watson, was pro/greenkeeper at the Minikahda Club in Minnesota. Robert Foulis was also a graduate of Old Tom Morris's shop in St. Andrews. He came to the Midwest with his brother James and promptly became involved with golf courses as professional and greenkeeper. Soon the brothers were laying out golf courses, but Robert retained his relationship with the Bellerive CC in St. Louis, Missouri as a pro/greenkeeper, doing architectural work on the side. He was an early member of both the PGA and the NAGA. At the Country Club of Cleveland in Ohio, Joe Mitchell was hired in 1898 as pro/greenkeeper. Soon the job of maintaining the golf course became a burden for Mitchell and the greenkeeping duties were taken over by Bert Sheldin. At the nearby Mayfield Club, Bertie Way was the pro/greenkeeper and his expertise as greenkeeper was always in demand. Bertie was considered the dean of greenkeepers in Northern Ohio.

By far the best-known Scot in golfing circles to land on the shores of America was Donald Ross. He arrived in 1899 with excellent credentials as a pro/greenkeeper and he accepted a position at the Oakley Club near Boston. From there he expanded his horizons and became the best-known golf course architect of his era. The American Society of Golf Course Architects considers Donald Ross its patron saint.

Golf professionals who served their clubs in the dual capacity as greenkeepers and as pros were by no means ignorant about the maintenance of golf courses. When we examine their beliefs and their theories in the early days, we cannot help but come away impressed. For instance, they believed in composting with a passion and at times they measured a man's competence by the size of his compost pile. Compost at the beginning of the twentieth century consisted of soil and sand, mixed with well-rotted manure or with leaf mold. Seeding the greens prior to composting was common practice. After a summer of busy play, September was the favored time to apply rich compost to stimulate growth of the worn greens. The compost served as a tonic to the tired turf. Even in the early days pro/greenkeepers knew that a seeded green

Joe Mitchell of the Country Club of Cleveland, Ohio.

resulted in a truer putting surface than a green that had been sodded. We must remember that sodding methods in the early 1900s
were very primitive by today's standards.

The Green Committee

There was one matter that greenkeepers, groundsmen and golf
professionals had in common and that was their reservations
about the value of the green chairman and his committee. "They
may be experts in their own field but they know absolutely nothing about the science of greenkeeping" lamented one golf
professional who also had to take care of the golf course, often
under the watchful eye of an interfering green chairman.

In the early days of golf in North America the green chairman
was a powerful voice at most golf clubs. Many chairmen were astute
businessmen with time to spare. They involved themselves with
obtaining information on the art of greenkeeping. They traveled to
other golf courses here and abroad and communicated among
themselves. Because of their position they often hired and fired the
greens staff, they made all the purchases and they formulated the
programs. It was the green chairman who decided with what and
when to fertilize. It was the green chairman who attended meetings
where decisions were made. It was the green chairman under
whose direction greens were rebuilt and bunkers installed.

Some of the enlightened green chairmen in the early days
included Samuel Ryder (of the Ryder Cup), Richard Tufts at
Pinehurst, James Standish, John Reid, and Robert Power from the
Westwood CC in Cleveland, Ohio. These men promoted the
greenkeepers and helped them along on the path toward
respectability.

One of the most powerful green chairman of his day was
Walter Travis at Garden City GC on Long Island. Travis had
gained legitimacy as an expert by winning the U.S. Amateur three
times in a four-year period. In addition he won the British
Amateur in 1904. One year he won eight of 10 tournaments that
he entered. Travis was opinionated and outspoken and he had a
soapbox from which to pontificate: He was the editor and publisher of the *American Golfer*, a magazine that frequently contained
articles on greenkeeping. In his magazine he promulgated his
thoughts on golf course maintenance long before any sources of
information were available. He advocated daily cutting and rolling

and admonished the greenkeepers to take down the height of cut long before the Stimpmeter was invented. The early greenkeepers were reluctant to cut the grass too short because they had inadequate water supplies and their first priority was the survival of the grass and not the speed of the green. Garden City GC greenkeeper Hugh Luke must have had a difficult time of it with such a prominent and opinionated golfer as his boss. But Luke survived and outlived his nemesis.

The powerful influence of the green chairman and his committee would continue for many years. It would not diminish until much later when finally the greenkeeper became superintendent with the help of professional associations.

Before that came to pass, some of the professionals, who also served the club as greenkeeper, began to realize that they had too much on their plate and that it was difficult to do justice to both occupations. The clubs increased their demands on the golf professionals, and they in turn found it difficult to wear two hats. At the same time some of the grounds men who had worked under the direction of the professionals as pseudogreenkeepers, developed their skills and their independence and became full-fledged greenkeepers in their own right. This transition did not come about overnight. It took many years and even today there are still some greenkeepers or golf superintendents who have accepted the role of golf professionals. The first greenkeepers who solely looked after the golf course and no longer had anything to do with the pro shop did not appear until the very end of the nineteenth century.

The First True Greenkeepers

John Pressler, "The Squire" of Pittsburgh

John Pressler in his office with golfing trophies on the mantle. Pressler, one of the first greenkeepers in America, started his career in 1897. In later life his colleagues called John "The Squire." He was held in high regard in his community and the golfing world.

One of the earliest greenkeepers in America was John Pressler. He began his career when he took charge of the Allegheny CC near Pittsburgh, Pennsylvania in 1897 and stayed there for the rest of his working life. Pressler may have been preceded by one G. E. Jacob, also from Pittsburgh, who is reputed to have started his career in 1895.

Prior to becoming greenkeeper, Pressler spent time out west where he was a cowpuncher, panned gold and handled a steam shovel. When the steam shovel fell on him and damaged his leg, he started greenkeeping. He became a leader in the industry who often contributed by writing for the *USGA Green Section Bulletin* and the *National Greenkeeper*. He also spoke at conferences and traveled a great deal in his region visiting other golf courses to learn from his colleagues. In the process he was one of the first advocates of the concept of the exchange of information between greenkeepers.

Pressler started the Greenkeepers Club of Western Pennsylvania, which later became the Tri-State GCSA and he was a founding member of the NAGA. John Pressler maintained experimental grass plots under the direction of the USGA Green Section at the Allegheny CC for most of his professional life. He was always looking for new answers to old questions and was forever experimenting with new methods.

John Pressler in a rocking chair, a gift from his colleagues who honored him for his contributions to golf. Pressler at the time (1940) had been on the payroll of the Allegheny CC for 44 consecutive years, making him the first full-time greenkeeper in North America.

John Sutherland, the Best Greenkeeper in All of Canada!

One of the most prominent greenkeepers in southern Ontario during the early part of the twentieth century was John Sutherland at the Hamilton GC. He came to work for the club as its greenkeeper in 1901 after a few years in a similar position at a Toronto course. Sutherland was an exceptional individual, much trusted and valued by the members at his club. When the Hamilton GC had to move to a new location, the directors instructed Sutherland, "to look over and inspect such properties as might be suitable for the purposes indicated and to gather such information as he could but taking care not to give out what the lands were to be used for." (From *100 Years of Golf*, Hamilton GC centennial booklet.) Sutherland did just that. Travelling by horse and buggy with his wife in tow, he toured the countryside and found just the right kind of property for the members. The club hired Harry Colt to lay out a course and on the recommendation of the great British architect, Sutherland built the new course, because in the words of Colt: "Sutherland is as keen as mustard." With that recommendation Sutherland went to work and was busy directing such individual work as bridge building, laying drain and water pipe, cutting trees, blasting roots, draining swamps, plowing land, and sowing seeds. He was indefatigable.

Sometime early in his greenkeeping days, Sutherland picked out of the ninth green a piece of sod, about a foot square, which he

Testimonials from greenkeepers were frequently used by manufacturing companies. Sutherland is featured in this 1920s ad from Universal Motors Hamilton Limited.

had transferred to the nursery and which had spread rapidly till it covered about two and a half acres. There were no weeds in this grass, which was of a velvet bent variety. It was suggested by the members at Hamilton GC and unanimously agreed that this grass be named Sutherland velvet bent.

Sutherland worked at Hamilton GC for more than 50 years. He died in 1958. Sutherland is fondly remembered at the Hamilton GC but largely forgotten in the annals of greenkeeping. Like so many before and since, he seems to have kept to himself and decided early on that his first priority was responsibility to his employer.

John Shannahan, Dean of New England Greenkeepers

John Shannahan was born in Tipperary, Ireland and came to America in 1887. He started work at Brae Burn CC in Massachusetts in 1901 and was one of the first to grow velvet bentgrass on a sandy loam soil. He is considered the dean of New England greenkeepers in the early days.

William "Rocky" Rockefeller

Unique in the early days, William Rockefeller, a veteran greenkeeper at the Inverness GC, Toledo, Ohio, in the early part of the twentieth century, was not only a master of his craft but also an entertaining essayist when it came to chronicling his everyday work on the golf course. One of the early *Bulletins* of the United States Golf Association contains an article about how he planned his work in the early twenties.

IN THE SPRING

Rockefeller and his crew had been busy all winter overhauling machinery and equipment. The tee boxes and benches had been painted and made to look like new. Tee boxes in the early days contained sand, not for divoting but to raise the ball in the absence of tee pegs, which came later. On the sides of the tee boxes was important information for golfers: the number of the hole and the yardage. New flags and poles were ready to be put out and plenty of sand had been hauled into the bunkers during the winter. All

JOHN SHANAHAN
Brae Burn's veteran greenkeeper

John Shannahan, dean of New England Greenkeepers, came to America from Ireland in 1887 and started to work at the Brae Burn CC in Massachusetts in 1901.

manner of supplies had been purchased for the season. "When gentle spring comes, we shall be ready," said Rocky optimistically.

Golf on regular greens at Inverness often started in March and always by the first of April, but Rocky had become cautious through years of experience and opined that "March may come looking like a lamb, but it is doubtful if any greenkeeper ever saw it otherwise than as a lion! The poor greenkeeper is lucky, especially in the spring, if he accomplishes the half of what he plans."

Just as soon as conditions permitted, Rocky and his crew were out hand-raking or scarifying the fairways to remove the dead material and to encourage early growth. Next the fairways were fertilized with well-rotted barn manure at the rate of four tons per acre. The previous fall the whole course had been top-dressed with mushroom soil at 10 tons per acre. If these rates and quantities stagger the imagination, it must be noted that Inverness at the time had a 1,000 cubic yard stockpile of compost near the barn for future use. Rockefeller and the green committee believed in the natural benefits of compost and manure and were not much given to the use of chemical fertilizers. At times, Rockefeller felt that they were putting on too much fertilizer or manure, resulting in luxuriant growth. Said Rockefeller:

"A course with perfect turf and no bad lies is more of a park than a golf course, but nothing pleases the members more than a soft, deep, heavy turf. Since they pay the rent, my theories must give way."

Burning the rough in early spring was standard practice at many courses and Inverness was no exception. As soon as the grass was dry enough it was torched, which made it easier to cut later and the burning of the old turf rejuvenated and invigorated the new grass. Next the approaches and the greens were raked and sliced and overseeded with South German bentgrass. Rockefeller favored doing this work in the spring, even though late summer seedings were the preferred method, but Rocky looked after his golfers first and then the grass, and freely admits that he did not want to "discommode" the golfers at the busiest time of year (late summer and fall).

DURING THE SEASON

Top-dressing the greens at Inverness was an important part of the maintenance program. The material was applied with shovels and raked in with the backs of wooden rakes. Rockefeller was fortunate to have "Old Matt" on his crew, who could do a better job than anyone else. "Any golfer," said Rockefeller "may well envy the ease of his backswing with a shovel and his follow-through is marvelous, the punch in his swing comes just at the right moment and his finish is beautiful. The topdressing goes on fast, smooth and even." Fifty years before mechanical top-dressers came into being, Rockefeller and Old Matt were doing the work to perfection with shovels and rakes.

With all the work done in an orderly manner, Rockefeller knew that he was as ready as could be but still very much at the mercy of the elements. With a very primitive watering system he was ill equipped to face the burning and destruction of a long, hot summer. Timely rains were his only salvation.

The greens crew at Inverness was kept busy from when the snow melted in the spring till after the leaves dropped in the fall. They cut the greens almost every day and the fairways once or twice a week. They kept the bunkers raked, fought dandelions, pearlwort, buckhorn, chickweed, grubs, moles, and ants, and even chased off the neighbor's hogs on occasion. They filled the tee boxes daily, patched leaky waterlines, listened to advice from members, and apologized for not having moved the tee markers.

THE USGA GREEN SECTION

At a time when much of the management of greenkeeping was still in the hands of the green chairman and his committee, Rockefeller was gaining the respect of his members and expanding his responsibilities. The USGA green committee, made up of "scientists and earnest amateurs," had just been formed and Rockefeller was encouraging his colleagues to lend support: "The professional greenkeeper should assist the USGA by putting at its service all the practical knowledge and experience he has. Both will benefit!" These were prophetic words, from a man who was ahead of his time. True cooperation between the USGA and the greenkeepers would not come for many years. At the time, the USGA was still uncertain how to deal with the greenkeepers. They had yet to learn to talk to these men at their level and in terms that were respectful. The greenkeepers in turn were often suspicious of the motives of the USGA, an organization that represented their employers and many were reluctant to take unasked-for advice. The gap would eventually be bridged but not for several years.

BACKGROUND

William J. Rockefeller had been born on a farm near Harford Mills, New York in 1864, not far from his famous distant cousin John D. He quickly tired of farm work and at various times he became an upholsterer, a musician, and a pharmacist in Binghamton, New York and later worked in an insane asylum in Toledo, Ohio. From there it was an easy step to the Inverness golf course when it was built in 1903. Except for a brief period, Rockefeller remained at Inverness for the rest of his days.

His greenkeeping practice was founded on the common sense of good farming and though progressive, he was not given to experimentation and believed that he should get good value for every dollar spent. His love for the game and his study of its requirements combined to give quality and style to his construction work, which met the practical test of the greenkeeper as well as the spirit of the game. During his lifetime he laid out several courses in Ohio.

"Rocky" played the game rather well, though he was left-handed. On his mantle was a considerable array of trophies, among them a cup won at Midlothian, which proclaimed him as the left-handed champion of the Middle West. He lived in a "capacious" (spacious) house along the course at Inverness, a house that he bought for a song when the golf course was started. He was frequently called upon to advise other golf courses in the area. His professional success must at least in part be attributed to "Mrs. Rocky" who was reputed to be an excellent cook and took good care of him.

"ROCKY" THE INVENTOR

Besides being an excellent greenkeeper, Rockefeller had an inventive streak. One time he purchased an old thrashing machine for $35 and converted it into a topdressing shredder, thus saving Inverness hundreds of dollars. The unit looked like a Rube Goldberg contraption but it worked like flint and the greens crew at Inverness were kept busy during idle hours preparing finely screened topdressing.

Lifting and laying sod in the olden days was a backbreaking job, when everything had to be done by hand before the arrival of machinery. A sod cutter of sorts was available. It consisted of a

Horse-drawn mower.

The roughs were rough in the early days. One way to cut the long grass was to use a horse-drawn sickle bar mower. Another way to eliminate the long grass was to burn it.

The worm eradicant was sprinkled from a short boom at the front. The worms quickly came to the surface, were scooped up and hauled away. The worm poison allegedly had some remedial effect on large and small brown patch.

device very much like a sled with slicing knives attached underneath. The device was weighted down by a small man or rocks. Another man held the handles and a third guided the cutter by taking hold of the cable. A team of horses provided the power to move the cutter through the soil. The strips of sod were cut in three-foot lengths and were 12 inches wide.

While Inverness had been the proud owner of a sod cutter since the beginning of their days, not all greenkeepers were as fortunate as Rockefeller. Many had to rely on the conventional sodding iron, still in use today. An experienced worker could cut squares of sod but these were seldom even on the bottom and had to be shaved down, using either a scythe blade or a draw knife, to the same thickness by means of a cutting box mounted on a table.

WINTERKILL

The Inverness golf course was located in the lee of Lake Erie and enjoyed a relatively mild climate. It is not surprising therefore to hear Rockefeller admit that in 19 years of greenkeeping he had never encountered winterkill. He had however, experienced the extremes of winter weather: Some winters are as cold as "Medicine Hat" (in northern Alberta), others mild and open without snow cover. The worst kind of winter, according to Rockefeller, was one where extreme cold was followed by mild spells, and warm and thawing one day and bitterly cold the next. Rockefeller knew there was a relationship between ice cover and winterkill. Any prolonged ice cover during the winter would set back the turf in spring but it would eventually recover. There must have been very little *Poa annua* on the Inverness greens. According to Rockefeller winterkill was the result of poor drainage, both subdrainage and surface drainage. He did not approve of mulching greens with straw as had been proposed by "inexperienced persons." The mulch might protect against temperature changes of the winter, but it would do more damage in the spring than it benefited all winter. Rockefeller believed that the mulch would stimulate a weak, spindly, unhealthy turf that was likely to perish shortly after the removal of the mulch.

"It seems to me that grass was intended to live out of doors unprotected and that it is more or less hazardous to improve on nature. But drainage is another thing and that involves merely reproducing the best conditions of nature. If grass growing in a well drained location is doing better than

that which is covered at times by water or ice, it seems reasonable to provide good drainage."

As simple as all that and the advice from this modest man is as valid today as it was many years ago.

ON WATERING

"If I were free to do as I wished, and had all the money and facilities necessary, I would water greens at night for the reason that it is cooler then and there is less evaporation. The difficulty is that there is no sprinkling equipment that distributes water evenly and I have been unable to find a man who could go around in the dark and place the equipment so that the green is watered evenly. Therefore, we have decided that it is most practical to water greens by hand, the first thing in the morning."

Some highly trained superintendents with very sophisticated irrigation systems do precisely that almost 75 years later. Rockefeller preferred watering by hand because he could see what he was doing. Having watered greens at all times of day and night, he did not think that it made a difference one way or the other. He had reservations about applying cool water during the heat of day because it would give the grass a shock. The most important consideration was to water evenly and sufficiently, according to the old pro.

Rocky suffered a calamity during the 1920 USGA Open that was held at Inverness in August of that year. His greens had been

Rocky, the inventor, converted an old thrasher into a top-dressing shredder.

devastated by "small brown patch" or dollar spot as the disease became known later. The greens were virtually unputtable. As a result of this disaster the USGA called an emergency meeting that led to the formation of the Green Section later in the year. Another offshoot of the 1920 greens disaster was that, from then on, the date for successive Opens was advanced to July, and later to June, when better course conditions prevailed.

William "Rocky" Rockefeller on his black stallion, inspecting the Inverness Golf Course in Toledo, Ohio during the early 1900s. Note that Rocky is wearing jacket and tie, as was common for supervisors in that era. Most greenkeepers walked the course to get around, some used a bicycle. Motorized vehicles for greenkeepers did not arrive until the 1930s.

ROCKY MADE AN HONORARY MEMBER

In 1925 William Rockefeller had reached the summit of his career. He had molded a sound design into a fine golf course and he had successfully prepared the Inverness golf course for several major championships. He was acclaimed as one of the best greenkeepers in the nation. Some cynical persons would say "self proclaimed" because Rockefeller had not done his work in obscurity. He had written knowledgeably in the turf journals of his time. He was often quoted and his advice was sought at other golf courses. He had been at Inverness since the course was started as a nine-hole layout in 1903, except for one brief period. He had helped Donald Ross create one of his greatest masterpieces when Inverness was expanded and refurbished in 1919.

Green committees had come and gone at the club but Rockefeller had remained year after year. He had taught new committees about the intricacies of greenkeeping so that they could better communicate with the golfers. When a problem arose, the members would automatically ask: "Well, what does Rocky think of it?" He was a dependable source of knowledge and had become a fixture on his tall horse trotting around the course. The club decided to show its gratitude to the greenkeeper and he was made an honorary member at a time when many of his colleagues were not even allowed in the clubhouse.

PROFESSIONAL ACTIVITY

The Cleveland District Greenkeepers' Association was formed in May of 1923 and Rockefeller quickly became a member. A few years later he attended the founding meeting of the National Association of Greenkeepers of America (NAGA) at the neighboring Sylvania CC. Not only was Rocky a charter member of the newly formed NAGA, he also became the association's first secretary. For a while he waited in the wings to become president, but founding president John Morley was well ensconced and there was no opportunity for Rockefeller to advance. He did, however, fully support the aspirations of the new association and was a frequent contributor to the *National Greenkeeper*.

RECORD KEEPING

The development of the USGA Green Section led to the inevitable budget comparisons between sections of the country and even individual golf courses, but there was no standard of comparison, no yardstick that could be used to compare one operation to another. Rockefeller realized that greenkeeping was in many ways a very inexact science, mostly because no two greenkeepers did things exactly alike. He had observed that: "Some greenkeepers are very particular and give the job of changing cups and markers to one man. Others permit that work to be done by the man who cut the greens. Every greenkeeper has his own way of doing his work and he thinks that way is better than any other. He thinks he is right and knows perfectly well that everyone else is wrong." Some semblance of order was needed, and Rocky created what must have been one of the first time sheets on golf course record keeping.

One of the early hole cutters.

Some only looked after the golf course proper, others were responsible as well for roads, clubhouse grounds, and even hauling firewood. The bottom lines of such operations bore no resemblance to each other.

APPLYING AMMONIUM SULFATE

Although Rockefeller for many years relied solely on compost, manure, and mushroom soil to fertilize his turf, later in life he did incorporate ammonium sulfate into his program, but very cautiously. Ammonium sulfate was a powerful fertilizer that could easily burn the grass, so Rocky took precautions: he used sprinkling cans and dissolved one-half the amount of fertilizer that he intended to use into 50 gallons of water. Let Rocky tell the rest of the story:

"We put this solution on with sprinkling cans, the men walking slowly backward, swinging the can from right to left and covering the green with the 50 gallons. We then use the other half portion in a like manner, only crossing the green in the opposite direction." For good measure he watered the green in well with a hose. Although sprinkling was a more expensive method of application, Rockefeller preferred it to mixing the sulfate with sand, which is how most greenkeepers at the time applied the fertilizer.

Not only was Rocky a fine turfman, he was also a teacher and graduated two prominent superintendents: Joe Mayo at Pebble Beach and Al Schardt at the Buffalo CC. Rocky worked hard to prepare his course for the 1931 U.S. Open. He died suddenly in 1932 at age 67.

Turfgrass in the Early Days

The North American conception of a fine sward of green grass at the turn of the century was often based on a typical English lawn of creeping bent, fescue, and bluegrasses. How did such lawns come about and how could they be created in America? The answer was simplistic: "First you level it, seed it and water it and then you roll it, for about 100 years." Few gardeners had the patience to make English lawns in America that way and they looked for shortcuts and found them on the golf courses. Ever since golf began, the greenkeeper has been the resident expert on the establishment and maintenance of fine lawns as well as golf courses. Their livelihood depended on their ability to produce quality turf for the playing fields and there is no better motivation than economic necessity. Greenkeepers learned quickly that they had to be good to keep their jobs and in the process they became the experts in their field.

The early greens were seeded to a mixture of bent and red fescue. The bent was imported from Germany and became known as South German bent, which contained variable proportions of colonial, creeping, and velvet bents. With the outbreak of World War I, trade with Germany ceased and another source had to be found. Rhode Island bent and New Zealand browntop became satisfactory substitutes. At the same time agrostologist Lyman Carrier, near Coos Bay, Oregon, found a true creeping bent which was initially called Coos County bent and eventually Seaside bentgrass.

With the prevailing methods of cutting the grass at one-quarter inch and higher, accompanied by regular watering and fertilizing and aided by the warm summer temperatures, the fescue soon disappeared from the mix, and around 1900 greens consisted mostly of a mix of a colonial and creeping bentgrass with the omnipresent *Poa annua* germinating naturally to form the turf. The greens were frequently quite rough for lack of regular cutting. The early greenkeepers protected the grass at the expense of the requirements of the game. With time they would learn that daily cutting at a lower height did not spell disaster for the turf, but the age-old conflict between what's good for golf and what's good for grass was discovered very early in the establishment of the game. Till this day that enigma has never been resolved satisfactorily to please both ardent golfers and professional superintendents.

Dr. Walter Harban on the green committee at the Columbia GC near Washington, DC, states in 1911: "For years it was impossible to get a greenkeeper to cut the greens close in the summer. After much insistence and finally absolute demand, the greens were cut not only every day, but very close. The improvement was so marked in quality, texture, and strength of grass after the hot weather was over that the greenkeeper now resents the suggestion even to let them go for a day." Dr. Harban further advises "to get the surface of your greens true by heavy rolling in early spring, followed afterward by frequent light rolling with the wooden roller." Dr. Harban did not live to see the Stimpmeter but if he had, he would have loved it. But long before the invention of the speed stick the roller was one of the most important greenkeeping tools. The first greenkeeper at Columbia GC was J. H. Links, an African-American.

The green committee had become all-powerful and the chairman of the committee was almost as important in a club's hierarchy as the captain. Whereas the committee members may have known a thing or two about golf, they knew very little about the culture of golf course grass on a day-to-day basis. The most important book about golf course maintenance was not published until 1917. Prior to that date, the authors, Drs. Piper and Oakley, had already become established as authorities on the subject. The need for qualified greenkeepers became more pressing as the game of golf grew in popularity and the maintenance of fine turf became more complex. Yet the profession was still in its infancy.

Three Eras of Greenkeeping

According to Fred Hawkins, longtime greenkeeper at the Lakeview CC near Toronto, the early days of greenkeeping can be divided into three distinct stages, and since there are no higher authorities, we gladly accept the opinions of our esteemed colleague:

1. The era of single horse machine or the pony mower
2. The triple cut machine era
3. The era of the tractor

1. In the single horse era, Hawkins states that: "All the implements they had was one single horse machine, three hand machines to cut the greens, one team of horses with two barrels on a wagon and a hand pump to water the greens when necessary and two heavy rollers. In the summer when the grass was growing good, they turned about 200 sheep loose on the course to help the one-horse machine. After a spell of wet weather, it seemed a race between the sheep making holes in the wet fairways and a steam roller rolling them out."

2. As golf became more popular we enter the triple cut machine era: single horse pulling a three-gang set of gang mowers. Many more new courses were built and more attention was paid to the construction of the greens. Instead of working the greens up out of old sod, they were slightly shaped and a few bunkers put in and the greens sodded with some of the finer grass mixtures. Play demanded closer putting surfaces. Water systems were installed for the greens, and fairway mowers were made in gangs of three instead of one but were still drawn by a single horse.

3. Now comes the era of the tractor, beginning in 1918. The greens have become boldly molded and heavily bunkered. The putting surfaces are seeded with one of the fine grasses instead of with a mixture of bent and fescue, or are put down with bent stolons. The size of greens increases from 3,000-4,000 sq. ft. to over 10,000 sq. ft. Tractors that started with three fairway gangs have increased to five and even seven. Fairway watering systems have become common on most new courses.

Hawkins's arbitrary division of the three different eras of green-keeping corresponds roughly to the end of the first era leading up to the turn of century. The second era covers the time period leading up to the end of World War I. The era of the tractor takes us up to World War II. There is of course plenty of overlap at different courses in various parts of the country. Some courses used horses well into the 1930s. Others used sheep to graze the fairways in the early part of the twentieth century. The essential matter is that the development of golf courses was on the move.

The Bible of Greenkeeping

When the book *Turf for Golf Courses* was published in 1917, scientific greenkeeping became the order of the day. Green committees and green chairmen realized that they needed better qualified greenkeepers and that golf professionals who doubled as greenkeepers would no longer do. The book by Drs. Piper and Oakley was a giant step forward but in terms of today's knowledge, the recommendations must be taken with a grain of salt, and bring faint smiles to our faces. The remedies for turf problems were quite primitive in today's terms but at the beginning of the century that's all the knowledge that was available.

Greenkeeping Remedies for Putting Greens in 1916

Crabgrass . . . . . . Pluck it
Clover . . . . Cut it out
Dandelion . . . . . Inject gasoline into the crown
Plantain . . . . Dig it out
Moles . . . . Trap with the harpoon trap
Field Mice . . . . . Poison with strychnine mixed with crushed
           wheat
Earthworms . . . . Spray with bichloride of mercury diluted
           in water
Ants . . . . Inject carbon bisulfide with an oil spout
Grubs . . . . Push a ¼" rod into the opening and spear
           the grub

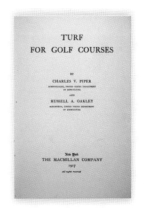

The book Turf For Golf Courses *by Drs. Piper and Oakley quickly became the bible of greenkeeping and lent esteem and credibility to its authors.*

Dr. Piper was an authority on turf culture at a time when very little scientific knowledge on greenkeeping existed. His sudden death in 1926 shocked the industry. It was said of Dr. Piper that "In Storm and in sunshine, he was the greenkeeper's friend."

Qualifications for Greenkeepers circa 1910

Hugh Wilson, green chairman at the Merion GC in Philadelphia, Pennsylvania, opines about the requirements for a greenkeeper in the era prior to World War I and emphasizes the need of budgeting:

"We have found that a greenkeeper should be a man who can diagnose any trouble quickly and who will nurse the grass with infinite care. He must watch the course every day and practically all day as changes come very rapidly in turf. One of the greatest failings of greenkeepers is due to the lack of thought on the part of the committees. They have never taught them thoroughly the question of cost. After careful study, one of the committee members has worked out a budget, which shows the detailed cost of the work month by month for the whole year. Of course this cannot be adhered to in every detail but the main object is to put the plan before the greenkeeper so that he can see just what he has to do and how much money he has to do it with. It is most important to make the greenkeeper think in dollars and cents. The usual answer to a question of, 'Do you think you can do this,' will be: 'Oh Yes, It is not a very big job.' But if you ask the same man what it would cost, it would be hard for him to give an answer. The cost of mowing fairways and greens in addition to all the general cost, becomes an interesting and most profitable study. It is a very simple matter for the greenkeeper to keep track of the cost of a new bunker or the sodding of a green, and each time he does it, he learns a little more about the cost question and why it is such an important factor in all work. It also gives the greenkeeper a new interest in the work and a basis for comparison. We believe that you will find that a greenkeeper is keener for knowing that the last bunker cost $20.80 to build and the next one will cost a little less because he figured out a way to do it more cheaply. We have obtained splendid results by sending our greenkeeper to as many courses as possible in order that he may see what other persons are doing and profit by their good results as well as by their errors."

Other Greenkeepers at the Beginning of the Twentieth Century

John Gray was born in 1885 on a farm near Aberdeen, Scotland. In 1907 he immigrated to Canada and worked with architect Harry Colt in the Detroit area. In 1913 he supervised the construction of

Essex GC near Windsor, Ontario. Then he went off to war, but missed all the action when he was assigned to train bagpipers for the trench warfare.

William Flynn was the first greenkeeper at the Merion GC when it was laid out by Hugh Wilson in 1911. He stayed for a short time and then became full-time architect. He was succeeded by Joe Valentine who was hired at the Merion Cricket Club in 1907 before there was even a golf course. He became construction foreman when the course was built. Valentine's talents as greenkeeper contributed much to the fame of that old course.

Emil "Dutch" Loeffler started his life in golf as a caddie and became greenkeeper in 1913 at the Oakmont GC in Pittsburgh at the young age of 21. He remained all his working days at Oakmont and at times he served both as professional and greenkeeper. He also dabbled in golf course architecture and construction as a sideline. Loeffler was an excellent golfer who won several tournaments but he is best remembered for the furrows he left in the sand bunkers at Oakmont, which helped make the golf course the toughest in the country.

In Ohio, John Morley and Fred Burkhardt were being recognized as established greenkeepers and were already dreaming of starting an association for greenkeepers. In Chicago, John MacGregor had the same aspirations. In the real world, away from the golf course, there were storm clouds on the horizon.

World War I

Trench warfare during World War I from 1914-1918 brought golf in continental Europe and England to nearly a standstill. The American involvement in the conflict did not start till 1917 and quickly led to the termination of the war a year later on the 11th hour of the 11th day of the 11th month. When the soldiers came back after the war, golf continued its unabated march forward and at an increasing rate involving all classes of society. The roaring twenties and the golden age of golf were about to start.

Chapter Three

Between the Wars

1919-1945

By Gordon Witteveen

Chandler Egan, well-known amateur golfer, advises Pebble Beach greenkeeper Joe Mayo in 1929 prior to the National Amateur Championship. Joe Mayo learned greenkeeping at the Inverness GC in Ohio under the tutelage of Rocky Rockefeller.

With the conclusion of World War I, Americans were anxious to put the great war behind them and to get on with life in peace and prosperity. The time that followed the European conflict quickly became an era of economic expansion on the North American continent. It resulted in mass consumption of manufactured goods, which included automobiles and radios, and the rise of the movie industry. It was also the era of prohibition and gangsters, and for some it was a decade-long dance party until the stock market crash in 1929 put a damper on things. The Roaring Twenties were the beginning of modern America. The era gave birth to suburban living as we know it today, and for the prosperous middle class that meant country club membership.

Like the rest of the economy the golf course industry was expanding. There was more leisure time for the wage earners, and where better to spend that time than on the golf course? Hundreds of thousands and eventually millions took up golf and quickly became addicted, as people have ever since. The new players demanded more and better golf courses. The demand was met by some of the greatest designers that golf has ever known and the era became known as the golden age of golf design. Some of the most famous and best courses of all times were constructed during this period, among them Pinehurst, Baltusrol, Westchester CC, Cypress Point, Florida's Seminole and California's Riviera, to mention but a few.

Public Golf

A contrast in dress circa 1930: on the left, greenkeeper Erich Paul of the Interlachen CC in Minneapolis. Paul is flanked by (LEFT TO RIGHT) Willie Kidd, the club's professional, National Amateur Champion Jimmy Johnston and Green Chairman Charles van Nest, with the bowler hat.

It was not only private country clubs that experienced growth. Public golf was also on the rise at a rapid rate. The first public golf course in the United States was the Cobb Creek Park course in Philadelphia, which was established in 1898. Twenty years later almost any city or town worthy of the name had at least one municipal golf course and the city of Toledo, Ohio had three courses. Most municipal courses offered free golf to its taxpaying citizens and others charged minimal amounts, ranging from 25 cents to one dollar. An annual membership could often be obtained for as little as 10 dollars. Nevertheless when the fees were doubled at the Van Cortlandt Park golf course in New York, the golfers rebelled. The disgruntled players were not just upset with the increase in dues. What really added to their ire was that course conditions had deteriorated drastically. Apart from the incident at Van Cortlandt Park, golfers flocked to the municipal courses in large and astounding numbers. The Lincoln Park 9-hole golf course in Chicago issued 107,600 green fee tickets in just one season. The 18-hole Jackson Park in the same city did even better: 125,000 golfers teed off in 1922 alone. At the nearby Olympia Fields GC, a private facility with three 18-hole courses, only 60,000 rounds were recorded. Private operators of public golf courses also flourished in these flush times. The Harlem golf course, also in Chicago, charged two-dollar green fees and cleared $43,000 after expenses in 1921. The following year the owners did even better. They profited $75,000 from their golf operations.

Certainly the boom of public golf was not limited to Chicago, but the fact that Gene Sarazen won the U.S. Open in 1922 at the Skokie CC in Chicago may have provided extra incentive for Chicagoans to take up the new sport. Sarazen also won the PGA Championship that year. This dapper man, dressed in plus fours and from humble immigrant beginnings, became an instant golfing hero in his time and added even more to the popularity of the game.

Greenkeepers in the 1920s

For the greenkeepers, the twenties were also an era of growth and development. Gradually the responsibilities of maintaining the golf courses were shifted from the golf professional and the green chairman to the greenkeeper. The twenties saw the establishment of the USGA Green Section, the arrival of the golf course tractor, turfgrass research at state colleges, winter courses for greenkeepers, the birth of our first regional associations or clubs for greenkeepers, and then the arrival of the National Association of Greenkeepers of America in 1926.

TOP AND MIDDLE: *Construction of golf courses was often primitive, involving much handwork and scrapers drawn by horses. Horses were gradually phased out and tractors took their place.*

BOTTOM: *Golf course construction at Squaw Creek GC in Texas included equipment and techniques from old and new methodology.*

The USGA Green Section

Stirrings for better playing conditions on golf courses can be found as early as 1906. Dr. Walter Harban, an avid golfer and the

The Arlington Turf Gardens were established in 1928 at the current location of the Pentagon. In the early years, meetings were conducted at the Gardens for greenkeepers and green chairmen.

green chairman at the Columbia CC, Columbia, Maryland, paid an exploratory visit to the United States Department of Agriculture (USDA) in the nation's capital. He was looking for scientific information regarding turf problems at his home golf course. It was fortuitous that he made contact with Drs. Piper and Oakley, who were experts in the culture of pasture grasses. Dr. Piper also happened to be a golfer and took an immediate interest in the grass problems that Dr. Harban presented. During the ensuing years Drs. Piper and Oakley and Dr. Harban continued to meet at regular intervals and were often joined by Dr. Lyman Carrier, a plant pathologist with the USDA. They discussed and developed the first attempts at scientific methods for greenkeeping. Piper, born in Canada and educated at the University of Washington State, was the expert on grasses. Oakley's expertise was soils, and Lyman Carrier's specialty was plant diseases.

In the early days of golf, greenkeepers and chairmen were often at the mercy of unscrupulous seed salesmen, who tried to sell seed of questionable origin and usually recommended far more seed than was needed. Drs. Piper and Oakley changed all that. With the cooperation of the USDA these experts worked together to look after the needs of a fledgling industry. They often tested samples of seed sent for germination and purity. They received inquiries by mail and answered without fail. Piper traveled widely in Europe and Africa checking grasses in pastures and on golf courses.

In 1916 the USDA established the Arlington Turf Gardens at precisely the same location where the Pentagon now stands. Drs. Piper and Oakley laid out the different plots of grasses and experimented extensively. One of the early managers of the Turf Garden was O.B. Fitts, who in later years became greenkeeper at the Columbia CC, where he served from 1928 till 1955.

When Piper returned from his travels abroad, he collaborated with Oakley to write a book titled *Turf for Golf Courses*. It was an extensive document filled with information that hitherto had not been available from one source. Not only were the pages filled with theory, but practical experiences of Dr. Harban at the Columbia CC added to the reader's knowledge as well. Work continued on the book throughout 1916 and it was finally published the following year with assistance from the USGA. It quickly became the standard reference for "scientific" golf course maintenance. While some practical minded greenkeepers might have been suspicious of book knowledge at first, they soon changed their minds. Green chairmen welcomed the treatise immediately as a source of indispensable information.

The most serious problem on golf greens in the northeast and central U.S. was large and small brown patch, both fungus diseases. What was then referred to as small brown patch became later known as dollar spot. There was no cure available, although some scientists and enterprising greenkeepers experimented with bordeaux mixture, used in apple orchards mixed with corrosive sublimate. Few greens escaped the invasion of this tenacious disease. On many courses, during late summer the greens were dotted with the pockmarks of small brown patch and became almost unplayable. Such was the case when the U.S. Open was played at the Inverness Club in Toledo, Ohio in August 1920. Even the talented Rocky Rockefeller, the greenkeeper at Inverness, had no answer for this serious problem.

The USGA, with the reputation of its major tournament at stake, went into action. At a meeting on November 30, 1920, the USGA Executive Committee responded by creating the Green Section of the United States Golf Association. Its purpose was to assist with proper maintenance and upkeep of golf courses. In order to accomplish this goal, Dr. C.V. Piper, was appointed chairman, while Dr. Oakley and Dr. Carrier from the USDA as well as

Hole cutting in the 1920s.

At first greenkeepers used flat-bladed spades to cut the sod into squares. The squares were then trimmed to obtain even thickness. When the horse-drawn sled was introduced, it was a great improvement that speeded the process.

13 club officials were appointed to the Executive Committee of the newly formed Green Section. There were great expectations of the newly formed Green Section but all realized that Rome was not built in one day. It would take time to improve course conditioning. Because of the disease problems at the Open in August 1920, the date for the 1921 Open was moved to July and later to June, where it has remained.

The Green Section was for many years an independent body. It was not until the Depression that the parent organization assumed full financial responsibility for the turfgrass advisory body. The mandate of the Green Section in 1921 was:

1. To collect and distribute information for the benefit of its members
2. To promote the proper maintenance and upkeep of golf courses
3. To establish a service bureau to help individual clubs with their problems
4. To help with the training of greenkeepers
5. To issue a bulletin filled with greenkeeping information for the benefit of Green Chairmen and Greenkeepers
6. To organize an annual meeting of the Green Section at which papers were to be presented and discussions on greenkeeping take place
7. To encourage the creation of regional green committees.

The annual dues for the Green Section were $15 for member USGA clubs and $20 for nonmembers. By the end of 1921 almost 400 clubs had signed up as members, including more than 25 from Canada.

By February 1921, just three months after the initial meeting, two issues of the *Bulletin* were published and widely distributed. They contained practical and scientific information for committee chairmen and for the benefit of individual greenkeepers. There were 37 pages filled with extensive and valuable information and no advertising. The *Bulletin* proudly announced that: "The Green Section wishes to maintain independence of thought." To this day, the same principle has applied.

The first greenkeeper to contribute to the *Bulletin* was William Rockefeller from the Inverness Club in Toledo. Not far behind was Rockefeller's former assistant Joe Mayo who had become greenkeeper at Pebble Beach in California. In the November issue of 1921 there was a featured article and photo of "Notable Greenkeeper" John Shannahan of Brae Burn CC, Massachusetts. Many prominent greenkeepers were quoted and had their experiences printed for all to read. We can assume that the greenkeepers most often quoted were from clubs with active chairmen on the USGA Green Section Committee or from clubs that hosted major tournaments.

The first annual meetings of the Green Section took place in September of 1921 at the St. Louis CC and the Merion Cricket Club. The meetings were addressed by Drs. Piper and Carrier and featured discussions on turfgrass identification, irrigation, fungus diseases, grubs and an exhibition of mowers and machinery. The meetings attracted as many as 350 club officials and some greenkeepers. The *Bulletin* subsequently reported that "The meetings will be to the greenkeepers' personal advantage, will enlarge his field of acquaintance, bring himself useful information and perhaps increase his earning power."

Applying bordeaux mixture for the control of large and small brown patch —with the duster (TOP), and with a grass seeder wheelbarrow. (BOTTOM)

Joe Valentine, America's Famous Greenkeeper

Much has been written about Joe Valentine, America's famous greenkeeper. The story of his life is best related by his granddaughter, Christina Valentine-Owsik, who wrote about her grandfather at the time of the 75th anniversary of the Eastern Pennsylvania GCSA. The following article was published for the *Bonnie Greensward*, a publication of the chapter.

"Born in Abruzzi, Italy in 1886 as Guiseppi Valentini, he felt his original calling was to the priesthood, and attended an Italian seminary for a number of years. But his continuing correspondence with relatives and friends, who had found their dream in America, inspired him to emigrate, which he did at age 19 in 1906. He Anglicized his name to Joe Valentine and took a job with a bank in Camden, N.J. He also enrolled at night school to learn English. Joseph Valentine embodied the enthusiasm and tireless drive of so many new Americans of his era.

"Then, at age 21, he was struck by tuberculosis. Doctors advised him to find a job working outdoors for the good of his health. In 1907 he became a grounds worker at the Merion Cricket Club, in Ardmore, PA. When Merion's East Course was laid out in 1912, Valentine became foreman under greenkeeper William Flynn. When the latter had to take a

*Watering fairways was a tedious
process with miles of hoses and
primitive sprinklers. By necessity,
much of the watering took place
in the daytime.*

*leave of absence to do war work in 1918, Valentine became temporary
greenkeeper. After the war Flynn returned briefly but then left to help
launch the famed golf course design firm of Toomey and Flynn.*

*"Thus, at age 32, Valentine was made Merion's greenkeeper, a position
he would hold for the next 45 years. During that time he earned prominence as one of golf's best-known turf experts. And Merion would earn
prominence as one of the best golf courses worldwide. Over the years
Valentine maintained a close working relationship with William Flynn,
partly because their skills were complementary: Valentine, an expert on
turfgrass and course maintenance and Flynn, a well-known golf architect
skilled in course construction.*

*"Deeply interested in agronomy and a student all his life, Valentine
persuaded Penn State College in 1919 to establish a formalized course for
greenkeepers, the first in the U.S. Also in 1919, Valentine married Adelina
Talone, the daughter of a prosperous Italian tailor in Bryn Mawr, PA.
Four of their six children survived childhood and all three boys worked on
the golf course. Ritchie, the youngest, eventually succeeded his father as
superintendent.*

*"Joe Valentine was a dedicated agronomist who continually searched
for new strains of grasses. The most famous of his findings was Merion
bluegrass. He discovered it behind the 17th tee at Merion. It was a hardy
grass that withstood low cutting at one inch and it was used for American
fairways, sports fields, and even for the White House lawns. In 1961 Joe
Valentine retired from the Merion Golf Club at age 75 and in 1964 he was
awarded the USGA Green Section Award for his lifelong service to golf.
He was the first superintendent to gain that distinction. Joe Valentine died
on March 18, 1966 one day short of his 80th birthday.*

*"He will be forever remembered, not only as discoverer of Merion
bluegrass and for putting the Merion Golf Club on the map, but also as one
of the earliest greenkeepers to gain recognition for the profession."*

Dean Hill, the Merion Green Chairman at the time of Joe
Valentine's death remarked that their superintendent had acted
"pretty much the part of course architect during his long years of
service." This statement confirms that Joe Valentine was largely
responsible for the prominent position of the Merion East Course
in the annals of golf. During Joe Valentine's 45 years of dedicated
greenkeeping, Merion hosted 11 USGA major events but never a
PGA competition. Joe Valentine gave much credit for his success
to the fact that Merion's green chairmen served for long periods of
time and were always supportive of his work. During his first 25
years of greenkeeping, Joe Valentine worked with only four green
chairmen. The most famous of Merion Green Chairmen was

Hugh Wilson, who often contributed to the *Green Section Bulletin*.

Because of his relationship with the famous Merion golf course, as well as his excellent professional reputation, Joe Valentine was often called upon to consult at other courses. After completing all the important work at Merion in the morning, he would take the afternoon to visit other courses. His wife Adelina, who liked drives in the countryside and along the ocean shore, would come along but frequently ended up sitting in the car patiently waiting for her husband to return. One time, waiting in the Merion parking lot for her husband, her patience ran out. She left the car and found Joe near the putting green in deep conversation with several Merion committeemen. She sternly approached the group and said: *"Look it, I am not his bitch! I am his wife and I am tired of waiting."* Joe left the meeting and went driving with his wife.

Adelina made no secret of the hardship of being a green-keeper's wife. She warned her daughter never to marry a greenkeeper, *"Or you'll become a golf widow for sure."* The Valentine's only daughter listened, but not their granddaughter, Chistina. She received the same advice from her grandmother but nevertheless married Joe Owsik, who is the superintendent at the Philmont CC in Pennsylvania.

Joe Valentine never forgot his Italian roots. He employed many new Italian immigrants and encouraged them to learn the English language. He was also a better than average golfer but he never played with the Merion members. It just was not done in those days. He did play in the annual Knights of Columbus Tournament.

Joe Valentine, highly regarded greenkeeper at the Merion Cricket Club.

Valentine points to the spot near the 17th tee where he discovered Merion bluegrass. Interested golfers are on the tee nearby.

The year this tournament was held on the Merion West course, Joe won the trophy. He also played in the competitions with his colleagues in the Philadelphia Greenkeepers Association as well as in the national event.

Joe Valentine attended many conferences during the winter season but his favorite was the annual Penn State Conference. Valentine and his buddies would rent the corner room at the Nittany Lion Inn and they would sit there for hours on end discussing grass and golf courses. Eb Steiniger was there, so was Marshall Farnham, and Burt Musser and many others including some young students, shyly listening in. Among the students was a young undergraduate named Joe Duich.

Rich Valentine followed in his father's footstep, attended Penn State College and worked at Merion for many years but received no special treatment. He relates how his father, a dyed-in-the-wool Republican, found Rich's car in the Merion parking lot with a Democratic bumper sticker. Rich was called on the carpet in his father's office and was given the choice of removing the sticker or being fired. The choice was easy and Rich remained.

The members at Merion treated Joe Valentine, their greenkeeper, with the greatest respect. This was brought home to Sherwood Moore, an aspiring young superintendent at the time, who visited with Valentine in the 1940s. For up-and-coming turf managers, a pilgrimage to Merion was essential and part of the education in becoming a superintendent. Moore was just a rookie at his craft when he made the trip to Ardmore. He found Valentine in the maintenance area behind the clubhouse dressed in his usual jacket, white shirt, and tie. Moore addressed his much older colleague by calling him "Joe" and was cut off almost immediately and put in his place. Valentine reminded his visitor that even the members called him "Mister."

USGA Green Section Expands

The powers that be in the Green Section quickly realized that more benefits could be derived from frequent regional meetings than from just one annual national meeting. The establishment of regional Green Sections was heartily encouraged and the first off the mark was the Philadelphia Green Section, no doubt with much encouragement from green chairman Hugh Wilson and greenkeeper Joe Valentine. Other regional Green Sections were established in Chicago, New York, and Cleveland. The early meetings of these regional Green Sections were presided over by the green chairmen, but it must be noted that many chairmen invited their greenkeepers to also attend the early meetings. At the Skokie CC in Chicago, in the summer of 1922, Dr. Piper addressed the meeting and was peppered with questions from all in attendance.

It was at these initial meetings of the Green Section that greenkeepers got to know one another. Up until that time greenkeepers in the same city or area often had not met personally. The common interests quickly led to friendships and the sharing of information. Groups of greenkeepers started to meet informally without the benefit of associations, and it was only a matter of time for formal greenkeeping associations to be formed.

The establishment of the Cleveland District Green Section is significant because it involved an interesting lady called Gertrude Farley who would play a role for some time during the ensuing years of the greenkeeping movement. Farley was employed as an administrative secretary to Mr. J. K. Bole, who was green chairman at the Mayfield CC in Cleveland. Together they established a regional Green Section in 1921. Their main emphasis was on cooperative buying and in early 1922 they secured a deal with a tractor company that resulted in great savings for the members of their group. They also purchased seed collectively and had it tested for germination and purity by Drs. Piper and Oakley in Washington. Membership in the association was by no means inexpensive: $50 per nine holes and $100 for 18 holes. At a time when green fees were often one dollar or less, this was a substantial amount. The money-saving benefits were obvious and the Cleveland group quickly grew in numbers. In 1922, 17 clubs belonged and the following year that number almost doubled. For the clubs the membership fees were an investment, which in many cases showed handsome benefits. Some clubs saved from $200 to $900 and one new course, during the process of construction realized a saving of $1,200. No wonder then that Farley and Bole found it necessary to open an office. They did so in February of 1923 for the purpose of handling the business on a larger scale. Gertrude Farley's position with the Cleveland District Green Section was firmly established. There is no doubt that during these early years she became acquainted with John Morley and Fred Burkhardt, two prominent greenkeepers in that area. She also knew Robert Power, who was the Green Chairman at Westwood CC. Power was president of the

John Morley in his stolon nursery at the Youngstown CC, Ohio in 1927. Morley often shared his stolons with other golf courses and encouraged his colleagues to start their own nursery. The lady in the picture is a green-keeper's wife: Mrs. Rees from New York. Almost certainly the photo was snapped by her husband.

Cleveland District Golf Association. Both Power and Farley were fond of the local greenkeepers. Farley, besides running the co-op, also wrote articles for the *Cleveland District Golfer* magazine addressing the plight of the greenkeepers. Power went a step further: he encouraged greenkeepers to become organized and form their own association independent from the Green Section. The seeds were planted and on May 12, 1923, the Cleveland District Greenkeepers Association was born under the leadership of John Morley. It happened at the Youngstown CC where Morley was the greenkeeper. Notwithstanding a cold rain, 40 greenkeepers and/or chairmen attended.

The first few meetings of this new association were all conducted under the auspices of the District Green Section Committee. For the first several meetings a green chairman chaired the meeting. It was not that Morley lacked confidence to take the chair. To the contrary, he was a fluent speaker but also a humble man, respectful of his employers. Eventually, John Morley took over the running of the monthly meetings. Fred Burkhardt from the Westwood GC became the first secretary. Support and encouragement were received from Robert Power, Westwood Green Chairman and the indomitable Gertrude Farley.

In the September 1924 issue of the *Green Section Bulletin*, Morley writes that he was elected on May 12th, 1924. This causes confusion because the Cleveland newspapers at the time reported that the meeting took place in May of 1923. Therefore John Morley was either mistaken or there was a typographical error in the *Bulletin*. More than likely the latter was the case.

Elmer Michael, back center with tie, with his crew at the Transit Valley Club near Buffalo, NY.

James Lyon, greenkeeper at the Flintridge GC in Pasadena, California, reported in the 1931 *Green Section Bulletin* that a greenkeepers association was established informally in Southern California in 1921 but later disbanded. The Southern California group reorganized in 1926. Similarly the Connecticut Greenkeepers Association met informally in 1923 but the New England Greenkeepers Club, under the chairmanship of John Shannahan, did not come to life until a meeting took place in February of 1924.

It is difficult to determine with certainty which was first, the local

green section or the greenkeepers club. In most cases, once the greenkeepers became acquainted with one another at the green section meetings, they took the initiative and formed their own associations. In rapid succession, greenkeepers became organized all over the United States and Canada. An interesting deviation took place in Ontario, Canada, when the greenkeepers became organized, with much prodding from their club managers, on October 4, 1924. A decisive William Sansom took the reigns and ruled the Ontario group with a firm hand for the next 10 years. In Ontario, green chairmen and golf professionals did not attend the greenkeeping meetings. Nor were they eligible for membership.

All regional organizations held regular monthly meetings at golf courses. Often they invited speakers from state colleges or representatives from the Green Section. Piper, Oakley, and Carrier frequently addressed these meetings. The Cleveland group added golf to the meetings in 1925, but they continued to invite outside speakers for educational purposes.

Spread of the Greenkeeping Movement

John Morley was an inveterate traveler. He was always on the go and mostly he visited other golf courses in Ohio and the surrounding states. It is said that he had visited more than 100 golf courses in the years leading up to the formation of the national greenkeepers association. In his travels he made many new friends. Both greenkeepers and club officials sought his advice. He was held in high esteem by some of the most important people in golf. Morley listened to his colleagues and he began to realize that the USGA Green Section did not have all the answers and all the solutions to greenkeeping problems. During his travels Morley related the success of the Cleveland Greenkeepers Association and by so doing inspired others to become organized. From this grass roots movement came a request, first from a few and then in increasing numbers, encouraging John Morley to inaugurate a movement that would lead to the formation of a national association of greenkeepers. William Rockefeller from the Inverness Club in Toledo was well acquainted with John Morley and he knew that Morley was hesitant to organize a national association. Only when he was firmly assured of the support of the greenkeepers in his own district, and those whom he had met in his travels beyond, did he make the decision to take action.

Greenkeeping Associations by Date of Establishment

Cleveland District Greenkeepers Association, May 13, 1923

New England Greenkeepers Club, February 25, 1924

Ontario Greenkeepers Association, October 4, 1924

Michigan Border Cities Greenkeepers Association, spring of 1925

Philadelphia Association of Golf Course Superintendents, September 1925

Greenkeepers Association of Westchester County, November 16, 1925

Greenkeepers Club of Western Pennsylvania, March 17, 1926

National Association of Greenkeepers September 13, 1926

Greenkeepers Association of New Jersey, October 1926

Midwest Greenkeepers Association, November 29, 1926

Indiana Greenkeepers Association, 1928

Mid Atlantic Greenkeepers Association, 1928

Western New York Greenkeepers Association, March 1928

Long Island Greenkeepers Association, 1930

Wisconsin Greenkeepers Association, 1930

Rhode Island Greenkeepers Association, May 26, 1930

The Lewis ballwasher was revolutionary when it first appeared on the golf market in the mid 1920s. Remarkably, 75 years later, it has not changed all that much.

Some of the early golf course tractors only had front wheels.

The First Meeting

John Morley called for a meeting of greenkeepers to take place at the Sylvania GC in Toledo, Ohio on September 13, 1926. A few dozen greenkeepers attended and sat down for a hearty lunch. They were welcomed by the president of the Sylvania GC. Words of encouragement followed from Dr. J.W. Hartshorn, the chairman of the local Green Section. Hartshorn emphasized that the greenkeepers would benefit by getting together just like other associations of businessmen did.

Then it was Morley's turn and he made a stirring speech. He began by stating that greenkeeping is both an art and a science and not a labor job, and that only those that were qualified should be responsible for the caring of the green. He espoused the following principles and asked for the support of his colleagues:

1. The Association was to be founded on justice, brotherhood and generous benevolence.
2. He maintained that greenkeeping was an art and a science and not a labor job.
3. Only those qualified should be responsible for caring of the green.
4. He wished to cement the greenkeepers of the United States and Canada into one organization.
5. He promoted the exchange of information between greenkeepers and the need for a magazine and an annual conference.
6. He wanted the new Association to provide financial benefit to the families of greenkeepers who died or became disabled.

The 31 men in attendance applauded Morley's speech and adopted all of his proposals. During the next weeks and months news of the new organization spread across the land and the meeting at Toledo was quickly followed by more meetings in Pittsburgh, Chicago, Cleveland, and Detroit. By the time of the first annual conference in Chicago in 1927, 72 men had signed up as charter members. (*See back of the book for list of charter members.*) This small, distinguished group was the nucleus that built the National Association of Greenkeepers of America (NAGA) into a respected organization. Its publication was the *National Greenkeeper*, published and edited by Robert Power. It was a monthly booklet that was first published in January of 1927. Although many experts contributed, it was a magazine for and by greenkeepers. Initially the magazine was distributed free of charge to as many golf clubs and greenkeepers as could be reached with the hope that greenkeepers would sign on and become members. Many did and the NAGA quickly grew in numbers. Later, the magazine became part of the benefits of membership and sending complimentary copies ceased.

John Morley, the Man

Born in Middleboro, England in 1867, Morley came to America and Ohio at an early age. He was a grower of vegetables, onions, carrots, and corn. Besides working hard to become established, Morley did not ignore social activities. He was quite active and belonged to a number of service clubs: The Elks, Moose, Owls, and the Sons of St. George, an English society. He was a highly ranked Mason (32nd degree), and a member of the local garden club. In the "panics" of 1893 and 1896, economic depression years, he was placed in charge of feeding the poor in Youngstown, Ohio evidencing his social involvement.

It is not clear how John Morley spent his working years prior to his appointment as greenkeeper at Youngstown CC in 1912. At a testimonial dinner in 1942 at the time of his retirement, he was thanked for his more than 40 years of contributions to golf. In President Theodore Roosevelt's time, John Morley became secretary of the Progressive Club. Because of his support for the cause, newly elected Ohio Governor Fox appointed him to the Board of

Sometimes the early tractors lacked front wheels. Note the engine crank, which injured many a greens worker.

Observations and Opinions of John Morley

- In the early days, before World War I, 75% of the golf courses were under the direct supervision of golf professionals. The British and Scottish professionals applied old country methods that did not work in America. At the time of the formation of the NAGA in 1926, green-keepers were in charge of 80% of the golf courses. Professionals were reluctant to give up their greenkeeping responsibil-ities, because it meant a reduction in their paychecks.

- The early greenkeepers were lacking in knowledge of the proper care of turf. The methods used for farming did not work. It required three to five years to produce adequate turf on golf courses, about the same length of time required to graduate a worker from pupil to greenkeeper.

- The early greens were a mixture of Poa trivialis, Poa annua, creeping bent, fescue and clover. Greens were cut every other day. With the passing of time, putting green mowers were perfected. The greens were cut much lower and more frequently and sometimes even twice a day!

- At first fairways were cut with horse-drawn mowers. The horses wore iron, aluminum, or leather shoes, or else their hoofs would dig into the soft turf and leave depressions. The first mechanized fairway mower weighed a ton, was huge and cumbersome and had only one cutting reel. It often broke down. Its successor was the sulky-type mower with three mowers, but drawn by a horse.

Equalization, a well-paying position. While waiting for the appointment to take effect, he was offered the greenkeeping posi-tion at the Youngstown CC. His only qualifications were that he had had somewhat related experience, that he was a known organ-izer, and an obvious leader. For 15 years he had managed the Bass Lake Hotel where wealthy people spent their summers. He had also managed a dining club. Because of poor health and defective hearing, Morley sought outdoor work and the opportunity with the Youngstown CC was just what he had been looking for.

Because he seemed to know very little about actual greenkeep-ing, he visited golf courses in Cleveland and Pittsburgh and the newly created Turf Garden in Arlington, Virginia. He became acquainted with Drs. Piper, Oakley and Carrier. Dr. Oakley sent Morley on a tour of golf clubs, such as: Baltusrol, Deal, and Hollywood in New Jersey; Whitemarsh Valley and Sunny Brook in Pennsylvania; and Lido and Garden City GC in New York. He attended several of the early USGA Green Section meetings.

Why was Morley able to take time off and visit so many golf courses, often at the height of the season? Possibly the answer could be because he was no ordinary greenkeeper. He had taken the position at the urging of his friends who were also members and directors at the Youngstown GC. Morley must have had means of his own other than his income from the club. Undoubtedly Morley had an excellent support staff, because his golf course, even during his frequent absences, was always in the "pink of condition" (a contemporary expression frequently used by greenkeepers to describe a fine-looking golf course). The great British golfers, Harry Vardon and Ted Ray, on a tour of America, stopped by at Morley's course and for more than two hours quizzed the expert about his greenkeeping methods. In later years he received compliments from Walter Hagen, Joe Kirkwood, and Gene Sarazen.

What did Morley learn from his many visits to other courses? He learned the rudiments of greenkeeping that were in vogue at the time and they were much different than they are today. He came to enjoy the company and camaraderie of his colleagues. He soon discovered that these hardworking men were humble and decent individuals. He also came to realize, in his own words: "That every golf course is an individual problem in itself."

He relates the story of a greenkeeper who, on the advice of an expert, treated his greens with hydrated lime to control crabgrass. The unlucky greenkeeper not only killed the crabgrass but also the rest of the turf. All that season the members of the club were compelled to play on a temporary green on a portion of the fairway. Morley realized very quickly that a little bit of knowledge could be a dangerous thing.

How did John Morley, the busy greenkeeper, the 32nd degree Mason, and a member of the local horticultural society, find time for the fledgling NAGA? There is no ready answer. Perhaps, like so many busy people, he found time to do even more. Morley surrounded himself during the initial years with quality people and most had experience in the makings of an association.

Vice president John McNamara, a greenkeeper from Pittsburgh, was a frequent contributor to the *USGA Green Section Bulletin* and well known as an activist. Rocky Rockefeller, fellow Ohioan with whom Morley had been acquainted for almost 10 years, became the secretary of the NAGA and Alex McPherson from nearby Detroit was the treasurer. In the background, but as a tower of strength, was reliable Fred Burkhardt from the Westwood CC in Cleveland. Burkhardt and Morley together were still involved with the Cleveland District Greenkeepers Association, but their primary interests were now diverted to the new national body. They turned the regional association over to other greenkeepers they had trained.

One more experienced person joined the group as the first paid secretary of NAGA. Gertrude Farley, who had worked for the Cleveland District Golf Association and the Cleveland Green Committee in the cooperative purchasing endeavors, now joined the greenkeepers association. Farley was paid $200 per month, a princely sum when many greenkeepers made less than $100 for hard physical work on the golf course. This remarkable lady, who often wrote doggerel for the *National Greenkeeper*, is best remembered for her book published in 1931: *Golf Course Commonsense.*

While the book was popular and lasted many years, Gertrude Farley did not. She had a falling-out with President Morley and she left the Association shortly after its first conference in Chicago in March 1927.

To gain nationwide acceptance, President Morley also surrounded himself with a bevy of vice presidents from all different parts of the United States and even from Canada, in accordance with the founding principles. All these vice presidents may have had aspirations to become leaders of the national body in their own right, but they had a long wait ahead and few were destined to make the presidential grade. Morley simply outlasted his col-

Observations and Opinions of John Morley—*Continued*

- During Morley's time watering systems were improved with high pressure and high capacity pumps making it possible to water all greens in one night.

- Morley was a great advocate of the water-soluble fertilizer sulfate of ammonia, which he believed lowered the pH on the greens to slightly acid, which he thought beneficial for the control of clover. Morley was in the forefront of those using sulfate of ammonia. Interestingly, he dissolved ammonium sulfate and applied it with a watering can, walking backward.

- He had seen many disasters from over-applications of sulfate of ammonia and he warned his colleagues: "Don't apply too much, only enough to keep the grass healthy during brown patch weather."

- The summer of 1928 was one of the worst on record regarding turf diseases and Morley comments that: "The greenkeeper of today knows no rest or contentment. They are at the mercy of Mother Nature."

- Morley was a sought-after consultant, even beyond the borders of his home state. The Canadian Department of Agriculture contacted Morley for advice as to what turf to grow in Winnipeg. Morley sent them a batch of stolons with detailed instructions on how to grow them.

leagues. Some died while waiting for their turn at the helm, others gave up and dropped out of sight. Still others like MacGregor from Chicago and Burkhardt from Cleveland persisted and were eventually rewarded.

Morley, meanwhile, continued his travels in an effort to drum up support. One of the most memorable excursions took place in the fall of 1928. Morley had MacGregor take the train from Chicago to Cleveland. Morley and Fred Burkhardt met MacGregor at the station. The three men then proceeded to Burkhardt's home on the grounds of the Westwood CC, where Mrs. Burkhardt had prepared a delightful supper. Many more delightful suppers and luncheons were to be enjoyed in the coming days. Leaving Burkhardt behind, the president and his deputy, "knowing that a trip on Lake Erie would be beneficial," in Morley's words, took the night boat to Buffalo. Robert Henderson, president of Western New York Greenkeepers Association, met them the following morning. Together they inspected the grand Statler Hotel, still a landmark in Buffalo many years later. The Statler Hotel and the Western New York Greenkeepers Association were seeking to host a national conference. The men found the hotel's beautiful ballroom just perfect for the golf show. Without making a decision they then took the train to Boston.

At the time of their visit, the Brae Burn GC in Boston was the site of the National Amateur competition and Morley and MacGregor wasted no time in getting to the course and catching some of the action. They also rubbed shoulders with USGA dignitaries. Also in attendance was Robert Power, publisher and editor of the *National Greenkeeper*. In the early years Power and the magazine operated separately from the NAGA. Most importantly Morley and MacGregor met with John Shannahan, greenkeeper at Brae Burn, dean of his peers and the president and founder of the New England Greenkeepers Club. Through the courtesy of Shannahan, the visitors were extended the freedom of the clubhouse. After a delightful luncheon, Shannahan then drove his colleagues to the nearby Woodland CC. The greenkeepers got down on their hands and knees and inspected the turf on the greens as they had done at Brae Burn. They found velvet bentgrass! As an ingredient of the South German bent mix, velvet bent had arrived in America and adapted well to the marine climate of the Northeast. In spite of *Poa annua* invasion, velvet bentgrass has continued to survive at many courses in the northeast region.

Was Shannahan, the Irishman, mistrustful of Morley, the Brit?

We shall never know but can only wonder why, under Shannahan's influence, New England greenkeepers took so long before joining the National Association.

Morley and MacGregor continued their visits to area golf courses and toured the Brookline CC, the Charles River CC and the Fall River CC, before proceeding to the Rhode Island CC on the shores of the Atlantic Ocean. From there it was a short train ride to Providence and another overnight boat crossing to New York City.

For the first time since departing, their travels were less than smooth. There was a brisk wind blowing on the waters, and these men of the land were not used to the waves of the sea. They were much relieved when during the early morning hours, they finally could observe the famous New York skyline while sailing under the Brooklyn bridge. After disembarking on terra firma, they found a suitable hotel and breakfasted before proceeding to visit their friend Hugh Luke, the greenkeeper at the Garden City GC. Under the care of Luke, they were motored around and visited the Cherry Valley Club and the Lido Links on Long Island. Mrs. Luke came along for the ride.

Morley and MacGregor also visited with Alfred Lundstrom who in those early days had achieved the title of superintendent at the Crescent Athletic Club of Brooklyn. Lundstrom was also chairman of the magazine committee and treated his VIPs to yet another delightful dinner. Then it was off to Captain David Rees who was the greenkeeper at the Progress CC in Purchase, New York. Captain Rees was not around but his energetic wife took charge of the situation. Mrs. Rees, who, according to Morley, "had all the qualifications of a greenkeeper," impressed Morley. Their next stop was at Fenimore CC, managed by Mr. Wilder, one of the youngest greenkeepers they had ever met. Morley was so impressed by the Fenimore golf course that he sketched some of its features, including a particularly striking green, which Morley hoped to duplicate at some time in the future.

Still in New York State, they visited the Apawamis CC, one of the oldest courses in the country. The greenkeeper Mike Vuehole, like all his colleagues, was anxious to show his old course to the visitors. Morley observed that because of its formations, the course was difficult to maintain but reported that: "Mike was equal to the task." The turf on the putting greens was above average and Morley cut out a piece to take back home for his nursery. Morley and Mike Vuehole hit it off immediately and agreed on most things, especially when it came to small brown patch. They were both convinced that too much fertilizer and water during the hot summer months increased the severity of disease.

To gain entrance to the exclusive Westchester CC near Rye, New York, the two greenkeepers had to do some talking. They were eventually allowed in with the understanding that they would not trespass in the clubhouse. They stood in awe of the practice putting green that contained 45 holes and was lit by electric lamps so golfers could putt in the evening.

On Saturday they left New York and took the train to Philadelphia for a visit to the Merion Cricket Club and Joe Valentine, who was a vice president of the NAGA and highly regarded as the dean of greenkeepers in Pennsylvania. The visitors were not disappointed: Merion was in the 'pink of condition' and its greenkeeper a gracious host who treated his company to lunch and then took them over to the nearby Cedarbrook CC to meet its greenkeeper Lewis Evans. For the first time Morley observed the destructive work of the Japanese beetle that destroyed the roots of fairway turf. In addition to the ravages of the brown patch disease, the beetles presented yet another problem for the greenkeepers of the era.

MacGregor and Morley had been on the road for more than a week visiting golf courses along the eastern seaboard. They were getting tired of all the luncheons, dinners, meeting greenkeepers, and visiting golf courses. They needed a rest! So before going home they decided to spend a day and a night in nearby Atlantic City to recover from their exertions. They walked the boardwalk and spent time watching bathers on the beach. The stern-faced Morley, who rarely cracked a smile, relaxed while he enjoyed the cool ocean breezes and the ambiance of the environment. That evening they took the train back to their respective homes in far-away Illinois and Ohio.

Success or Failure?

Had the results of their journey reached their expectations? In terms of signing up new members for the NAGA, it was a dismal failure. Shannahan and his New England greenkeepers were hospitable but apparently reluctant to give up their independence. Few signed on with the national Association. Many years later in a letter to Clinton Bradley of New Jersey, Morley advised his colleague: "If you succeed in getting New England interested in our association, you will have done what no other has done." Eventually the New Englanders did join and became an important chapter of NAGA.

There was another purpose for the trip. Morley and MacGregor wanted to find out more about the small brown patch disease for which as yet, no cure had been discovered. They interviewed their colleagues at every course they visited and they soon discovered that there was no common method of preventing the disease nor reducing its severity once it became established. Some thought it was brought on by too much water or fertilizer, or not enough lime. Others thought that sulfate of ammonia caused the disease but veterans MacGregor and Morley pointed out that Columbia CC used no ammonium sulfate at all and it got the disease, eight years prior, at the time of the Open.

Morley came back to Ohio more perplexed about brown patch than he had been before leaving. Unbeknownst to the two friends, relief was in sight: Dr. John Monteith Jr. of the USGA Green Section was about to reveal his methods of controlling the dreaded disease.

The first logo of the National Association of Greenkeepers of America appeared in the early 1930s.

Another Journey, Across the Border

In the summer of 1930, Morley and his committee traveled to Toronto to check out the city as a possible conference site. They stayed in splendor at the majestic Royal York Hotel. The group now included vice-president-in-waiting, John MacGregor from Chicago, Fred Burkhardt from Cleveland, John Quaill from Pittsburgh, Lewis Evans from Philadelphia, George Davies from Kentucky, Robert Davies from New York and Robert Power the editor/publisher of the *National Greenkeeper*. Morley had been appointed Honorary Colonel of the State of Kentucky at the time of the winter convention in Louisville and forever afterward became known as Colonel Morley, sometimes as the "little colonel."

The Colonel and his retinue were guests of William Sansom, greenkeeper at the prestigious Toronto GC and another vice-president-in-waiting of the NAGA. The Americans visited seven Toronto area golf courses and after an inspection of the Toronto course, the manager and the green chairman of Toronto's oldest course hosted them for lunch. Morley also took advantage of the

Final Words of Wisdom
from the Little Colonel

*It's the little things that we neglect that
cause us so much trouble. The big things
seem to take care of themselves.*

*Don't do your experimenting on fairways
and greens. Use the nursery instead.*

*When you know that you spend the club's
money more economically than your own,
you are on the way to executive ability.*

*One great trouble in life is that we always
remember what we ought to forget.*

*Let our membership be mellowed by
good fellowship, humanized by charity
and dedicated to service.*

opportunity to visit with his cousins from England, who had immigrated to Toronto instead of the U.S.

After the lunch an animated discussion ensued about the poor condition of the fairways at the Toronto GC. It was an awkward moment and a delicate subject. Without hesitation the Americans sprang to the defense of their Canadian colleague. They spoke freely but the exchange became somewhat heated. John Quaill hit the nail on the head when he said that the topsoil was very sandy and did not hold water or fertilizer very well. Poor Sansom had to make do with terrible waterlines and the creek, which flowed through the golf course, often ran dry.

Morley and his group continued on their trip to Chicago and meetings with the club managers and PGA officials. Sansom remained behind. Although Toronto did gain the convention in 1935, Sansom's days as greenkeeper at the Toronto GC were numbered. The fairways continued to deteriorate and at the conclusion of his term as NAGA president, scant months after the conference in his home city, he was released from his job. He thereby became the first but not the last of future leaders of the national Association to suffer the same ignominy.

The End of an Illustrious Career

Morley was 45 when he became greenkeeper at the Youngstown CC in Ohio. He was 57 when he started the Cleveland District Greenkeepers Association. In the fall of 1926, when Morley was 59, he became founder and president of the NAGA. Six years later at the age of 65 he finally turned the reigns of the association over to John MacGregor who had been patiently waiting on the sidelines, often going along with Morley on his frequent trips. The end of his presidency was by no means the end of Morley, the greenkeeper. He served for at least another 10 years.

In 1940, at the New York Conference, Colonel Morley received the "Man of the Year Award" from William Richardson, Golf Editor at the *New York Times*. In the spring of 1942, the "little colonel" retired from active duty at the Youngstown CC. He was 75 years old, his wife was ailing and he felt it was time to stop working and traveling. By this time he had visited over 200 golf courses.

The members at Youngstown feted the colonel at a testimonial dinner in appreciation of his 43 years of service to the golf industry. William Guthrie from the Mahoning CC in San Antonio,

Texas succeeded Morley. Guthrie was of course a member of the National Association of Greenkeepers of America.

The colonel died four years later in April of 1946. He was 79 years old and was survived by his wife Emma and his two sons, neither of whom had taken up the greenkeeping profession. Both sons were strong union leaders instead, possibly under the influence of their father's social consciousness and humanitarian philosophies.

The USGA Green Section Continuing Growth

The Green Section did not sit by idly while the greenkeepers organized themselves. They continued with regular issues of their *Bulletin*, encouraged the formation of regional Green Sections and organized a summer meeting each year, usually in connection with an important tournament such as the U.S. Amateur or Open. The summer meetings provided a platform for Piper, Oakley, Carrier, and whoever else had something of importance to say. Often these meetings also featured equipment and machinery exhibitions. Green chairmen and greenkeepers alike attended the meetings, except that the latter found it difficult to leave their courses at a time when they were most needed. Then, a severe blow struck the well-being of the Green Section.

Dr. Charles Vancouver Piper died unexpectedly in February 1926. Born in Canada, educated at Washington State College, Piper came to the USDA in Washington, D.C. at the turn of the century. By training and predilection he was a botanist, but his study and research covered other areas of biology as well. Piper was a better than average golfer who frequently qualified for club events. Because of ill health he gave up golf, but that only increased his love for greenkeeping. His active work in golf turf investigations began in 1912. He was the senior author of *Turf for Golf Courses* which he wrote in collaboration with Dr. Oakley. He preached the gospel for better turf from 1912 till his death in 1926. It was his fondest dream to make the game of golf less expensive and bring it into financial reach of all. Piper directed the USGA Green Section from its inception in 1920 till his death. In fact, Piper was the Green Section. His desire was that the Green Section would be placed on a permanent basis and that its function would endure.

Fifty-nine years of life was a short span to be allowed so well-loved a man as Dr. Charles Vancouver Piper. His was a forceful, distinctive character, quick to see the right and diligent in correcting a wrong.

His achievements were many, among them the discovery of Sudan grass, a forage crop which has since added millions of dollars to the wealth of agricultural America.

His interest in the improvement of turf led to the establishment of the Green Section of the United States Golf Association in 1921, of which he was Chairman until his death. His unusual knowledge, strength of purpose and high intelligence compelled the admiration of the entire golf world, and his love for his fellowmen embraced those in every walk of life.

Few men have lived so usefully, so richly endowed in friendship, and so tenderly held in the memory of all who knew him.

Dr. C.V. Piper passed away on February 11, 1926. "In storm and sunshine he was the greenkeeper's friend."

The George Low Rake, named after its inventor, left deep furrows which forced golfers to use a niblick rather than a putter. The rakes were originally used at Oakmont CC, Pittsburgh. Greenkeeper Emil Loeffler caused a stir by raking the bunkers in this manner for an important tournament. Later the furrows were eliminated.

His colleague Dr. R.A. Oakley succeeded Dr. Piper. The latter tried valiantly for two years to keep the Green Section on an even keel, but he himself suffered from ill health. He gave up the work in 1928 and passed away in 1931. With the departure of Drs. Piper and Oakley came the end of an era in golf course maintenance in North America. Drs. Piper and Oakley wrote *the* book on green-keeping; they organized meetings; they published the *Bulletin* and wrote most of the articles. They exposed unscrupulous seed merchants. They answered all questions and visited many courses. They introduced the practice of stolonizing greens, which for more than 50 years became universally accepted as a sound method to grow in new greens. But Drs. Piper and Oakley did not solve their most vexing problem: how to control large and small brown patch disease.

The USGA Green Section and the Greenkeepers Association

With the passing of Drs. Piper and Oakley, the greenkeepers in North America lost two precious friends. In the aftermath it took some time before a workable relationship between the two groups became established. There may have been some apprehension on the part of the USGA about the upstart Greenkeeping Association. Possibly some may have suspected that the new organization was a guise for a labor union. At a time when there was much confrontation between management and workers, that suspicion could easily arise. However, the NAGA and President John Morley frequently reminded the members that the profession was an art and a science and not a laborer's endeavor. A few in the ranks of the NAGA may have had aspirations to deal collectively with their employers, but those that advocated a labor union never gained the upper hand, nor did they wield much influence.

In time both groups began to realize that in many ways they had identical goals, which was first and foremost to improve conditions for golfers. The national greenkeepers intended to accomplish that goal by means of the mutual exchange of practical information in their magazine and at the annual conference. The Green Section took a more scientific approach through research and support of state colleges and at an annual conference. These findings were reported in the *Bulletin*. Both aims were mutually supportive. Unfortunately the quality of the *Bulletin* with the departure of Drs. Piper and Oakley began to decline, a process that was accelerated by the economic depression when the Green Section became strapped for money. During the Roaring Twenties, the *Bulletin* had become the voice of golf course maintenance, with a steady monthly diet of page after page of information reliably presented and without advertising. After the stock market crash in 1929 the magazine shrank in size and for a time during the mid-'30s no *Bulletins* were issued. In 1936 the name was changed to *Turf Culture* and in 1940 it was published under the name *Timely Turf Topics*.

In 1928 Dr. John Monteith Jr., a trained plant pathologist, took over as chairman of the Green Section and he would be the guiding light through a very difficult period. He was well acquainted with the greenkeepers. In fact he had addressed the first conference of NAGA in 1927 in Chicago and would do so again at many conferences in the future.

After several disasters on greens infected with large and small brown patch during USGA competitions, Monteith was given the mandate to find a solution. His research led him to identify the causal organisms for both forms of brown patch. Since different organisms caused both diseases, small brown patch was named dollar spot in 1932. Next, Monteith experimented with several chemical formulations and found that a mixture of calomel and corrosive sublimate, both mercury related compounds, proved an effective antidote. Various rates of applications were tried with different quantities of water. Dollar spot, although always a threat, became controllable. The success of this treatment must be one of the greatest contributions that Monteith and the USGA Green Section have made to fine turf on our golf courses. In conjunction with Arnold D. Dahl, Dr. Monteith Jr. issued a summary of *Turfgrass Diseases and Their Control*. It became the classic treatise on that subject for many years and even today contains solid basic information.

Dr. Monteith continued his work with the Green Section and the greenkeepers until 1942 when he joined the war effort overseas. After the war he pursued other interests.

Educating the Greenkeeper

Professor L. S. Dickinson started a winter program at the University of Massachusetts for young men in the science of

The travelling salesman during the Roaring Twenties. Einer Brown covered the Eastern seaboard for the Jacobsen Company.

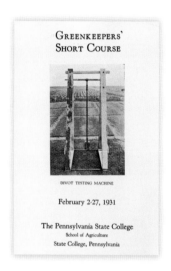

GREENKEEPERS'
SHORT COURSE

DIVOT TESTING MACHINE

February 2-27, 1931

The Pennsylvania State College
School of Agriculture
State College, Pennsylvania

The University of Massachusetts was the first to start a winter program for greenkeepers. With the urging of Joe Valentine, Pennsylvania State College was not far behind.

greenkeeping in 1927. That program has continued yearly till contemporary times. Initially many of the old-time greenkeepers resented college-educated greenkeepers coming into the field. The older generation was scared about losing their jobs in a time when jobs were hard to get. The combination of Professor Dickinson's reputation and the quality of graduates from the Massachusetts program lessened that resentment. Other state colleges soon followed suit and programs sprang up in Iowa, Pennsylvania, Michigan, and New York. The NAGA even conducted a correspondence course for its members that helped members become better educated. The correspondence course was ahead of its time but programs at state colleges continued to grow because the quest for knowledge was inexorable.

Not only did the old-time greenkeepers fear the competition of college-educated men, the professional/greenkeeper felt likewise threatened. Many pros did not want to give up their greenkeeping responsibilities because it meant less money in their pockets. But the trend became irreversible. Many young men of the thirties augmented their practical experience with knowledge gained at the state colleges and would become the leaders of the future. Most prominent among them were Robert Williams and Sherwood Moore, classmates in 1936 and 1937 in Professor Dickinson's program. They were both destined to become president of their professional association and remain lifelong friends.

The Depression

The Great Depression affected everyone's life. For many there was no money and no jobs and to compound matters the North American continent suffered a disastrous drought that lasted several years. The midcontinent became a dustbowl. With the economic downturn came reduced revenues and smaller budgets for golf courses. Members resigned and green fee play diminished. Courses closed up and greenkeepers lost their jobs, among them William Smith of the Silver Lake GC in Ohio, a charter member of NAGA. Smith overcame this period of economic stress and fathered a son named Colin who in turn became superintendent at Shaker Heights CC in Cleveland. He served his club for 27 years and among his disciples was John Spodnik, a future president of GCSAA in 1969.

The Great Depression was a period of belt tightening and

The New York greenkeepers and their wives decked out in finery on the occasion of their third annual Dinner Dance at Bonnie Briar CC in 1930. Some of these prosperous looking men were destined to lose their jobs in the economic hard times that would grip the nation for a decade.

reductions and even loss of wages. Hourly wages for greens workers were reduced from 50 cents to 35 cents per hour. On many courses overtime was not allowed. Only the richest and wealthiest courses could continue their maintenance standards, all others had to cut back. Only the essential work could get done on many courses. Greens and fairways were cut less frequently and roughs were neglected. Amazingly, in spite of the cutbacks, many talented greenkeepers continued to provide superb conditions for their few remaining golfers.

Both the Green Section and the NAGA were affected by the economic hard times. The Green Section shrank its bulletin in size and frequency. The NAGA had its funds ($16,000) impounded when President F. D. Roosevelt closed financial institutions all over the country to prevent a run on the banks. The NAGA was without funds at a time when it most needed money.

The association had purchased the *National Greenkeeper* magazine from its publisher/editor Robert Power in 1933. The magazine was rechristened as the *Greenkeepers Reporter*. A talented greenkeeper/writer, Leo Feser from Minnesota almost single-handedly produced the new magazine. Feser had to deal with dwindling advertising revenue and very meager financial resources. Fortunately, two prominent chapters, the Minnesota and the Midwest groups came to the rescue. They loaned money to the NAGA and both the Association and the magazine survived. Eventually the money that had been impounded was released and

After golf the men often played cards.

the chapters had their loans repaid. However, when John MacGregor from Chicago took over the presidency in 1932 he summed up the situation as follows: "I began my term with a bankrupt treasury, not one dollar to carry on the affairs of the association." A succession of presidents faced a similar fate: a dwindling membership and scant resources. Eventually and very slowly conditions did improve. The yearly conference brought in revenue and former members came back to the fold. In 1938 the association organized its first golf tournament. Registration at the 1940 conference in New York City exceeded 700.

The Golfing Greenkeepers

When many greenkeepers were just fresh from the farm, few played golf, but not for long. Once exposed to the game they quickly became addicted as everyone else had before and ever since. Soon after the formation of the regional and the national associations, golf became a regular part of the greenkeepers' monthly meetings. The early professionals, who also served their clubs as greenkeepers, were always avid players but full-time greenkeepers enjoyed the game just as much. Rocky Rockefeller and John Pressler were both accomplished golfers and they spoke out about the necessity to play golf to test the course. The early greenkeepers also knew their place and stayed away from the club-

In April of 1934 a group of Indiana greenkeepers practice their putting prior to tee-off at the Country Club of LaFayette. On the far right is Carl Bretzlaff from the Meridian CC in Indianapolis. Bretzlaff was to become president of the NAGA in 1949.

house. They rarely played with members, unless asked. This class distinction was eventually broken down when greenkeepers and superintendents gained respect and esteem. Many of the early photos of greenkeepers in the 1930s show that they were dressed as golfers.

In 1938 the NAGA organized its first tournament for greenkeepers in Ohio. Ernie Jacob won it. The next year the tournament was staged in Chicago and was won by Don Boyd. Emil Mashie won in 1940 and 1941. There were no competitions during the war years. In 1946 Emil Mashie won again. He won three more times in 1948, '49, and '50 for a total of six victories and a feat that has not been repeated since. Emil Mashie was almost certainly the greatest golfer to have come from the ranks of the greenkeepers. He once fired a course record 64 to beat his colleagues. Mashie also played in professional tournaments. In a particular tournament, he found himself comfortably in the lead going into the final round but Emil Mashie, the greenkeeper, did not want to embarrass his friends, the professionals, by beating them at their game. He ballooned to an 81 and the pros escaped ignominy.

The playing greenkeepers/superintendents hastened the advancement of the profession. By their ability as players these greenkeepers/superintendents increased recognition and respect not only for themselves but also for many others in the profession who were much less proficient at golf.

America was regaining its confidence; slowly the economy started to improve and

LEFT TO RIGHT: Alex Miller of Put-in-Bay GC, Ohio / Herbert Shave, Birmingham, MI / Emil Mashie, Chicago, IL / William Chinery of York Downs GC, Toronto.

A sand green in Georgia circa 1930, surrounded with bermuda turf.

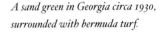

The annual conference and show at the Carter Hotel in Cleveland, Ohio in 1936.

a mostly positive state of mind affected the populace. Everyone was trying to forget the horrible depression years and felt good about the future, but there were storm clouds on the horizon. Both in the east and the west aggressors were on a war footing. A conflict of terrible violence was brewing and about to erupt. It would kill millions of innocent people. Continental America was not directly affected by the hostilities of war, but the country's economy was put on an all-out wartime footing. Golfing activity at first stagnated and then virtually stopped. Victory gardens began to sprout where fairways and roughs had been. Young men joined the forces to fight overseas, including some superintendents. Sherwood Moore from New Jersey became a meteorologist in England. Eb Steiniger built grass tennis courts and baseball fields for the troops going overseas. Still others, with their knowledge of grass, managed the many airfields at home and thereby avoided conscription. Only one Greenkeeping Superintendents Association (GSA) member became a casualty: Sergeant Edward Roach, a tail gunner, was lost on a mission over Germany. Roach had been the greenkeeper at the Crystal Lawns GC in Joliet, Illinois.

The NAGA, which in the meantime had undergone a name change to the GSA, conducted one final conference in 1942 in Chicago, just months after the Pearl Harbor attack and then GSA went into a kind of hibernation during the war years. Harold Stodola, president for four years and a tower of strength during that period, with the help of Gus Brandon, executive secretary of GSA and superintendent at St. Charles CC, Illinois, kept things going. There were no meetings and once again revenue was down but the association survived to rise in a new age to heights never imagined by its founders.

Other Key Players Between the Wars

Frank Maples

Frank Maples was the patriarch of the Maples clan that included several generations of greenkeepers, professionals, architects, and club managers. It all started in 1901 when Frank began his work on the golf course at Pinehurst, North Carolina. The resort included 27 holes. Practically all golf was played during the winter months on mostly dormant turf. As the play was heavy at times, the greens became sparse and thin. Maples found it impractical to grow grass on the greens. Instead he crafted wonderful sand greens, on a sand-clay mixture, firmly compacted and topped with fine sand on which golf balls rolled smoothly. Surprisingly, Maples maintained grass tees, overseeded with ryegrass in the fall. The fairways during the active winter months were composed of dormant bermuda. Maples's greatest contribution to golf must be his work with Donald Ross. The artistry of the old greenkeeper made the architect look even better.

Leo Feser, right, in conversation with Charles Erickson, one of the early Minnesota greenkeepers.

"Feser Philosophies"
Excerpts from a monthly column in the Association's magazine:

"A dull razor gives a poor shave."
Speaking about the need for sharp mowers.

"It is better to pay ten dollars more for a machine originally, than to pay twenty dollars for repairs later."

"Next to an efficient crew, the greatest asset is to have efficient equipment."

"There is a place for everything and the men need to be educated to put tools in the right place."

Leo Feser

At a young age Leo Feser was struck by polio, which crippled him for life. He walked with the help of two canes and with great difficulty. On the golf course he often used a horse to get around, just as Rockefeller did at the Inverness Club in Ohio.

Feser was born in 1899 in Minnesota of German stock. He attended a university to study law but changed direction and became a greenkeeper in 1921 at the Woodhill CC in Wayzata, Minnesota. Woodhill encompassed more than just an 18-hole golf course. There was also a 150-acre farm on the property. Feser not only took charge of the course, he harvested hay for the animals, chopped wood for the fires, and cut ice for the coolers. He employed from 18-20 men and hired green weeders in addition. He also had three teams of horses to help with his chores.

It was a remarkable operation taken care of by a man who was severely handicapped. Feser was extremely motivated to overcome his affliction. In his own words: "Polio won my legs and back, but I won the rest." Besides greenkeeping, Feser took an interest in his community and served on the school board. He was a founder of the Minnesota Greenkeepers Association and a longtime secretary of the group. Feser served on the National just when the association needed him most. Ownership of the *National Greenkeeper* had been transferred to the NAGA and the magazine had been renamed the *Greenkeepers' Reporter* and report Leo Feser did! He almost single-handedly wrote the magazine for a three-year period. College-educated and a voracious reader, he had become a thinker as well as a doer and in his writing style he expressed a philosophical bent to the art and science of greenkeeping. In earlier times Leo Feser had contributed several well-written articles to the *Green Section Bulletin* that had captured the attention of the readers. He was a charter member of the NAGA and invariably attended the annual conferences.

After a day of lectures, Feser would retire to his hotel room followed by his friends and acquaintances. He would take off his shoes, throw his canes under the bed and hold court with his disciples. Conversations about greenkeeping would drag on past midnight and one could learn more in a few hours with Leo Feser than in two days at the lectures, according to Bob Williams who often listened to Feser hold court.

Leo Feser helped immensely to put the *Greenskeepers' Reporter* on solid ground. In 1936 he turned the magazine over to a new regime but he continued to contribute articles in many future issues. An award in Leo's name was instituted at the urging of the old philosopher, for the best-written article by a greenkeeper or superintendent. To this day the Leo Feser Award is a sought-after distinction that is coveted by superintendents with writing skills.

Feser retired from the Woodhill CC in 1951 because he needed major surgery on his back, but he recovered and continued to work on golf courses. While he was at Woodhill he had established his own 9-hole course—Orono Orchards, still in existence today. That course was maintained with the help of his children. At various times Feser constructed and operated golf courses till his death in 1976. He was 77 years old and left behind two sons and two daughters. Both sons, Bob and David Feser, became successful superintendents in their own right.

Harold Stodola

He was born in Hopkins, Minnesota, and attended high school there. He caddied during the summer months and was promoted to fairway cutter. Then, Stodola's career took an interesting twist—he moved to Washington, D.C. to work in the post office department. His love for golf continued unabated and he caddied at both the Columbia CC and the Chevy Chase CC during his spare time. After two years in the nation's capital he returned to Minnesota and for the next three years he attended agricultural college and also became the golf champion at the University of Minnesota in 1926. During the summer months he worked as a locker-room man, caddie master, night waterman, green cutter and eventually assistant greenkeeper the Oak Ridge CC. Upon graduation he accepted a position as greenkeeper at the Keller Park GC.

Stodola was elected to the executive committee of the NAGA in 1937. At the 1941 conference in Detroit there was a rare runoff for the presidency between the incumbent John Gray from Canada and Harold Stodola from Minnesota. The youthful, handsome, college-educated Stodola won easily and guided the association through the war years, when meetings and conferences were suspended.

Harold Stodola, a young man with a bright future, at his golf course in Minneapolis in 1933.

Eberhard Steiniger

His mentor Norman Mattice brought Steiniger to Pine Valley from Long Island. Mattice quickly made a name for himself with his flamboyant presence. He wore a large Stetson, cowboy boots and carried a .45 caliber Colt. Dressed in that manner he rode across the course and in the village. But his glory days did not last very long. He was fired and Steiniger took over as head greenkeeper in 1935 and quickly became a man of influence in the industry. Armed with a German education in plant science, Steiniger tackled greenkeeping problems in a scientific way. He had a professional presence and a winning smile. He was also a golfer, but when he ran for election to the GCSA board in 1941 in Detroit, he lost. That did not stop this jovial man from reaching the height of his profession many years later. Eb Steiniger remained a well-known personality in the golf course industry till the end of the twentieth century.

Pine Valley's Eb Steiniger, one of the all-time greats.

Gradually conveyances for greenkeepers became motorized. The horse, and the bicycle were discarded in favor of the "knockabout," manufactured by the Toro Company in 1930.

Greenkeeping Practices Between the Wars

Cutting greens was mostly done with push mowers without engines. If the mower was set easy, an operator could cut four to five greens before noon. If the mechanic or, as was often the case, the greenkeeper, tightened the reels to the bed knife, cutting greens became a bear of a job that took much longer. Generally, four men were employed to cut 18 greens and the practice putting greens before noon. When self-propelled mowers with engines were introduced in the mid-twenties, the work became easier but took just as long. In the 1930s the triplex Worthington Overgreen was invented, three units pulled by an engine on a frame. The Overgreen speeded up the cutting process but caused complications with turns on the green. These triplex units survived on some golf courses for many years till they were replaced by riding triplex mowers. Almost every greensman used bamboo poles to whip the greens prior to cutting or sometimes instead of cutting. The main purpose of poling the greens was to break up worm casts, which, if left unattended, would disturb the golfer and clog the mower reels. Greens were rolled at first with a heavy roller in the spring followed by frequent light rolling during the season to obtain a smooth putting surface.

After World War I, horses on golf courses were still commonplace and used to cut fairways with gang units. When motor cars became a popular conveyance, tractors replaced horses on the golf course. The first golf course tractors were modified cars on Ford Model A frames. The Staudt tractor was capable of pulling five gang mowers and sometimes even seven. Tees were generally hand-cut, until the National Mower Company brought out their triplex mower in the mid-twenties. The National Mower Company was founded in 1919.

Roughs in the olden times were as difficult to keep trimmed as they are now. In the days before municipal bylaws, rough was often burned in spring or fall. That got rid of a lot of vegetative matter on the surface and the flush of potash seemed to give a boost to the new seedlings that were regenerated. The practice of burning the roughs decreased and became almost nonexistent at the start of World War II. Sickle bar mowers, at first drawn by one or two horses and later by a tractor, were very effective in keeping the rough in a manageable state.

The water wagon, used in the very early days of golf at the turn of the century, had made way for a system of pipes and hoses. Often only the greens were watered and the grass on fairways would become dormant and turned brown. On clay-based courses deep cracks developed that could and usually did swallow golf balls. That was an undesirable situation and as an intermediary step, pipes were installed along one or both sides of a fairway and the grass was watered, again with hoses and sprinklers. The watering men of the thirties had to have strong backs and not be afraid in the dark. They had to be able to drag hoses, often filled with water, from one outlet to another. Thus hoseless irrigation systems looked very promising. Concealed sprinklers, or 'pop-ups' had already been introduced in California. Some enterprising greenkeepers and superintendents experimented with the pop-ups on one or two greens or tees and thus convinced their committees of the desirability of hoseless irrigation. In 1929 the Glenview GC in Chicago used a system of underground sprinklers that were turned on by a manual valve. It was considered state of the art and way ahead of the times. But Glenview was not alone. The Midlothian CC in Chicago and the University of Michigan Golf Course near Ann Arbor had installed similar systems. At first there was resistance to the new hoseless systems. Greenkeepers maintained that sprinkler patterns were inconsistent and resulted in poor water distribution. Others complained that their lugged tractor wheels damaged the pop-ups. Pacific Coast greenkeepers laughed at the fuss that their colleagues in the East were making. California superintendents were way ahead of their more conservative eastern counterparts when it came to irrigation. They were already using part circle sprinklers when greenkeepers elsewhere were still dragging hoses. Be that as it may, the conversion to hoseless irrigation was very slow in the rest of the country. Funds had dried up because of economic hard times and greenkeepers made do with what they had.

The original Toro Dumpster as it appeared in 1930. It was powered by a Ford Model A engine.

BELOW LEFT AND RIGHT: *The Worthington Overgreen was the first triplex greens mower on the market circa 1930. It cut a swath of either 36" or 50" and could complete an average green in less than 10 minutes. Its price was $425. The Worthington five-gang fairway mower was drawn by a tractor with a Model A Ford motor. Its cutting width was 12' and it cost $360. The tractor sold for $650.*

John Anderson from the Crestmount CC in New Jersey started the New Jersey Greenkeepers Association. In 1936 he became NAGA's fifth president.

In 1922 the readers of the *Green Section Bulletin* were asked how often greens should be cut. The answers were as follows:

Columbia CC, Dr. Harban: "Every day and short!"

Detroit CC: "Every day of the week except Sundays."

Druid Hills GC, Atlanta, Thomas Hinman: "Every other day."

Dallas CC, C. Buxton: "At least once a day."

Minikahda CC, Minneapolis, Charles Erikson: "Every day including Sundays, but when you do cut every day, there is no need to remove the clippings."

Weeds had been a horrendous problem since the beginning of golf in North America. All golf courses without exception suffered the harm of weeds, which often spoiled otherwise perfect turf. Dandelions and plantain were difficult if not impossible to eradicate from fairways. Clover was a serious problem on greens. Many greenkeepers experimented with various applications of lead arsenate and sodium bichloride. Their sprayers were primitive and the effectiveness of these chemicals was questionable. Thus the results of these formulations were mostly below expectations. At a time when fairways were rarely, or at best, sparsely fertilized, the weeds retained the upper hand.

Many greenkeepers used ammonium sulfate (21-0-0) on their greens. Others preferred various organic formulations. Some enterprising greenkeepers mixed their own formulation from nitrogen, phosphorous and potash. Top-dressing the greens with compost not only smoothed the putting surface but also provided nutrients for the grass plants. Those courses that had access to manure from stockyards used it in ample quantities on the fairways. Others used mushroom soil or common soil augmented with leaf mold.

The only form of aerating on greens was a four-pronged fork, which was inserted and wiggled and then removed. It took the better part of a day to aerate just one green. The putting greens remained rough for several weeks after aerations and required much rolling and top dressing to make them smooth again. On the fairways the ground received some form of aeration from the lugs on the steel tractor wheels.

The greatest plague on greens was crabgrass. On greens in the transition zone, golfers were often destined to putt on crabgrass during most of the summer when *Poa annua* had died. But crabgrass was not limited to the transition zone. It was found on greens all over North America and even in Hawaii. Some tried chemicals, including sprays of the fertilizer ammonium sulfate but they did not know the rates and often the beneficial grass was burned along with the crabgrass. Therefore, hand-weeding the greens was a common practice and many greenkeepers hired extra hand-weeders during the summer season. Small groups of men, women and children, on their hands and knees, could be seen crawling across greens—and sometimes even fairways—digging the pesky weeds.

Earthworms and their casts had been a big problem on the early greens but various formulations of Mowrah meal were an effective worm killer. Corrosive sublimate worked equally well. When diluted with water and dumped on the greens, the chemical solutions brought the worms to the surface. They were then scooped up and hauled away. To control grubs, greenkeepers used sodium cyanide or lead arsenate, both highly poisonous but effective in killing the grubs. Mole crickets on southern turf were also controlled with lead arsenate.

Greens construction was often primitive and not based on scientific principles. The earliest greens were built in low-lying areas for ease of watering. With advent of water pipes, hoses and pumps, the principles of green construction changed. One of the earliest modified greens was referred to as the 'layer cake green.' As the name indicates, it was constructed from layers of differing materials that included sand, cinders and clay. Not surprisingly the layer cake greens were a disaster. Greenkeepers simply could not grow grass on this medium for any length of time. The Green Section and the nation's greenkeepers soon discovered that drainage on greens, both internal and surface drainage were of the greatest importance. Clay tiles were laid in hand-dug trenches in the bases of the greens. A layer of cinders was spread on the tile and a sandy loam mix completed the most modern greens at the time. Suffice it to say that the vast majority of greens were of the push-up type, constructed by pushing up surrounding soil and contouring it as desired.

Either seeding or stolonizing was used for establishing turf on new greens and the latter method became more and more prevalent as time progressed. Stolonizing resulted in a cloned turf whereas seed contained impurities, consisted of more than one variety and resulted in a mottled effect. Seed merchants largely promoted the practice of overseeding existing greens, tees, and fairways. It was soon discovered that scattering more seed on old turf was largely a waste of time and money. Southern greens were likewise improved by the introduction of the Atlanta strain of bermudagrass. In many places in the South, sand greens were common.

Disease control on greens was in a very primitive state. Golf greens that survived crabgrass invasions during the summer were often knocked out by either large or small brown patch. Both were serious diseases for which there existed no cure. Applications of the bordeaux mix that contained copper sulfate and was used in apple orchards, was only partially effective. Until Dr. Monteith Jr. identified the causal organisms and applied corrosive sublimate

TOP: *C. A. Tregillus was born in Canada and educated at the Ontario Agricultural College. He moved to Illinois and a superintendent's position at a Chicago area golf course. He frequently reported on Midwest happenings and was often a speaker at annual conferences.*

BOTTOM: *Doctor Sprague established an experimental garden at the New Jersey Agricultural Station. He was highly respected for his research and a friend of the greenkeepers.*

solutions to the affected turf, brown patch remained the scourge of greens. The same remedy as for brown patch also controlled snow mold, a serious winter disease on northern greens. Fairy ring, which was common on greens, had to be dug out to a depth of 6-12 inches. The soil was then replaced. Some claimed to have success with drenchings of iron sufhate, but 70 years later fairy ring remained an enigma. For worms and grubs most greenkeepers used lead arsenate. It was inexpensive and also effective as a weed killer. It was applied monthly at five ounces per thousand square feet.

The greenkeeper in the olden days often worked in isolation and became secretive and protective of his knowledge and experience. He felt that he had to guard his knowledge to secure his position. The story that is related is about two greenkeepers, one an old-timer, the other a rookie. They met at the fence that separated their courses. The rookie asked the old-timer what he was doing to his greens and the old-timer replied: "That's for me to know and for you to learn." End of conversation. The Green Section and the greenkeeping associations changed that, not at once but gradually over the years and much of the old mystery and secretiveness was overcome in time.

Scientific knowledge was not accepted universally in the golf course industry and many of the old-timers remained skeptical. Witness one old greenkeeper's remark: "This fuss about different grasses and different strains of grasses is just some more of that scientific tommyrot. They can talk about grass strains all they want, but, after all, grass is grass."

Michigan Border Cities greenkeepers relax in the grass at the Roseland GC in Windsor. From left to right: Jim Provan, Clarence Wolfrom, Herb Shave, John Gray and David Kennedy. John Gray became NAGA president in 1940. He was never much of a golfer and he is the only one not wearing spikes.

Fabulous Feats During the Roaring Twenties and the Depression Years

In 1922 the 9-hole Hillsdale GC in Michigan hired a man and a horse for $100 per month. It was their biggest budget item.

In 1923 greenkeeper Erickson of the Minikahda CC in Minneapolis dragged a bed spring across the greens to work in the topdressing. He built wheels under the bedspring so it could be moved from green to green.

In 1923 greenkeeper John Inglis of the Savannah CC in Georgia used peanuts to kill moles. Inglis inserted crystals of strychnine into the shell and placed the peanuts in the underground runways of the moles.

In 1925 Wm. Chinery, greenkeeper at the York Downs GC near Toronto, fashioned pieces of lard to resemble white grubs. The look-alike grubs were soaked in strychnine and placed into the greens. Skunks, feasting on the fake grubs during the night, quickly died. Over a period of a week Chinery counted 17 dead skunks. On the few remaining skunks, Chinery used his shotgun with great accuracy.

A St. Louis greenkeeper in 1927 completed the building of a 45-hole course in the record time of 90 days.

In 1930 C.O. Bohne at the Audubon CC in Louisville, Kentucky, reconstructed a green and had it ready for play in five days. On Monday the green was stripped, tile was laid, cinders placed on the tile and the top mix added. The following day sod was cut from the nursery and laid on the new green. On Wednesday the green was rolled, topdressed and watered. The job was completed by late Wednesday afternoon. Thursday and Friday were for rest and grow-in. On Saturday and Sunday 315 golfers played on the new green with no apparent signs of injury to the turf.

Martin Rasmussen, a greenkeeper in St. Paul, Minnesota (1928), relates how he got rid of large rocks that pop to the surface by frost in the spring. He dug around the rock and started a fire that he kept going for several hours. Once the rock was good and hot, he threw several pails of water on it. The rock will soon start to crack and crumble, according to Rasmussen.

Harry Pryke, greenkeeper at the Calgary CC in Alberta claimed to have been the inventor of the cup puller. It consisted of a piece of two-by-four with a hook attached. The device was also used as a tamper. In addition, Harry fashioned a sleeve inside the cup to hold the pin upright. Neither of these inventions was ever patented.

Early Greenkeepers Between the Wars

The following is a partial list of greenkeepers between the wars. There are many whose names have been forgotten and for others we have only limited information. Wherever possible the course where they worked and the years they were employed has been included. In many cases the date and place of birth of these men is unknown as is their greenkeeping history. Their names cropped up somewhere, often in an article or on a list of attendees at a meeting or a conference. Lest we forget their contributions, their names are mentioned here:

Abbott, John: *Rosedale GC, Toronto 1935. National Director and regional president of the Ontario Greenkeepers Association.*

Bain, Christopher: *Oakwood CC, Cleveland Heights, Ohio.*

Boyd, Don: *Portage CC, Akron, Ohio 1940.*

Brandon, Gus: *St. Charles CC. Also secretary of NAGA and editor of the* Reporter..

Bretzlaff, Carl: *Meridian Hills CC, Indianapolis, Indiana 1926.*

Burke, Mack: *Scioto CC, Columbus, Ohio 1927.*

Burton, A. D.: *Mountain Ridge CC, New Jersey 1927.*

Cale, Ed: *Canoe Brook CC, Summit, New Jersey 1940.*

Campbell, J.O.: *Eastridge CC, Lincoln, Nebraska.*

Casey, Ed: *Rye CC 1926. Wykagyl CC, New Rochelle, New York 1940 and Baltusrol GC.*

Chinery, Wm.: *York Downs GC 1925-1935. Frequent writer for the Golf Course Reporter.*

Cornwell, Ward: *Walnut Hills CC, Lansing, Michigan 1940.*

Creed, A. W.: *St. Charles CC, Winnipeg, Manitoba 1930.*

Cunningham, George: *Pine Valley GC, New Jersey 1930-1935.*

Darrah, John: *Beverley CC, Chicago, Illinois 1940.*

Davies, George: *Louisville, Kentucky, Director NAGA.*

Dearie, Edward: *Ridgemoor CC, Norwood Park, Illinois. Also secretary of the Midwest Association. A greenkeeper who became a golf course architect.*

Erickson, Charles: *Minikahda GC, Minnesota 189?-1930, Founder and President of the Minnesota group in 1926.*

Evans, Lewis: *Cedarbrook GC, Philadelphia, Pennsylvania. President of Philadelphia Association and National Director of the NAGA.*

Farnham, Marshall: *Philadelphia CC. One of the first college-educated greenkeepers and a spellbinding speaker.*

Farrant, Howard F.: *The Country Club, Brookline CC, Maine 1928, 1931.*

Feser, Leo: *Woodhill CC Minnesota 1920. See pp. 89-90.*

Fitts, O. B.: *Arlington Turf Gardens 1924-1927. Columbia CC 1928-1955.*

Frazee: *Hyperion Field and Motor Club, Grimes, Iowa.*

Flynn, Wm.: *1907-1918 at the Merion GC. Became a golf course architect. See p.57.*

Godwin, Hiram: *Redford GC, Detroit, Michigan. A greenkeeper who became a sod grower and a propagator of stolons.*

Graham, John: *Needham CC, Maine. 1920(?)-1930.*

Guthrie, William: *Mahoning CC, San Antonio, Texas 1922. Succeeded Colonel Morley at Youngstown CC in 1942.*

Hawkins, Fred: *Lakeview GC, Toronto 1907-1950. See pp. 54-55.*

Hayes, Robert: *New York. NAGA director.*

Henderson, Robert: *President Western New York Greenkeepers Association 1928.*

Huber, Lawrence: *Elks CC, Worthington, Ohio.*

Huddle, Charles: *Crestview CC, Wichita, Kansas. Died of a work related accident 1927.*

Inglis, John M.: *Country Club of Montgomery, Alabama, Savannah CC and the Country Club of Virginia, Richmond. Inglis had been at the Montgomery CC for more than 20 years where he developed bermudagrass putting greens, which gave him a national reputation. He died suddenly 1925 after only three months as greenkeeper at the Virginia CC.*

Jensen, Arthur: *Fargo, North Dakota.*

Johnson, W.H.: *Griffith Park, Los Angeles, California 1940.*

Lloyd, Howard: *Old-time greenkeeper at the Rosedale GC in 1928 and a bosom buddy of William Sansom. NAGA past president.*

Loeffler, Emil: *Oakmont CC, Pennsylvania, 1920. Chiefly responsible for the grooved bunkers at that famous course. See pp. 57.*

Luke, Hugh: *Garden City GC, Garden City, New York.*

Lundstrom, Alfred E.: *Superintendent 1928, Crescent Athletic Club of Brooklyn, New York.*

Lyle, Sam: *North Hills CC, Normandy, Missouri.*

MacPherson, Alex: *1925 Detroit CC, Michigan.*

Mattice, Norman: *Long Island and later at Pine Valley, New Jersey 1934, still later at the Canoe Brook Club.*

Mayo, Joe: *Pebble Beach, California 1927.*

McClenahan, Tom: *Mayfair CC, Edmonton, Alberta 1924. National Greenkeeper Sept. 1927.*

McNamara, John: *Born in Ireland 1871. Built nine holes for the Country Club in Pittsburgh in 1902 and stayed on as greenkeeper for 16 years. He then moved to the Pittsburgh Field Club, where he remained till his untimely death in 1929. He was the second secretary of the NAGA.*

Meister, Spence: *Aurora CC, Illinois 1941. Died suddenly from work related accident.*

Mendenhall, Chester: *Wichita, Kansas. Charter member.*

Michael, Elmer J.: *Transit Valley CC, Amherst, New York 1927.*

Miller, Riggs: *Richmond CC, Staten Island, New York.*

O'Grady, Michael: *CC of New Bedford, Massachusetts 1927.*

O'Keefe, Charles: *Myopia CC, Hamilton, Massachusetts 1940.*

Pahl, Erich: *Interlachen CC, Hopkins, Minnesota.*

Parsons, M. M.: *Wooster CC, Wooster, Ohio 1927.*

Picha, Emil: *Minnesota. President of the MNGA in 1940.*

Pickering, F. G.: *Myopia Hunt Club circa 1925.*

Pressler, John: *Allegheney CC, Pennsylvania 1897. See pp. 42-43.*

Rees, David: *President of the Metropolitan Greenkeepers Association 1930.*

Robb, George: *Hillcrest CC, Kansas City, Missouri.*

Rockefeller, Rocky: *See pp. 44-52.*

Rolfs, Ray: *North Hills CC, Menomomee Falls, Wisconson.*

Sargent, George: *Scioto CC, Columbus, Ohio 1928.*

Schardt, Al: *Wanakah CC, Hamburg, NY. Protégé of Wm. Rockefeller at Inverness, 1926.*

Schnapp, Jake: *Country Club, Toledo, Ohio.*

Scott, Robert: *Baltimore CC, 1925.*

Seaman, John: *Cherry Valley CC, Long Island 1928.*

Shannahan, John: *Born in Tipperary, Ireland. He came to America circa 1887 and worked initially as a stone mason before adopting the greenkeeping profession at the Brae Burn CC, W. Newton, Massachusetts 1902-1930s. He was the founder and president of New England Greenkeepers Club in 1924. See p. 44.*

Shave, Herbert: *Oaklands Hills CC, Birmingham, Michigan 1920.*

Sheldin, Bert: *Cleveland CC, 1924.*

Smart, Jimmy: *Dutchess GC, Poughkeepsie, New York during the 1930s and 1940s.*

Smith, William: *Ohio. Charter member and the patriarch of four generations of greenkeepers.*

Sutherland, John: *Hamilton GC, Ontario 1901-1937. See pp. 43-44.*

Valentine, Joe: *Merion GC, 1907 – 1961. See pp. 65-68.*

Vuehole, Mike: *Apawanis CC, New York 1928.*

Wilborn, Jim: *1928 at the Redway GC in Gaberville, California.*

Wilder, Albert: *Fenimore CC, 1928.*

Wilson, Frank: *Charles River CC, Massachusetts 1928.*

Wolfrom, Clarence: *Maple Lane GC, Michigan 1938. President of the Michigan Border Cities 1939-1940.*

Chapter Four

Recovery
1946-1960

By Bob Labbance

For anyone who lived through World War II, the memory of returning to normal life after a five-year wartime disruption is as fresh as if it were yesterday. For those who weren't around then, it's nearly impossible to imagine.

As if swept along in a raging current, North Americans had lived the high life of the Roaring Twenties, fallen to the greatest depths of despair the country had ever known during the Depression, galvanized all their resources to fight a planetary scourge during World War II and then reveled in the exhilaration of victory—all in the course of 25 years. It was hard not to expect another round of monumental changes as those involved in the war effort returned to North America and anticipated what was next.

Families that had been torn apart by the war were reunited, others were formed at a record pace. Home and business budgets that had been pared to the bone were unexpectedly flush with funds and looking for outlets. Technological improvements that had all been part of the military buildup were now being applied to modern life and the changes they produced were enormous.

Greenkeepers had ridden the same waves, reached the same highs and fallen to the same lows as society as a whole. Courses that had flourished in the 1920s and held their own in the 1930s were lucky to survive in the 1940s. Many others did not. North America lost nearly a thousand golf courses during this time and many others were kept alive only by the efforts of one or two people. But the challenge that faced greenkeepers as millions of players began to think about golf again in the fall of 1945 was as great as any other they had faced—as were the stresses.

Greenkeepers had employed many labor- and time-saving devices to keep their courses intact during the war. Few considered improvements and many merely hoped to preserve the status quo. As the war years dragged on, most were content merely to survive. To do so they had cut grass less frequently, used fewer control agents, employed a reduced staff and put in longer hours themselves. After World War II, it was time to reverse those trends.

Catch-22

Some greenkeepers recognized a Catch-22 that was affecting their jobs. After the war there would be competition between private clubs for members and for the number of rounds played at the public facilities. The clubs that recovered their courses the quickest would have the best opportunity to sign up new members and lure new players, but to do so required bigger budgets. Persuading the boards and owners to ante up additional funds after years of tight budgets was a challenge for course managers.

One prominent East Coast superintendent who was afraid to be identified for fear of losing his job or being criticized for revealing the truth of the matter put it best when quoted by Herb Graffis in *Golfdom* in May, 1944. "We are now running the course with five men and myself," he said, "and I used to think that 12 men was the absolute minimum. I know I never was wasteful in handling labor. So it is a sure thing that with half the men on the job we are doing just half the work that should be done to maintain a course in the condition our members have been educated to expect. At present they are making no complaints, but right after the war's over I think they again will be asking for perfection on the greens, fairways and tees, and in the traps."

After years of penny-pinching, superintendents knew what a tough position they would be in as expectations suddenly skyrocketed. "That means I am going to have to jump from a course force of six men up to 18 to 20 men to put things back into pre-war shape," the superintendent continued, "and that may mean an argument that can cost me my job. About the only thing I see that I can do now is to make notes of everything that has been neglected because of war conditions so I can put the entire record before the chairman and let him fight it out with the board."

The smartest greenkeepers kept journals of the work that had not been performed and wrote memos about what would be needed. These journals included discussions of every phase of their job and the consequences. Greens had been cut smaller to save time and gasoline. Many had gone from large, irregularly-shaped surfaces to small, round putting areas. The proper size needed to be restored, as well as the tournament pin placements areas tucked behind bunkers or near adjacent mounding. Many fairways had been cut to start 75 to 100 yards off the tees, rather than immediately adjacent. Restoring these pathways often meant brush removal and reseeding. Numerous bunkers had been filled in to save time and materials, often making the course easier to both play and maintain. If the integrity of the original design was to be recaptured the bunkers would need restoration. Often, one tee had been forced to serve the golfing needs, where once three were present. These teeing grounds needed to be leveled and recovered. During the war, weed control in fairways had slipped due to manpower shortages and attention was needed there as well.

Equipment had depreciated and many machines were kept together with homemade parts. With increased usage would come more frequent breakdowns and the need for professional repair or replacement. Some irrigation systems had fallen out of use; repair would be costly and advances in irrigation technology made complete replacement a possible option. Stockpiles of chemicals and fertilizers were nonexistent and once the availability of such was assured, orders were massive. The result of all these shortages, combined with the forces of nature taking control of the course, was a greenkeeper who appeared to neglect his duties.

Though there was an initial surge in appreciation for the fact the course was still operating, there was little patience among members in waiting around for the recovery. Albany (NY) Country Club pro Willie Ogg echoed the sentiments of many that the technological advancements of the war would make life easier for the greenkeeper. "We can look forward to better conditioned golf courses after the war as many clubs have formulated programs with this in view," Ogg wrote in 1945. "The depression period plus the war period has had an adverse effect on many courses and it is generally realized that much will have to be done to bring them back to shape. There will be many mechanical improvements in upkeep machinery and we will see hand labor more and more eliminated until it approaches the vanishing point."

Expectations High, Wages Low

If the superintendent thought his job was tough during the war, the prospects of higher expectations and a surge in golf participation brought on new anxieties. Just as baseball had soared in popularity after the Civil War, many expected golf participation to skyrocket following World War II. Scientists such as Dr. Gerald Wendt predicted that, "Whether we like it or not, we are going to have to get used to the greater leisure that will be made possible by the new science of atomic energy and electronics."

Don Thomas, president of the National Association of Travel Officials, also felt that expanded leisure time would result in increased travel and subsequently in many more golfers. "Travel is no longer a pastime for the rich," he wrote. "The tourist, the man with the golf bag, fishing tackle, riding boots, the man who leaves his job for two weeks to become a loafer, the man who stops being a producer to become a spender, to demand services he usually doesn't get at home, the man who takes money made in Peoria to spend in Maine, Florida, Georgia, Michigan or New Mexico is a highly essential and vital factor in the distribution of buying power." The greenkeeper had to be ready for transient players as well as members.

Compounding this problem was the pay scale for greenkeepers—one that was consistently below many other professions. Few men were being attracted to the job in supervisory roles and even manual laborers were hard to come by. Herb Graffis often wrote that a caddie at a reputable private club could make more than the greenkeeper, and with far fewer responsibilities.

While many courses that remained in play during the war years were successfully recovered in 1946, those that had ceased operations entirely took longer. The clubs that had been commandeered for military use suffered the worst fate, such as Glen Oaks CC in the Great Neck area of Long Island, New York. At first Glen Oaks was used by the army to launch balloons, then the $2 million clubhouse was turned over to the navy for atomic research. The lavishly furnished facility was gutted to make room for more than 2,000 scientists who worked on the atomic bomb 24 hours a day. When the job was done and the navy returned control of the club back to the members, the course was difficult to discern, the once-elegant clubhouse not more than a shell and club officials estimated half a million dollars was needed for restoration.

At nearby Glen Head, the Women's National Golf and Tennis Club was a casualty of the times and shut down for lack of funds. Veteran greenkeeper Fred Grieve was brought in to reopen the highly regarded layout following the war. "When we stepped in at Woman's National it was, frankly, a sorry mess," said Grieve. "The place was dormant for five years and the only hole of the 18 that was cut during the war years was the 10th. That was cared for because it lent beauty to the clubhouse." Grieve reseeded the greens, burned the fairways and roughs and resumed weed control and fertilization programs by early in 1947.

"The course had been attacked by the Japanese beetle and we also found that worms infested the course and that plantain and crabgrass were other problems facing us. We first applied sodium arsenate and after that went to work with arsenate of lead. Our soil analysis showed that far from the ideal of [a pH of] 5.6, we had 4.0.

That meant a treatment of ground limestone. We made three such treatments within a six-week span. We made replacement seeding of the grass greens and top-dressed them with 1-1-1 of topsoil, humus, and sand. We fertilized the greens once a month and top-dressed every two weeks. We used 2,4-D for weeds and the results were obvious in September. We did replacement seeding, using a mixture of bluegrass, fescues, and red top, with a large percentage of the latter on the fairways and tees," he said, documenting his extensive efforts. Grieve predicted that when his program was completed, the renamed Glen Head CC would be one of the best courses in the country.

Other Long Island courses were not so lucky. The Lido Club was recognized as one of the finest in the country before the war, but after being seized by the military and used for its purposes, the club was never reopened. Once the showpiece of the design work of golf course architect Charles Blair Macdonald, the layout which had taken three years and an immense earthmoving effort to construct, was trashed by the military. The carefully sculpted fairways were leveled to make way for amphibian landings. Little trace of the elegant design was left after a very short time, and at the end of the war there was no money to rebuild it.

2, 4-D and the Promise of New Chemicals

The postwar years saw advancements in all areas of a greenkeeper's life—from new chemicals to mechanical inventions to improved grasses—and the job was changed rapidly as well. To many, the lifeline of the Greenkeeping Superintendents Association (GSA) was their only connection to the type of education that could possibly keep them abreast of the changes they were facing.

The first major advancement in weed control came just as the war was winding down with the introduction of 2,4-dichlorophenoxyacetic acid, better known as 2,4-D. Experiments conducted by the USGA Green Section under the direction of Dr. Fanny Fern Davis, in collaboration with the Bureau of Plant Industry of the Department of Agriculture were first published in November, 1944. Physiologist John W. Mitchell wrote that the application of 2,4-D "in preliminary exploratory tests on Kentucky bluegrass have given excellent control of clover without any apparent injury to the bluegrass."

Davis was the glue that held the Green Section together during the difficult years around World War II. As the men departed to support the war effort, Davis became Green Section director and started to move the turfgrass trial plots from the Arlington Turf Gardens to a new facility in Beltsville, Maryland, in order to make room for what later became the site of the Pentagon. As she walked to the turf plots for daily inspections, Davis passed through the fruit tree areas. Here she noticed that the broadleaf weeds beneath the fruit trees were being controlled while the grass was thriving. Learning that researchers had treated the trees with growth hormones to regulate the setting of fruit, she initiated a study that applied various mixes of the same hormones to turfgrass. Through two years of formulations and observations she developed a new concept of control and the first modern tool in the greenkeeper's arsenal.

Fanny Fern Davis served as director of the USGA Green Section during World War II. Experiments conducted under her direction in 1944 led to the introduction of 2,4-D, the first modern tool for the control of broadleaf weeds.

The first tests were conducted on four-by-four-foot plots of Kentucky bluegrass at the Chevy Chase Club in Maryland, under the auspices of greenkeeper Richard Watson—a highly-regarded turf man who served that club from 1929 to 1966. Stands of fairway grass were identified containing approximately 75% clover and growing in somewhat shady locations. The 2,4-D was applied in a 0.1% solution with a 3-gallon knapsack sprayer, at a rate to give uniform coverage. Application was made August 28, 1944, and 25 days later the treated plot contained less than 1% clover, while the untreated control plot showed an increase to 80% clover. Meanwhile, according to Mitchell, "The darkened clover stolons which remained on the treated plot were apparently dead while the bluegrass had continued growth without distortion, discoloration or any other apparent indications of injury."

Davis inspects turf plots at the new Beltsville turf testing facility.

The discovery of a plant growth regulator that could selectively control certain plants without injuring other vegetation was revolutionary and just what the superintendent needed at the time. The fact that the 2,4-D compound controlled turf weeds of many botanical families, including such vicious weeds as dandelion and buckhorn in the North and pennywort and dichondra in the South, while having little effect on both warm- and cool-season turfgrasses was more than could be hoped for. Although it did not control crabgrass, goosegrass, paspalum, or *Poa annua*, optimistic researchers felt the next miracle regulator soon would be found.

Testing began in earnest during the summer of 1945 at several locations. On the Mall in Washington, D.C. the USGA Green Section in cooperation with National Capital Parks division of

Davis directs spraying of 2,4-D in experiments on the Mall in Washington, D.C., during the summer of 1945.

the U.S. Department of the Interior tested 2,4-D on more than 50 common turf weeds under all conditions using formulations from several different companies. Weeds were eradicated on turf at fairway and rough heights, in full sun or full shade and in moist and dry locations. Affected weeds included those previously mentioned plus sheep sorrel, henbit, chickweed, veronica, pepper grass, mustards, milk purslane, cinquefoil, false strawberry, ground ivy, moneywort and others. The only question about the compound was the timing of release, which varied by locale for individual plants. Spring and fall were the ideal times in the D.C. area, with summer applications showing less effectiveness.

Tests in Iowa were conducted in a joint effort of the Iowa Agricultural Experiment Station and the Iowa Greenkeepers Association at the Turf Garden in Ames and at several area courses. In January of 1946, assistant research professor H.L. Lantz wrote, "The reported results as to the preliminary experiments were so overwhelming as to lead some of us to wonder whether 2,4-D was not too good to be true." But Lantz and the superintendents verified the earlier work, treating plots on a close-cropped fairway where five to 15 dandelions per square foot were noted. "Within a week the foliage took on a purplish brown coloring, began to droop, and the flower buds did not expand and open thereafter," wrote Lantz. "In about three to four weeks, practically all dandelion plants had disappeared leaving only their blackened and disintegrated remains."

In Cleveland, Malcolm McLaren—president of the Cleveland GSA and superintendent at Canterbury GC, site of the 1946 U.S. Open—had area greenkeepers greatly interested in his experimental 2,4-D test plots. McLaren made applications of 2,4-D from June 27 to September 11 on different stands of grass. "The tests were made on one of our regular fairways, the grass being chiefly bluegrass with a sprinkling of Astoria bent," wrote McLaren in late fall that year. "The last application, made on September 11, had the dandelions in the first stages of wilting, but not much damage to clover. There was no effect on the grasses. In the application made on September 5, the dandelions were badly wilted and the clover almost completely eradicated. There was a slight discoloration of the grasses. In the application made on August 14 no clover was left in these spots, and only holes where dandelion roots had been. The grasses were completely back to their normal state."

Every greenkeeper observing these experiments knew they needed 2,4-D to bring their course back from weed infestations, and by 1946 many companies were marketing the product. The year was a pivotal one for greenkeepers, and the introduction of 2,4-D was only a part of it.

GSA Conventions Resume

The first annual convention of the GSA since the war was a gala affair at the Carter Hotel in Cleveland in 1946. More than 600 greenkeepers attended despite the fact that this was the first time a registration fee was charged. At the time membership in the association was $10 annually, and another five dollars allowed a member to attend any of the 21 educational seminars that were conducted during the three-day national convention. Programs included "Modernization of the Golf Course for Efficient Mechanized Maintenance" by T.T. Taylor of the Westchester CC, "Preview of New Materials for the Control of Turf Diseases" by Dr. Harry Keil, "New Developments in Weed Control" by Dr. Paul Marth, "New Horizons in Turf" by Dr. Fred Grau and "Sources of Technical Information" by Dr. H.B. Musser.

More than 25 exhibitors also were in attendance, including Toro, Jacobsen, National Mower, O.M. Scott, Dupont, Stumpp & Walter, Skinner Irrigation and the Milwaukee Sewerage Commission. O.J. Noer, midway through a career that touched the lives of more superintendents than anyone, often contributed at the annual conventions. Although Noer was a lifelong employee of Milwaukee Sewerage, his pitches for their Milorganite product were always conducted with class, outside the convention atmosphere. His conduct set an example for other manufacturers that helped to elevate the profession.

The association hadn't met since 1942, and attendance surpassed the 1940 New York meeting as the largest gathering yet. Networking with fellow turf managers, sharing recovery stories and work nightmares brought the profession together. Listening to the promise of the new technologies brought optimism, hope and pride. The attendees left charged with enthusiasm and in search of new members to join them.

At the start of 1946 it was estimated that only 16% of the

Malcolm McLaren, superintendent at Canterbury GC in Cleveland was one of the first greenkeepers to test 2,4-D during the summer of 1946.

An early homemade sprayer.

Dr. G.N. Hoffer's demonstration of plant tissue testing at the 1946 conference drew a rapt audience.

TOP: *Tom and Tony Mascaro developed the "aerifier" which was marketed by West Point Lawn Products, and ushered in a new era in surface cultivation.*

BOTTOM: *Aerification technology advanced rapidly in the 1950s.*

country's 4,795 golf courses had superintendents who were members of either the national GSA or local greenkeeping associations. Newly elected GSAA secretary A.L. Brandon of St. Charles, Illinois, was committed to helping greenkeepers to organize local chapters and instrumental in increasing national membership, calling for "a vigorous move to get more greenkeepers together for comparing experiences and applying findings." The profession was on the rebound following years of difficulty, though few had any idea of how far the ride would take them.

Superintendents Themselves Advance the Profession

In the years following World War II, more than any other era in the history of greenkeeping, advances in the profession were brought on by greenkeepers themselves. Superintendents contributed by selecting grasses that were tested by scientists and then distributed by suppliers, as well as by developing equipment that made the job easier.

Thomas C. Mascaro fit into the latter category. Mascaro was disabled by polio as a child and classified 4F for military service, so during the war years he found other ways to support our troops and advance cultural practices in his profession. "I managed to get a defense contract as a subcontractor," wrote Mascaro. "I purchased some equipment and fabricated steel struts for wooden gliders. After the war, we found that they were used in the Allied invasion of Normandy to land troops behind enemy lines."

Mascaro also found a way to drill valve tappets for airplane engines—a task that many others had failed to accomplish—but his greatest contribution to greenkeeping came in 1946 when, in conjunction with his brother Tony, he unveiled a device that the West Point Lawn Products company immediately marketed as the "Aerifier."

Greenkeepers had previously recognized the need to introduce air and moisture in the soil beneath their greens, but lacked a practical method to do so. In an article entitled "Fifty Years of Progress in Aerating Established Turf," veteran superintendent Chet Mendenhall of Mission Hills CC in Kansas City, Missouri wrote,

"As air and moisture are retarded in their movement in the soil, the root growth is also retarded. This means the turf becomes less productive; the stand of grass becomes thinner and thinner, allowing the turf to become infested with all kinds of weeds which have a more sturdy root growth and can withstand these conditions better than turf grasses."

Mendenhall continued by noting, "The potato fork or the manure fork was introduced as a means of opening the soil to a greater depth to allow for good root penetration. A fork of this type can be forced into the ground to a depth of six to eight inches and by working the handle back and forth the soil can be broken between the fork holes." The process was slow and with 18 greens to cover, the time involved was too great for the average crew.

The other concern specific to golf courses was a minimal disruption to the surface of the green. Mascaro himself noted, "The job of loosening soil without destroying the grass cover presents a problem. The hollow tine fork, imported from England around 1926, came a little closer to the present day concept of aerating tools. Needless to say, all these early tools were slow to use. So spikes were mounted on discs or drums to cover more ground." But hollow tines that fed the cores to hollow drums quickly became clogged with soil, and the machine needed to be stopped frequently to clear the plugged tines.

"The Aerifier was developed to meet the need for a rapid, effective tool to cultivate under soil. It was first marketed in 1946," notes Mascaro. "It cultivates by means of curved, open 'spoons.' The concave spoons remove soil as the full-round hollow tine does, but the open spoons have the advantage that they can't block up with soil. Spoons are curved to minimize tearing as they enter and leave the turf. Not only greater speed, but also greater effectiveness is obtained with the new principle."

The machine was versatile as well, with hydraulic lifts that could adjust the depth of penetration and a cultivating action beneath the surface leaving loose-walled, easily penetrated openings. Superintendents used the machine before planting greens, to introduce seed into a protected pocket for better germination, to deliver lime or fertilizer beneath the surface and to relieve compaction. In October 1948, less than two years after the Aerifier's introduction, greenkeeper Mal McLaren of the Oakwood Club in Cleveland commented, "The time is not too far off when we may well look back and puzzle over how we were able to get along without it."

Tom Mascaro never let his childhood bout with polio stand in the way of a distinguished career in greenkeeping. His introduction of the aerifier in 1946 was the first of many innovations he brought to the industry. Mascaro traveled far and wide, talking to turf people around the country and documenting turf issues with his ever-present camera. He also wrote a monthly column of turf tips for the Golf Course Reporter *for more than 20 years.*

LEFT TO RIGHT :

O.J. Noer, agronomist with the Milwaukee Sewerage Commission was the most traveled man in golf, visiting hundreds of greenkeepers throughout the world.

Jim Haines of the Denver CC was an innovator whose many time-saving devices improved the tools at a greenkeeper's disposal.

Frank Maples was another greenkeeping innovator who brought many advanced ideas to the grounds at Pinehurst in North Carolina.

Joe Valentine, superintendent at Merion GC in Ardmore, Pennsylvania, was one of the first greenkeepers to aerify and top-dress championship greens.

H.B. Musser's contributions included books, research and lectures.

Advances in equipment, both by astute superintendents and enterprising companies, were rampant in the technological great leap forward that coincided with the conversion of the wartime economy to domestic production.

Denver Country Club (DCC) greenkeeper Jim Haines was blessed with a multitude of cottonwood and elm trees on his Colorado course, but maintaining the grass beneath the canopy was always a challenge due to the effects of the surface feeder roots. When he visited DCC, O.J. Noer found Haines "handicapped by a lack of sufficient manpower and the necessary time to do an adequate job of trenching," so Haines "designed and made an ingenious device called the Haines Tree Root Pruner and can now cut feeder roots to a depth of 16 inches and do it in the time it takes his tractor to travel along the border of any given turf area needing treatment." The cutting knife was soldered to a beam fastened to the hydraulic lift of his tractor, and when the ground was moist Haines could operate in second gear, quickly trimming offending roots, while carefully avoiding water pipes and tile.

Haines had previously unveiled a crabgrass removal apparatus as well as a leaf rake that featured rabbit wire enclosed bins to capture leaves scraped from the surface by a beveled-toothed, 11-foot-wide rake.

At Pinehurst, Frank Maples contrived a device to overseed the fairways with rye seed. Two lime spreaders, mounted on their own axles 15 feet apart were pulled by a tractor. This enabled "two men—one driving the tractor and the other controlling distribution of the seed—to do a job formerly requiring 15 workers," according to an April 1947 description in *Golfdom*.

Both Mal McLaren at Canterbury in Cleveland and Jim Morrison at Hershey CC in Pennsylvania developed vertical mowers and turf slicers. Bob Scott at the Five Farms Course in Baltimore created a fertilizer distributor, a square greens plugger and a homemade duster. In Florida, Stan Clarke developed the first motorized sand trap rake.

Other greenkeepers fiddled with spraying devices to replace knapsack sprayers, fairway sweepers to pick up leaves and debris, power scythes for knocking down overgrown areas, verticut slit seeders and rotary blade mowers.

Top-dressing a Hot Topic

The advances in equipment, specifically the aerator, initiated a discussion of top-dressing techniques and materials. At the 1947 GSA Annual Meeting in New York, Joe Valentine, superintendent at Merion GC in Ardmore, Pennsylvania and the first greenkeeper to aerify and top-dress championship putting surfaces, spoke about his experiences. "The topdressing material should contain a good portion of organic matter, granular sand and well-prepared topsoil. In our club, we have been rather fortunate in that we have been able to purchase a spent mushroom soil. Our mixture has been 40% mushroom soil, 40% sand and 20% prepared soil." This mixture was calculated by volume rather than weight.

"Top-dressing will encourage the expanding nodes and buds of all the grass plants," continued Valentine, "and it will promote beneficial bacterial action. The topdressing material creates a wealth of food for the grasses regardless of where it is used. Work the topdressing into the crown of the grass as evenly as possible by using either a drag mat or a drag brush. Take out the debris by using available implements, follow up with a roller, and finish with an application of gentle watering."

In "Making Proper Topdressing for Bent Greens," O.J. Noer elaborated on Valentine's remarks and offered additional recommendations. "The ratio of soil and sand is not a fixed one," wrote Noer. "It varies at different places because of the diverse character of the soil and sand obtainable in the locality. There is less leeway with respect to the content of the organic material. The quantity should be 20 to 30 percent by volume. The importance of selecting the right kind of sand, and obtaining a suitable organic material is always stressed. The necessity for a careful choice of the soil fraction is either overlooked or ignored. Texture of the soil is vastly more important than its color or organic matter content."

Keeping up with the new technologies and the new methods was challenging for greenkeepers, but without education at the

Noer (RIGHT) *received almost every award in the industry during his lengthy career.*

The leaf rake was one of Haines's inventions.

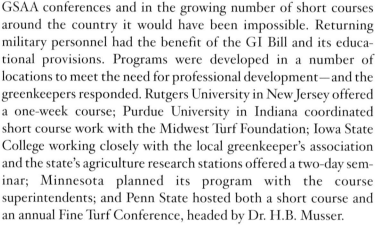

Two lime spreaders, mounted on their own axles 15 feet apart and pulled by a tractor, enabled two workers to overseed fairways with ryegrass seed in a fraction of the time it had taken manually.

GSAA conferences and in the growing number of short courses around the country it would have been impossible. Returning military personnel had the benefit of the GI Bill and its educational provisions. Programs were developed in a number of locations to meet the need for professional development—and the greenkeepers responded. Rutgers University in New Jersey offered a one-week course; Purdue University in Indiana coordinated short course work with the Midwest Turf Foundation; Iowa State College working closely with the local greenkeeper's association and the state's agriculture research stations offered a two-day seminar; Minnesota planned its program with the course superintendents; and Penn State hosted both a short course and an annual Fine Turf Conference, headed by Dr. H.B. Musser.

The 1947 meeting of the national organization at Hotel New Yorker was "by a considerable margin the largest business meeting ever held in golf," according to Herb Graffis, with more than 1,200 attendees. With the now-mammoth PGA Merchandise Show then in its infancy, who could dispute him? The greenkeepers had initiated a membership drive the previous year and the ranks were growing—slowly but steadily—while interest in education was skyrocketing. Graffis noted, "Attendance at the educational conference was almost 100%, a much higher percentage than is usual at the business conventions club officials attend. Discussion was so lively following some addresses that it had to be halted lest it throw the time schedule far off. Business of the exhibitors generally was good beyond expectations."

No two nongreenkeepers did more to advance the greenkeeping professional than Herb and Joe Graffis. Herb served as editor of *Golfdom* magazine for more than half a century, while Joe established and guided the National Golf Foundation—an information clearinghouse that has grown steadily ever since. Through their untiring efforts to bring respect and recognition to greenkeeping the brothers armed turf managers with a positive self-image and satisfaction with their contribution to the golf industry.

Even the Grass Changes

In almost every facet of a greenkeeper's life, the familiar tools of the trade employed during the years before World War II were being replaced with new implements. It happened with equipment, with chemicals and even with the grass they stood on.

As with equipment, many of the advances in turfgrass began in the field at the hands of the superintendents themselves. They selected grasses, cultivated them in their own nurseries, tested them on their own golf courses and then shared them with nearby colleagues before passing them on to agricultural experiment stations, state universities, the USDA and the USGA Green Section. One prime example of this scenario is the work of Joe Valentine at Merion GC in Ardmore, Pennsylvania.

Valentine replaced course designer Hugh Wilson as the greenkeeper at Merion in 1918 when Wilson left for World War I. It was a position he would remain at until handing the reins over to his son Richie in 1963. In 1932, Valentine spotted an unusual patch of bluegrass behind the 17th tee of Merion's East Course. The grass was a darker green than the surrounding turf and its vigorous growth seemed to crowd out competing grasses. Valentine observed the progress of the grass for five years before turning it over to the USGA for testing.

The development of Merion, a grass the USGA would code as B-27, was delayed by the war, but even though other Green Section activities were curtailed, Dr. Davis continued to work with the Department of Agriculture Division of Forage Crops and Diseases. Together they carried on the cloned stock and planting observations. By the late 1940s the grass had been closely observed at the Arlington Turf Garden for more than a decade and the results were quite impressive.

The performance was markedly superior to other common bluegrasses in several areas. First and foremost it was resistant to helminthosporium leaf spot, the bane of other bluegrasses.

The Graffis family (LEFT TO RIGHT: *Herb, Joe Jr., and Joe Sr.) did more for the golf and turfgrass industry than any other family in the business.*

Valentine selected Merion bluegrass, a turfgrass that, after extensive testing in Beltsville. Maryland and at Penn State, would be widely planted throughout the United States and Canada in the early 1950s.

The Arlington Turf Garden was a proving ground for turfgrass throughout the 1940s and 1950s.

Fred Grau's work with turfgrass diseases assisted superintendents for decades.

Secondly, it tolerated lower mowing heights, producing a carpet-like appearance while keeping its robust color. Merion also spread at an accelerated rate, showed increased rhizome vigor, was resistant to weed invasion and was heat and drought tolerant. It flourished in partial shade and, most importantly, the plant produced seed that remained absolutely true to the parent plant.

Initial tests were conducted in Arlington, as well as in Milford, Connecticut; Lexington, Kentucky; and Ames, Iowa. Tests were so positive that in 1947, with 100 pounds of foundation seed donated by Lloyd Arnold of the Associated Seed Growers of Klamath Falls, Oregon, trials were established in 14 additional states. Researchers were furnished with two pounds of seed and were encouraged to plant it in direct comparison to common bluegrass with the first report due to the Green Section in November 1948. Of the 16 replies returned, 11 were highly favorable, prompting officials to call for more detailed observations by September 1949.

The results of the second reports were nearly unanimous. "In spite of the severe weather Merion has been outstanding," wrote the Ohio scientists. "Commercial bluegrass will suffer for water before Merion shows signs of needing any. Merion is far superior at either half-inch or one-and-a-half-inch height of cut," reported Colorado researchers. "It spreads out closer to the ground and takes less mowing for this reason. It forms a very dense, tight turf and it may be more resistant to weed invasion," noted observers in California. Equally impressive was the fact that Merion thrived in loam in Missouri, sandy soil in Colorado and adobe clay in California's desert region.

At the second annual National Turf Field Day in Beltsville, Maryland, on October 19, 1949, researchers noted, "One of the features of B-27 bluegrass is its ability to grow and persist in combination with bermudagrass and Japanese lawn grass, giving the turf excellent fall, winter and spring color when these summer-growing grasses are dormant and brown." By 1950, approximately 20,000 pounds of Merion seed had been produced by growers and sold in one-, five- and 25-pound lots for prices ranging from $3.50 to $4.00 a pound, while common bluegrass seed sold for 80 cents a pound. Despite the high price, demand was strong and supply continued to be a problem for years. In July 1952, Fred Grau commented on Merion by noting, "The greatest handicaps at present are scarcity of seed and high price per pound."

Eventually commercial production of Merion reached 100 million pounds, but its genetic uniformity due to asexual reproduction proved to be its downfall. Rust, striped smut, unknown patch diseases and mildew devastated stands—and the resulting fairways grew up in *Poa*—forcing many superintendents from their jobs. Seed companies learned a lesson from Merion: No matter how promising one bluegrass variety seemed, blends of multiple varieties were safer choices for turf managers.

Further north, another greenkeeper who made contributions in both equipment and grass selection was quietly going about his business for half a century. Manuel L. (Manny) Francis was born aboard a Brazilian steamship while in route to Portugal. He would come to America in 1919 at the age of 16 and find work with a Mamaroneck, New York-based developer who was building golf courses for Donald Ross. Francis migrated to northern New England where he constructed layouts until business dried up during the Depression. He took work as a superintendent at the South Portland (Maine) Municipal and his lifelong interest in plants led him to experiment with the German bentgrass that covered much of the course.

"I always picked up plants as a kid," Francis remembered. "I'd take them apart, study them and learn about them. Back then, you couldn't read it in a book like today. Greenkeepers always have to read the plant because the soils don't talk," he quipped.

In 1948, Francis signed on at the Vesper GC in Tyngsborough, Massachusetts, where he planted a grass he had identified and cultivated several years earlier. "Vesper velvet bent is a dwarf minicreeper, a strain that I propagated through selection for its winter hardiness," Francis said. "No other grass will withstand the low cutting that my Vesper will. In comparison to other creeping bentgrasses it doubles and triples its stems and blades."

Vesper velvet produces a luxurious growth of upright grass, while remaining remarkably disease and cold tolerant compared to similar grasses. Despite years of experimentation, Francis never was able to produce a genetically accurate seed crop of his Vesper velvet. But through his architectural and consulting work with fellow superintendents throughout New England, the grass spread vegetatively to many fine courses. From Val Halla in Maine to Belmont in Massachusetts and Lake Sunapee in New Hampshire, Vesper was cultivated by superintendents and appreciated by golfers.

Francis contributed to the profession in many other ways as well. He was one of the first greenkeepers in the north country to remove snow and ice from his greens when the winter snows suf-

When funds for materials are low, innovations run high.

Dr. Ralph Engel harvesting seed with the help of his son.

TOP: *Superintendent Joe Burham directs overseeing at East Lake CC in Atlanta.*

BOTTOM: *Manny Francis selected Vesper velvet bentgrass, developed a rudimentary verticutter and pioneered clearing northern greens of snow to prevent winter damage.*

focated the grass. In the 1940s when Francis drove his Willys Jeep out onto the Vesper greens and cleared most of the snow, allowing the sun to infiltrate to the putting surface, people considered him crazy. But winterkill at Vesper was always considerably less than surrounding courses and Manny's golfers were always playing their course before others were ready—a luxury that endeared him to his members. When he witnessed his greens yellowing, Francis questioned top-dressing wisdom, moving the composition away from soil and organic material and more toward a mixture heavily weighted with sand. "It's hard to give an exact formula to follow," Francis said. "I feed according to the needs of the plant. Common sense will tell you when there's been enough feeding."

By inserting flat, carbon steel blades onto a round drum and propelling the spinning wheel over his greens, Francis also developed a primitive form of verticutting before such commercial machines were marketed. He developed bunker rakes with 12-inch spikes to loosen hard-packed pot bunkers, and used organic fertilizers whenever possible. He was the ultimate do-it-yourself, self-taught, hard-working greenkeeper with a positive attitude and a love for his job.

Francis nearly lost that job in the late 1950s when he used tricalcium arsenate for crabgrass control. Following the label instructions, Francis killed all the *Poa annua* on Vesper's fairways—an unintended consequence of his application. He took Chipman Chemical Corporation to court, claiming the material was mislabeled, and won, forcing Chipman to overseed for a complete grassing renovation. Francis saved his job, and later served as a spokesperson for tricalcium arsenate as an effective control of *Poa*.

Francis remained at Vesper until 1968, eventually opening his own club, Green Harbor GC in Marshfield, Massachusetts, which remains to this day a testament to the beauty and playability of the Vesper velvet bentgrass.

Grasses Selected in Every Quarter

In the South there were other superintendents working with grasses that would improve upon common bermuda. At Ormond Beach in Florida, Gene Tift was responsible for selecting a fine-leafed strain of bermuda from his course, as was T.R. Garlington of the Atlanta Athletic Club. In Savannah, Les Hall cultivated another that gained renown as bermuda U-3—one of the most

widely used southern grasses for a long period of time. The
Southeast Turf Research Center in Tifton, Georgia, was established in 1947, offering research, extension programs, and teaching
services and as interest grew, the Southern Golf Association
stepped in with the USGA Green Section, the University of
Georgia and the USDA to fund the project. By 1952, 116 strains of
bermuda were being tested for use on putting greens, fairways and
lawns, with Dr. Glenn Burton at the helm.

Burton began his bermudagrass research in 1942 and continued
refining his results and improving warm-season grasses for golf
courses for more than four decades. Tifton 57, officially released as
Tiflawn in 1952 proved too coarse for golf greens and was supplanted by Tifton 127, or Tiffine, which demonstrated a softer,
finer texture. Tiffine was also replaced in short order by Tifgreen,
a selection from the fine-bladed grass in evidence on the fourth
green at the Charlotte CC in North Carolina. Tifgreen was
released in 1956, and was widely planted until the next improvement at the hands of Dr. Burton.

Released in 1960, Tifway was a darker color than its predecessor and featured greater frost tolerance, greater pest resistance
and stiffer leaves. Finally in 1965, Burton released Tifdwarf,
another advancement of the Tif strain with finer stems, shorter
internodes and smaller, softer, darker leaves. Burton's work has
been the critical link in assisting superintendents to establish
world-class putting surfaces in the southern climates.

Art Snyder is another legendary superintendent who left his
mark on turf selection. Starting his golf career as a caddie at
Oakmont CC near Pittsburgh in 1907, Snyder worked at various
clubs in Pennsylvania before assuming the superintendent's position at Alcoma CC in 1927. He helped to establish the turfgrass
research program at Penn State in the 1930s, working with Drs.
Musser and Grau. While driving home through Arizona after
attending the GCSAA conference in Los Angeles in 1949, Snyder
vowed to leave the North for the beauty and climate of Phoenix,
moving there in 1953.

Snyder established a commercial turfgrass nursery with his
brother Carl and developed one of the earliest fine-leafed bermudas,
first known as A-53, and later renamed Snyder bermuda. The grass
gained a widespread acceptance in the Southwest, until Tifgreen
largely supplanted it with its superior disease-resistant characteristics. Snyder also dabbled with bentgrasses in the Phoenix
environment, searching for one that would withstand the desert

*Dr. Glenn Burton tested hundreds
of strains of bermudagrass at the
Southeast Turf Research Center in
Tifton, Georgia, before offering
Tifgreen and Tifdwarf to the golf
courses in warm climate zones.*

TOP: *Art Snyder and other longtime superintendents remember the days when few precautions were taken when applying chemicals.*

BOTTOM: *Art Snyder and his sons introduced bentgrasses to the Southwest and were at the forefront of the industry for much of the twentieth century.*

heat, at a time long before such varieties were considered possible.

Zoysiagrass was another tool for superintendents in the transition zone. Known as Korean lawn grass and Japanese love grass, the seed from Japan was originally banned from this country in the 1920s due to its reputation as a carrier of fungus diseases. In the early 1940s, O.J. Noer was impressed with the grass found in use at the Louisville (KY) Municipal Course, planted by park employee C.O. Bohne from stock provided out of the Arlington Turf Garden by Dr. John Monteith Jr. Right from the start, the best results with *zoysia* were obtained with sod, as vegetative stolons were slow to take root and slow to spread.

Emerald—a hybrid of *Zoysia japonica* and *Zoyzia matrella* exhibited a finer leaf than previous cultivars—and was introduced by Department of Agriculture research agronomist Ian Forbes in 1949. In trials at Beltsville, Maryland in the early 1950s, this variety recorded the best score for its winter hardiness, nonfluffy growth habits, color, density and faster rates of spread. Meyer Zoysia, cultivated from a seed introduced from Darien, China in 1941, was released in April 1951 after testing at Beltsville. It featured a more rapid establishment and spreading, and a better color, but the finest leafed variety has proven to be *Zoysia tennufolia*.

From the time he first started teaching botany at what is now Washington State University in 1892 until his death in 1926, Charles Piper's contributions to turfgrass research are legendary. His selection of Washington bentgrass in 1920 from the Arlington Turf Garden gave superintendents a grass moderately resistant to brown patch with good tolerance to heat stress, a light green color and medium texture. With Piper's reputation and commitment, it was well received and utilized until other vegetatively planted bents with greater disease resistance were discovered.

Greenkeepers received one more grassing tool in the middle of the century, though widespread usage did not occur until the modern era. Paspalum, thought to be indigenous to Africa, was used as bedding in slave ships that arrived in the United States in the 1700s on the coast of Georgia and South Carolina. The most salt tolerant of any warm-season turfgrass, the plant was identified along the fairways at the Sea Island GC, shortly after its construction in 1925.

In the early 1950s, O.J. Noer selected the grass from that site and began promoting it for bank stabilization and transition zones between bodies of salt water and cultivated fairways. At about the same time, Charles Wilson of the USGA Green Section selected

Pucinillia distans—another warm-season, salt tolerant grass from the fairways of a golf club in Magna, Utah. In 1953, Noer delivered paspalum to golf course architect Mark Mahannah in Coral Gables, Florida, where it was established in experimental plots. After a sufficient period of testing the grass was exported to other locations in Florida, as well as to the Netherlands, Venezuela, Australia, Hawaii, Texas and California. In the modern era, testing for the USGA has been conducted at the University of Georgia Agriculture Experiment Station under the direction of Dr. Ron Duncan. The use of the grass has been expanding rapidly in the last few years.

The Growth of the Conference and Show

The new grasses were yet another ever-changing facet of the greenkeeper's job. Some in the GSAA felt that the name, the by-laws and the breadth of the organization should also be changed. The Turf Improvement Association was one suggestion and admitting turf specialists who were not greenkeepers was another idea that gained favor with some. A "Name Your Association" contest in 1946 had led to no change of the name despite dozens of suggestions, and when the executive committee met in 1948 they tabled the idea of admitting nongolf personnel. They did suggest the addition of National to the association's name, creating the National Greenkeeping Superintendents Association (NGSA), a proposal that was approved by the membership the following year.

The 1948 meeting was held in Detroit, with official registration down to 700, in part because of difficult weather conditions that prevented substantial southern attendance. James Standish, chairman of the USGA Green Section, addressed attendees. He encouraged them to continue to sign up USGA members and work cooperatively with the Green Section and Tom Crane, executive secretary of the PGA, who paid tribute to the greenkeepers "for the excellence and scope of their educational work and their advances in course management." Crane also noted that fewer and fewer pro/greenkeepers—men who took responsibility for both jobs—were in evidence as the demands of the jobs increased, but that, "the club pro who is on the job knows that the results of the greenkeeper's work has a definite, important relation to the pro's income. Hence pro cooperation with the greenkeeper is urgent and sound good business for the pro."

One of the main topics of conversation at the Detroit meeting related to rough on golf courses. During the war, rough was frowned upon for its potential to gobble up valuable golf balls, which were in short supply. Many courses had continued to cut down their rough after the war to speed up play by the many new converts and returning players. Now, some felt that courses had lost their character with the alteration. "Veteran greenkeepers of better courses generally were of the opinion that cutting down the rough has brought some formerly distinctive private courses to the point where there isn't much difference between them and public courses," summarized one correspondent.

Also at the 1948 gathering, Dr. James Tyson of Michigan State conducted "Importance of Water and Air Drainage on Turf Production and Maintenance," Dr. Karl Dressel of the Forestry Department amazed attendees with information on the specialized needs of the 862 species of trees found on golf courses in the United States and Col. W.N. Baird of Ft. Leavenworth (Kansas) CC entertained members with an inside look into Army golf. The Colonel concluded by noting that a wise greenkeeper understood things that others merely saw.

Over the next five years the sophistication of the conference would advance substantially, both as a reflection of the change in the profession as well as the change in society. For the 20th annual meeting in February 1949, greenkeepers convened in Los Angeles at the Memorial Coliseum, the first time the event had been staged on the West Coast. Attendance of more than 700 people proved that Easterners would journey across the country, despite the concerns of organizers. Of particular interest was the first outdoor demonstration of equipment at a national conference. The largest number of exhibitors ever to attend had brought their wares, and companies were contained in two tents while demonstrations were conducted on the open football field. President Chet Mendenhall had expected typical California sunshine, but the week featured an unusual burst of wet weather—though certainly greenkeepers would not expect stubborn old Mother Nature to cooperate with their needs. When the rain ended, the football field dried brick-hard and created additional problems for eager demonstrators.

Movie star Randolph Scott, also a green chairman at Bel-Air CC, lauded the attendees, giving them credit for the growth of golf. He anticipated that the visiting authorities would help the area's own experts solve nagging turf concerns and applauded his own superintendent, Vince Vidal, as the epitome of the new generation of turf managers.

Leo Feser of Woodhill CC in Wayzata, Minnesota, was chair of the opening session and introduced George Hjelte of the Los Angeles Department of Recreation who spoke on the need for more public golf. He explained how Los Angeles began with one nine-hole sand green course in Griffith Park and had grown to seven public courses supported solely by green fees received from golfers. Hjelte noted that even if the city doubled its facilities it still would be turning away golfers looking for a place to play. The administrator was concerned that the construction of additional public courses had been flat in the United States since 1938 and that more than half the cities with populations above 20,000 had no public courses.

W.E. Langton of the National Lead Company, and a former greenkeeper, spoke on "Practical Psychology in Golf Course Management," noting "the greenkeeper frequently is handicapped by being inarticulate." He advised the greenkeeper to "write up his ideas and make sketches, sign them and display them on the club bulletin board or in formal reports." He went on to say that greenkeepers needed to "extend their contacts in securing recognition for their achievements and in building their own confidence." Never a boastful lot, and always knowing that forces outside their control could put asunder all they had accomplished, the majority of greenkeepers had to learn when, where and how to promote themselves and their successful work.

While equipment has changed, the beauty of golf settings has not.

The following year the conference was back on the East Coast at the Hotel Statler in Boston and attendance neared 1,000. Herb Graffis summed up the change in the profession succinctly when he said, "Course maintenance had developed from farming, through greenkeeping, into science and business and now is an operation in which an overall management attitude is essential." He continued by noting that "the technicalities of course maintenance today were too many and too specialized to be understood by most chairmen, but that chairmen understood results, money and management, therefore the superintendent-chairman relations had to be on those terms." Graffis continued to bemoan the low pay scale that most superintendents were trapped in and the scarcity of qualified young greenkeepers learning the trade.

Samuel Mitchell of Ponkapoag Golf Course in Canton, Massachusetts, and part of the famous greenkeeping Mitchell family, spoke on the process of making a public course outstand-

TOP: *Bob Williams inspects his home-made spray boom.*

BOTTOM: *The innovative spray boom in action.*

ing. Despite the damage inherent in hosting nearly 700 rounds a day at times at Ponkapoag, Mitchell felt that the appropriate grass varieties, sufficiently sized tees and greens, a vigilant program of fertilization, good drainage and proper cultural practices could present players with a course that would rival the privates.

Also on the agenda in Boston, Professor Lawrence Dickinson of the University of Massachusetts spoke on the continuing need for "Education for Greenkeepers;" O.J. Noer of the Milwaukee Sewerage Commission—and quite possibly the most traveled man in golf—gave "Tips on Maintenance," illustrated with slides from his vast collection; H.B. Musser of Penn State College lectured on "Use and Misuses of Water;" Henson Maples, superintendent at Pinehurst CC, spoke on "Turf on Golf Courses for Winter Play;" and William Glover, superintendent at Fairfax (Virginia) CC covered "The Behavior of Named Strains of Bent under Actual Play."

In 1951, for the 25th Anniversary of the founding of the organization, members gathered at the Sherman Hotel in Chicago. In the interim since the last meeting the United States had entered the Korean Conflict and superintendents were apprehensive about the possibility of a prolonged conflict and a return to wartime restrictions, just six years after rebuilding their courses. Surprisingly, the exhibitors recorded strong orders placed during the show, and except for steel pipe and some pieces of heavy equipment, availability was still good.

Superintendents were warned to plan ahead. Arthur Snyder, then of Longue Vue Club in Pennsylvania recalled, "Most of my headaches during World War II came from inability to get replacement parts when breakdowns occurred. New equipment was, of course, unobtainable. So buy the equipment that is needed; see that all old equipment is in good condition. Put into stock those replacement parts that are most likely to wear out. Then take the best possible care of every piece of equipment."

John McCoy of the Cincinnati (Ohio) CC noted that "Clubs have tried to improve course conditions through drainage, aerification, fertilizing, changing to better strains of grass and so forth. There will undoubtedly be some stockpiling of fungicides and fertilizers, but what any individual club can do will depend on finances."

At the conference, educational seminars were expanded, overall attendance reached 800 and Chick Evans—former U.S. Open and U.S. Amateur champion—addressed the assembled, showing a remarkable understanding and insightful appreciation for the work superintendents perform. Officials surprised the 71 charter members of the association with commemorative pins, and Noel Wysong, Cook County forester, sounded a note of warning when he concluded the session with a caution on the spread of Dutch Elm Disease.

During the meeting the executive board voted to once again change the name of the organization, this time to the Golf Course Superintendents Association of America (GCSAA), a change that would take effect the following year when ratified by the members. One activity that did not go as planned in 1951 was a scheduled tour of Chicago area courses. The week featured subzero temperatures and a thick blanket of snow. Wives of the superintendents were treated to a performance of the musical, *My Fair Lady*.

Golf Participation Skyrockets

By 1953, a cease-fire had been declared in Korea; Lew Worsham's hole-out for an eagle two from the fairway in the country's first televised golf tournament at Tom O' Shanter in Chicago had entertained thousands; and America had elected Dwight D. Eisenhower, the golfing president. While the growth of the game had been noteworthy since the close of World War II, the popularity that followed was unprecedented.

Courses had weathered the Korean Conflict restrictions without major upheaval and suddenly the attention of everyone was focused on the game. Eisenhower played two or three times a week when he was in Washington, D.C., at Burning Tree in Bethesda, Maryland. He also played wherever he traveled, as well as at his favorite course, Augusta National GC, where he owned a cabin next to the tenth tee. Despite calling himself an "ordinary duffer," Ike did show some talent at the game with a handicap that ranged between 14 and 18, and he once posted a 79 at Augusta.

But Ike brought the most attention to the game by practicing around the White House. Just four days after taking the oath of office, Eisenhower was spied hitting iron shots on the lawn and the following spring a 1,500-square-foot green with a tiny sand bunker was constructed just outside the Oval Office. The GCSAA offered to help install the feature for the president. However, it was the USGA, under the direction of Al Radko, and working in conjunction with the National Park Service that arranged the

University of Massachusetts professor Lawrence Dickinson pioneered turfgrass education and inspired more of the first generation of American greenkeepers than anyone else.

landscaping. Beside a clump of trees a tee was also built and Ike could slap iron shots in the direction of the fountain and ornamental pool where secret service agents waited to retrieve them.

Eisenhower practiced at every opportunity and he began to draw crowds of onlookers whose rubbernecking caused traffic problems. Reluctant to be the cause of a pileup on Pennsylvania Avenue or have his sessions analyzed on the evening news he would retreat to putting on the Oval Office floor or hitting balls into a net he had installed in a West Wing gym. "You know, once in a while I get to the point, with everyone staring at me, where I want to go back indoors and pull down the curtain," the president admitted.

The green remained in play throughout Ike's tenure and was also used by closet golfer John F. Kennedy, but disappeared during the Nixon years. Though both Gerald Ford and George Bush wanted to restore it, the green remained dormant until Bill Clinton reopened it in conjunction with the USGA's centennial celebration in 1995.

The son of a Pennsylvania greenkeeper also contributed to the new high profile of golf in the middle of the 1950s. Milfred J. (Deke) Palmer was the keeper of the green at Latrobe CC for 51 years, and a member of the GCSAA for 39 of those years. His son, Arnold, came into competitive golf at a time when the country was looking for new stars, and Arnie's swashbuckling style played perfectly for television. By mid-decade, the combination of Palmer, Eisenhower and Augusta National was indelibly etched on the minds of golfers and turf managers.

The exposure of golf on television and in the print media was a double-edged sword for superintendents. As magazines progressed from black and white affairs with fuzzy photos to full-color showpieces with inviting professional images of greens in distant places, the stature of the superintendent who produced such lush lawns rose. At the same time, greenkeepers realized the need to keep the course neat and trim was paramount, lest they be portrayed in the wrong light.

As green committee chairmen, club presidents and course members watched the drama unfold at the perfectly maintained Augusta National, they wondered why their course couldn't look like that. What they didn't realize was that Augusta had a budget outside the realm of possibility for the average club, and that the course was brought to its peak for one week out of

Dwight D. Eisenhower, "The Golfing President" installed a green on the White House lawn, drawing attention to golf and course maintenance in the early 1950s.

the year—and to expect such standards year-round was ridiculous. Nevertheless, many superintendents were called to task for the gap between what was possible there and what was reality at home, and some lost their jobs over it.

Costs Soar with Construction

The desire on the part of people everywhere to get in on the hot sport of golf began as early as 1953, when *Golfdom* reported, "Active participation by President Eisenhower and his love for the game has been a

Arnold Palmer developed an appreciation for golf course maintenance from his father Deke, who served as pro/greenkeeper at Latrobe CC in Pennsylvania for many years.

healthy stimulant and a contributing factor in creating new interest. A most noticeable increase in women's play is another noteworthy barometer giving support to spot-check reports that play in general is up from 10 percent to as much as 30 percent in some areas. The most significant trend, however, is the genuine interest and activity all over the country in planning and building new golf courses."

In 1953, 48 new courses opened nationwide, while 115 others were under construction and 224 were in the planning stages. In 1957, 160 new courses were opened for play, 289 courses were under construction and 758 courses were being planned. In 1959, 202 additional courses were opened, 317 were under construction and 1,178 were listed in planning. Finding qualified people to manage the new crop of courses was a challenge for owners and led to the greatest amount of job movement inside the greenkeeping profession since the 1920s. Those who had stuck with their employment situation through the thick and thin of the 1930s and 1940s now enjoyed a little more breathing room. Qualified turf managers were in demand in every quarter, and finally, after 20 years of waiting, wages were beginning to rise as well.

Membership in the GCSA had been stagnant during the 1930s and 1940s due to the Depression and World War II, but the 1950s changed all that. As industry wages began to rise, so did interest in the profession and membership in the organization. At the start of the decade paid membership hovered around 500, but by mid-decade it had risen to 848. In the spring of 1957, the rolls passed 1,000 members—a goal that had been sought for many years —with many of the new members coming from the Southwest. The decade closed with nearly 1,500 members—a threefold increase in just 10 years—and a clear indication that the industry was healthy and the organization was providing the services its members needed.

Since the formation of the American Society of Golf Course Architects (ASGCA) in 1947, superintendents had been working closely with architects in recovering courses and remodeling old layouts. Now the ASGCA turned its attention to designing new courses and there was a new role for superintendents who enjoyed the construction process. Golf course architect A.H. Tull summarized the partnership this way: "Sometimes, when the club has available a competent construction man or contractor, the club's own committee supervises the work. In other cases the construction work can be carried out by the club's own superintendent. But if the golf course architect supervises the entire operation of building the course, he supplies his own superintendent paid by the club. This superintendent would carry on the work by 'force account,' by which is meant that the club meets the payroll and pays for materials, or he acts as the club's agent in dealing with contractors who do work by lump sum contract."

Supervisors who knew how to maintain a course, and understood long-term money saving and ease of maintenance factors to be considered when building a course, were highly sought after in the 1950s building boom—but there was still a massive shortfall in personnel. In 1957, the USGA noted, "New golfers are pouring into golf, creating a constant demand for new courses which for years to come will far outweigh the supply. Golf course architects and construction firms are assured of perpetual work in the immediate and even distant future, and they are working wholeheartedly to try and cope with the demand."

New players, new courses, and new interest led to new pressure. Writing in *USGA Journal*, Army Navy CC superintendent James Thomas said, "The constant increase in the number of rounds played per year results in the game being played from early morning until late evening. Tees, fairways and greens are in constant use and get very little rest. This creates a serious and growing problem for the golf course superintendent. He is confronted with the question of how to get his routine work accomplished, and not interfere too much with play." Increased play meant more wear and tear to the golf course, bringing with it the need for more labor, more equipment, more storage, shorter downtime for equipment repair and more stockpiling of pesticides, fertilizers and raw materials.

TOP: *As golf participation soared in the 1950s, some course installed lights and opened for night play, putting additional stress on superintendents and course management. Fortunately the trend was short-lived.*

BOTTOM: *Night golf was initially restricted to par-3 layouts, but eventually included regulation-length 18-hole courses.*

According to a 1957 study conducted by *Town & Country* and published by accountants Harris, Kerr, Forester & Co., maintenance costs had risen in every year of the 1950s. The one-year rise in 1957 included a 3.5% rise in salaries, a 4.2% rise in supplies, a 6% rise in equipment repair and a 5.3% rise in all other expenses. The overall rise between 1951 and 1957 was approximately 33%, with maintenance costs reaching $2,632 per hole nationwide.

Resources for Superintendents

The rise in play and in costs sent greenkeepers scrambling for information, resources and advice to improve efficiency and lower expenses. The need for sound advice was pervasive. While the international GCSAA show was well attended, many professional turf managers couldn't get there, giving birth to regional associations, shows and newsletters. In addition to the regional *Turfletters* published by the USGA Green Section, publications available included *Turf Clippings* in Massachusetts, Oklahoma *Turf News*, Rhode Island's *Turf Maintenance Tips*, the *Bull Sheet* in the Midwest, *Tropical Turf Tips* in Florida, *Turf Topics* in Pennsylvania, *Newsletter for Greenkeepers* in Iowa, the *Pocono Golf Turf Association* newsletter, *Midwest Turf News*, *Turf News* of Texas, Mississippi Valley Golf Superintendents' *Heart of America*, *Green Master* in Ontario and publications from the University of California in Los Angeles and the Southern Turf Foundation, just to name a few.

In addition, field days were springing up at extension services throughout the country, and conferences were planned for local, regional and sectional groups. University courses were full, and many would-be superintendents had to wait until the classroom crowding created by the GI Bill subsided. Transcripts of many lectures were reproduced by West Point Lawn Products and distributed through their salespeople.

The USGA Green Section responded to the demand by establishing its first Regional Turf Service in 1953—in the Western Region and headed by Charles Wilson—three years later there were four offices located throughout the country and by 1957 services were available nationwide. Since its founding in 1920, the Green Section sought to connect green committees with superintendents, seeking to educate both and build bridges that would permit better communication. By the 1950s its primary role was offering site visits by USGA agronomists to subscriber courses.

*Dr. Montieth (CENTER) one of three
USGA agronomists to receive the
GCSAA Distinguished Service
Award, helped to bridge the rift that
had developed between the USGA
Green Section and the GCSAA.*

Though the Green Section mission included research, education, publishing of relevant information and site visits, it was the direct contact through inspections that had the greatest impact.

The Mid-Continent region was the last office opened, headed at its debut in 1957 by Dr. Marvin Ferguson, with assistance in Chicago from James Holmes and in Texas by John Monteith. The Southeast office was headed by James Latham Jr., the Mid-Atlantic office was run by Charles Hallowell, the Western Director was Bill Bengeyfield and Alexander Radko of the Green Section directed the show in the Northeast.

Clubs with an 18-hole course paid $110 for membership, with no extra charges levied for travel. Though the charge was substantial for the time, it was significantly below the actual cost of providing the service, with the difference being made up by the USGA. In 1956, 126 new clubs joined, bringing the nationwide total to 539 courses. During that same year more than 1,000 visits were made to help solve turf problems.

A typical visit started with advance notice in the form of a letter to the superintendent and the green chair, inviting anyone who wished to accompany them on an inspection of the course. If there were serious problems the team might go to the trouble spot first; otherwise a tour of the entire links, starting with the first hole would commence. In the early going, many superintendents were reluctant to show their problem areas for fear of retribution or criticism by the green committee, but slowly they recognized the value of the service as a way to correct problems, not to ridicule them.

The director took notes during the tour and at a future date produced a written report for the club. Recommendations were noted and a permanent record established to track problems in subsequent visits. Greenkeepers used the suggestions to implement solutions and also as a basis for budgetary requests. Reports would include the positive aspects of course maintenance as well as the problem areas, and many times the results would serve the superintendent well. Rather than being critical of substandard areas, the reports often cited manpower shortages or budget constraints that prevented areas from being properly maintained. Slowly, superintendents learned to appreciate and embrace this critique of their facility.

When the Green Section was established the greatest thrust of the work was in research and education. Slowly, universities, extension services, seed and chemical companies and laboratories filled the void that had existed in that arena. The field visits became the greatest contribution of the Green Section to the development of course maintenance, and a networking tool that spread the positive and negative discoveries being made by the superintendents themselves.

In 1956, the GCSAA board of directors went on record as opposing the Green Section Services, creating an uncomfortable rift between the two organizations. Private conversations and gentle persuasion resulted in a reversal of that position the following year under president Paul Weiss. Mending of the fences was complete by 1959 when the GCSAA board bestowed Distinguished Service Awards upon Dr. Monteith, Richard Tufts and Joe Dey, all of the USGA.

The Next Challenge: Golf Cars

Prototypes had been around for decades. As early as the late-1920s senior members at the Biltmore Forest Golf Course in North Carolina had been seen in them. In 1930, Curtis Willock, a green committee chairman with a wooden leg at the Annandale Golf Course in Pasadena, California, had designed one. In 1938, Dr. R.A. Richardson at the Indian Hills GC in Kansas City converted a motorcycle to serve the purpose. The earliest models offered for sale appeared in 1948, but golf cars didn't really have an impact on the game until the early 1950s. From that point on, purists felt like the little Dutch boy holding his finger in a dike. Unfortunately the story would not have as happy an ending.

The subject of using motorized transportation on the fields of play was one that divided clubs, angered members and gave superintendents both another maintenance headache and, in many cases an added responsibility as well. The added responsibility came in the fact that at many courses it was the superintendent who stored, maintained and administered the cart program. In some cases this allowed them jurisdiction over where and when the carts were allowed on the course, but in other cases it did not. The headaches came from the damage the carts did to the golf course.

Initially, members bought their own carts and drove them to the course, using them as they pleased. This ignited disagreements on whether or not they had any place on a golf course, an argument won by using medical excuses, speed of play defenses and the

Golf cars (referred to as carts though the proper golf terminology is cars) brought a new set of problems for greenkeepers in the 1950s. Though their introduction was controversial, superintendents embraced their use for their own purposes.

first amendment. Next came battles over where they could go; who would store and service them; if private ownership should be allowed; what the club should charge to rent them; and who would pocket the revenue. The use of golf carts was the major topic of discussion at the 19th hole for years. USGA executive director Joseph Dey Jr., once noted "The subject of mechanized transportation for playing golf has evoked deep soul-searching by club boards throughout the land. It is a subject which must be dealt with, regardless of one's personal preferences."

To superintendents the issue went beyond the debate over whether or not driving to your golf ball was in keeping with the rich traditions of the game, and went right to the heart of their livelihood. The vehicles compacted turf and destroyed grass—should this be allowed after decades of working so hard to cultivate it? One area in which the superintendents' input improved the cart was in tire size. Originally the narrow, hard tires considerably compacted soil. As suggestions from workers were considered, tires became wider and softer, spreading the weight of the vehicle out over a greater space and reducing the compaction. Dr. Glenn Burton's study on tire size and compaction was a major contribution to the discussion and together with greenkeeper input, started to change the way tires were designed for such usage.

Although many superintendents opposed the appearance of carts on the course, they also adopted them for their own use. "Put wheels under your crew," was the battle cry, and the utility cart that followed the introduction of the golf cart became an essential tool in the transportation of workers, equipment, topdressing, fertilizer, and other necessities.

The GCSAA recognized the threat to the proper maintenance of the course, but could not deny the economic boost to the industry, as the dozens of companies that manufactured the vehicles began to reserve floor space at the annual shows, support programs with generous donations and advertise in *Golf Course Reporter*. The magazine devoted a special section to the carts, detailing their use, safety concerns, proper driving etiquette and the effect on turf quality. The USGA on the other hand, with little to gain from the carts, came down firmly in opposition, banning them from USGA-sponsored events and running editorials against their use.

Citing additional labor for crews, increased budget for fertilizers, need for additional aeration, development of wear-tolerant grasses and construction of asphalt pathways, Alexander Radko of the Green Section explained that, "Cool-season grasses, such as bluegrass, fescues and bentgrasses, which predominate in the Northeast, are in their danger period during the hot months of July and August, when electric cart owners would use their cars most. At some time during that period unwatered cool-season turfgrasses are at the wilting stage; if they are in a state of wilt, the use of many electric cars may mean the difference between turf and no turf."

In a study at Penn State, Dr. R.B. Alderfer found a quadrupling of runoff as the result of compaction similar to that created by golf carts, no matter the soil type. This prompted a recommendation of frequent aerification to overcome the effect carts would have on the soil. Other USGA and GCSAA suggestions included dense, tight turfgrasses which would wear better than open turfs; a more frequent fertilization program; elimination of low spots where wet ground would be severely damaged; regrading of steep slopes that may be traversed by cart drivers; paving of small areas where turf is subject to high volumes of traffic; training of drivers on proper operation; additional signage to prevent travel in restricted areas; increased maintenance budgets to implement needed changes; and documentation of the changes to the golf course for future committees to ponder.

Fortunately, the decision on when to deny members the use of carts due to inclement weather was nearly always left with the superintendent. Realizing the income stream they generated, the superintendents did not abuse their power. Sherwood Moore recalls closing Winged Foot after a period of heavy rain, prompting the pro to comment, "You closed the course to carts, but your own crew is out there with heavy equipment." To which Moore replied, "Yes, but they know where the high areas are to travel and the low wet areas to avoid, whereas the golfer would go anywhere."

Although it took years to play out completely, one eventual negative effect of carts became the number one issue in golf, something no one envisioned at the onset of the debate: slow play. Originally, committees allowed carts to travel anywhere golfers needed to go. In the 1980s, when the call for perfect playing surfaces butted heads with the damage caused by roaming carts, courses were built or retrofitted with continuous cart paths from the first tee to the 18th green. The resulting increase in the time needed to play 18 holes of golf—while golfers parked their carts on one side of the hole and slowly walked across fairways to the other side where their balls lie—contributed substantially to the number-one nemesis of golf in

James Thomas, Fred Grau and Lou Strong examine Grau's special putter at the 32nd Conference.

the modern era—the increase in the average time needed to play a round of golf from three-and-a-half hours to nearly five.

A Solution Worse than the Problem

The 1950s were a confusing time for superintendents regarding the use of chemicals on the golf course. While considerable progress was made in all fields of research, there also were setbacks. Coming from the 1940s when greenkeepers used mercurials for disease, arsenate of lead for insects and arsenicals for weeds, the new generation of control agents were a dream. Previously, the application of mercurials could result in severe burning and weed killers could stress the turf so radically that it would be susceptible to disease.

The difficult part of the new products was knowing which ones had been properly tested in the rush to produce better tools for the greenkeeper. The result of less-than-stringent requirements could mean that a product would perform one way in one circumstance, and differently elsewhere. Spencer Davis Jr. cited numerous examples of this in a 1953 review of the 10-year 1942 Fungicide Trials. "The use of Actidione was discontinued in the Pennsylvania turf tests in 1951 due to its poor showing against dollar spot in that state in 1950, and yet the same fungicide responded so well in Michigan tests in 1951 that it was given top rating."

Application rates and the proper combinations of fungicides were also under exploration by greenkeepers. In the same article, Davis noted that a 50/50 combination of two products may work better than either product singularly. He quoted Sherwood Moore of the Hollywood GC in New Jersey, who recommended half the rate of both Calo Clor and Tersan in the same tank for the control of copper spot. This duo outperformed the control groups of either one separately.

The earlier discovery of the herbicide 2,4-D had produced unbridled optimism, but Dr. Harry Keil summed up the reality best by saying, "As the investigation progresses, the Utopia of discovering one fungicide which will control all the diseases all the time is gradually fading." He went on to explain that, "At present, the development of turf fungicides is largely an empirical, or trial and error method." Unfortunately superintendents could not afford many errors on the properties they maintained, for fear of losing their jobs. Unable to understand or participate in the science that created the new agents, their reliance on the integrity of the company and its sales force was closely tied to the performance of their products in the field. One trial that didn't go as promised and the company might not get a second hearing.

One infamous product that superintendents relied on until it was outlawed was DDT. First described by a German chemist in 1874, its insecticidal value was not known until 1939. In 1943, the chemical was first manufactured in the United States for use by the military, and in 1946, at the conclusion of the war, it became widely available for civilian use. "Probably the most revolutionary of the new insecticides is DDT," wrote George Caskey, superintendent of the Winnetka Park District in Illinois. "With this, it should be possible to eliminate the common house fly and mosquito from the clubrooms, garbage disposal areas, dumps, etc. It is a wonderful product and one that answers a long-felt need."

Many years later, while in his 90s, superintendent Art Snyder summarized the naiveté of many greenkeepers when handling the new chemicals in the 1950s. "I could go on and on telling how we mixed calomel and bichloride of mercury with sand and Milorganite, breaking up the lumps of mercury with the aid of the family rolling pin. The mixture was then applied to the greens with a cyclone seeder. Or, how we handled DDT and 2,4-D dust until our faces were coated with the powder. Old-time greenkeepers did many things in a reckless haphazard way, but it was because no better way was known."

Despite nearly 75 years of experimentation, and sky-high hopes, few suspected DDT's persistence in the environment would be deadly, and that many years in the future the product would be banned. Most swallowed the promise of new products and the belief that science could solve all the problems. "There are approximately ten times as many investigators in the field of turfgrass research today as there were ten years ago," wrote Dr. Marvin Ferguson in 1956. "There is a greater awareness of the value of turf than ever before. As greater pressure is brought to bear upon state institutions in behalf of turf research, more effort is going to be directed to the solution of turfgrass problems." Little did they know that 50 years later, researchers would still be searching for that golden bullet.

One friend of the researchers was Eb Steiniger, a German immigrant who arrived at the Clementon, New Jersey-based Pine Valley GC in 1927, just six years after its construction, and remained for 53 years. Serving five years as the assistant before taking the reins from greenkeeper Norman Mattice, Steiniger tested new products, equipment, grasses and techniques on his own 12-acre experimental plot adjacent to the course. His lifelong friendship with Tom Mascaro resulted in a proving ground for Mascaro's inventions, and Steiniger's love of his profession and desire to advance it benefited many of his contemporaries. For many years he served as the Association's official ambassador at international meetings. He shared not only his findings, but also his facility—by hosting numerous superintendents' meetings— and most importantly, his good fellowship—by his active role in his church, the military, and causes such as the nearby veterans hospital and Boy Scout campground.

Steiniger landscaped Pine Valley with a vast array of native plants that, many years before it was mainstream, demonstrated how a golf course could fit its native environment. He built greens at Fort Dix for the use of the troops during World War II, conducted nature walks identifying trees for the Boy Scouts, served as an elder in his church, was active in the Lions Club and believed that superintendents needed a life outside the golf course. His relationship with Pine Valley—a club that appreciated his work and rewarded him for it both during his tenure and after his retirement in 1980—still stands as a model for the industry today. His professionalism, desire to achieve the highest standards, and conduct on and off the golf course made him a paragon for the thousands of superintendents who would follow him.

Breakthrough in Bentgrass

Although turf managers in the northern climates had a variety of bentgrasses at their disposal, researchers at Penn State offered them an exciting gift in 1954. At the time, few involved in scientific research or the cultivation of grasses realized how long the gift would keep on giving.

Prior to this time there were at least a dozen varieties of creeping bentgrass, as well as several locally known velvets, but all were planted vegetatively and all had shortcomings. Some of the favorite creepers included: Arlington (C-1), selected in Virginia by the USGA—it was slow growing, required a high level of soil fertility and was susceptible to brown patch. Old Orchard (C-52), selected and produced by Ralph Bond in Wisconsin—it tended to thin out in hot weather, but remained a popular choice in the

Midwest, especially for the manner in which it successfully competed with *Poa*. Cohansey (C-7), selected by Eb Steiniger at Pine Valley—it was yellowish-green and tolerated a wide range of conditions, but was especially vulnerable to dollar spot. Congressional (C-19), selected at its namesake in the DC area—a popular variety with few major drawbacks in its local environment. Metropolitan (C-51), selected in Arlington, Virginia—the turf tended to become fluffy and grainy and was very susceptible to melting-out. Toronto (C-15), selected at the Toronto GC in Ontario—well adapted to central-eastern Canada and the Great Lakes district, but it required careful management. Washington (C-50), selected by Charles Piper at the Arlington turf plots—one of the first bents identified and an excellent grass with some disease tolerance, but a short growing season. Many considered Washington the best solution to the *Poa* problem, as it was compatible with the annual bluegrass in the Midwest and was a strong deterrent to its spread in the coastal areas of the Northeast.

It was in July, 1954, that Penn State introduced another vegetatively planted bent—Pennlu, selected from the 17th green at LuLu Temple Golf Course near Philadelphia in 1937. First planted for testing as a golf green in 1939, the grass showed favorable results in 1940 and 1941, before testing was suspended for the war years. From 1947 to 1952 the grass outperformed all the other bents under evaluation. At the same time, H.B. Musser introduced Pennlawn, a strain of creeping red fescue that was more tolerant to leaf spot disease than other fescues.

While these grasses were welcomed by greenkeepers, their usage has faded over time and few of today's superintendents are familiar with them. This is not the case with the other bentgrass that Penn State and Musser offered in 1954: Penncross. At the time, the only creeping bentgrass that was available for greens in a seeded variety was Seaside. While that creeping bent was in use by many, it was characterized by extreme variability. The turf it produced was lower quality than most of the vegetatively planted alternatives. It ranked below average in disease resistance and showed a total lack of uniformity. Individual patches with marked differences in color, graininess, texture and disease susceptibility were common on Seaside greens. Despite the ease in establishment, the grass was far less than ideal. It was in this environment that Musser delivered Penncross creeping bentgrass.

"The seeded group of creeping bentgrasses consists of two varieties for which seed is commercially available," Musser wrote.

"These are Penncross and Seaside. Critical observations and comparative tests indicate that the Penncross will produce materially better turf than Seaside over most of the area where creeping bents are used. The former is more uniform, has better density, is more disease resistant, and is adapted to a wider range of growing conditions." When you consider that Penncross is still the most widely used bentgrass in the world, 47 years after its introduction, this was one of the biggest understatements in the history of greenkeeping. Nevertheless, Musser backed up his announcement by adding, "The seeded bents are less expensive to establish, both because of the first cost of seed vs. stolons, and the difference in the time and labor required for planting. An added advantage is the greater simplicity in making overseedings on established turf when renovation is needed."

In the early going Penncross seed was obtained by planting three separate vegetative creeping bents side by side and letting them go to seed. Cross-pollination took place and the result was Penncross seed.

In the short time following its introduction, Musser's claims for the new grass were confirmed by other scientists. O.J. Noer wrote, "Penncross is the new designation for Polycross developed by H.B. Musser at State College, Pa. Pennlu is one of its three parents. The original Polycross gave a good account of itself. Its performance at Edmonton, Alberta, has been very good. Penncross should be just as good because it is from the same parent stock. The seed is expensive, but turf can be developed with a seeding rate of one pound per thousand square feet. On that basis the actual cost of turf development is cheaper than for use of purchased stolons. Penncross is not apt to produce a turf of one color and uniform texture. Separation should be something like the separation in Seaside bent turf." But Musser's continual improvements in Penncross proved those words false, and by the 1960s the grass had become the standard throughout the northern climates. Today, despite a new generation of boutique bentgrasses, Penncross remains the most widely grown bentgrass in the world.

Final Fifties Fling

As the decade drew to a close, the GCSAA was on a roll. Membership was at an all-time high; superintendents had more tools than ever before at their disposal and golf courses were being groomed to standards hardly imagined just a decade previously. Although the pressures for perfection were greater than at any time in the past, budgets were growing, more young people were entering the profession, mechanization was making some jobs easier and the country was at peace. All these factors contributed to an unbridled optimism, and a hope among greenkeepers that the setbacks of the past were finally behind them.

At the 1958 fall board meeting in Pinehurst, North Carolina, it was decided to terminate the services of secretary-treasurer Agar L. Brown, and hire an executive director. After an extensive search the organization chose Dr. Gene Nutter, a professor at the University of Florida and also voted to move headquarters from St. Charles, Illinois, to Jacksonville Beach, Florida. By hiring Dr. Nutter, the Board felt it could better serve the Association's membership with a turf-oriented educator at the helm. This philosophy proved its value in the following years.

The last national meeting of the decade took place in Chicago and more than 1,700 members attended, an increase of nearly 25% from the year before. The size and scope of the conference had more than doubled in the decade with exhibitors and educational programs keeping registrants busy. More and more, presentations were being made by the superintendents themselves, a fact not lost on president Bob Williams during his opening address, who noted that all seven chairmen of the conference were superintendents, and three-quarters of the speakers, as well. While many of the seminars were geared toward the latest developments in turf management, there was a growing need to address the other aspects of the job—managing employees; interacting with committees, boards and club members; record keeping; preparing comprehensive budgets; motivating workers; leadership, enthusiasm and professional training. These traits were in demand by both the established courses, and by developers who were building the rash of new courses each year.

A film by O.J. Noer and Charlie Wilson entitled *Progressive Superintendents and Their Practices* was well-received. It detailed new techniques, new chemicals and new equipment, and how the advanced superintendent incorporated the march of progress into his long-standing routines and long-held beliefs. Coming from such a respected figure as Noer, the presentation opened the eyes of many.

The discussion that drew the biggest crowd was moderated by Herb Graffis, with a panel of superintendents discussing "Living

TOP: *As recently as 1960, registration could be accomplished at one counter.*

BOTTOM: *Turf Tours, such as this one at the 1960 conference in Houston became a popular part of the annual gathering.*

with Golf Carts." The most common complaint from those in attendance, and those who had responded to a questionnaire distributed prior to the meeting, was irresponsible use of the golf cart by players. After five years of usage nationwide, it was concluded that the cart was here to stay, much to the dismay of most in attendance. But many issues connected with their use were raised.

Jim Haines of the Denver CC believed that the problem started with rental carts, since the lack of ownership led to a devil-may-care attitude in their handling. Other greenkeepers called for improvements in the manufacture of the vehicles, with larger tires that would do less damage to turf. Many agreed that carts represented a sizable source of income for clubs, but that in most cases the revenues were not being returned to the turf maintenance budget as they should be.

Gordon Brinkworth of Olympia Fields CC spoke on the need for blacktop pathways. Although not a complete solution, he believed that although fairway damage so far was minimal, siphoning carts off approach areas would save greenside areas that are easily damaged. Paul Addessi at Tamarisk GC noted that rules infractions should be reported, and that at his club two infractions meant loss of driving privileges. He felt signs had little effect, but marking gypsum lines made a positive improvement. Graffis summed up by encouraging golf architects to plan for carts in their course drawings in the future, a concept that was just being considered in the late 1950s.

In his turf roundup, Fred Grau called 1959 "one of the worst seasons for course maintenance that anyone remembers." A summer of excesses in nearly all parts of the country followed a long ice-covered winter in the north and a cold wet spring everywhere. "Diseases appeared to be at an all-time high. Much of what happened simply was not supposed to be in the books. When the chips were down it took all the research results of past years, together with huge doses of old-fashioned horse sense and practical knowledge to figure out what to do next."

Grau noted that many of the old standard grasses were susceptible to the adverse conditions, but that "the ability of Penncross to withstand excesses gave practical evidence of the soundness of the test results which helped to launch it in the golf course field." He concluded by saying "It is safe to say that we are at the beginning of a great change in procedures wherein more and more of the management practices will be based on careful technical analysis of the existing conditions before action is taken."

Poised at the threshold of the modern era, golf course architects were also examining what lay ahead. Just after the war they had been concerned with recovery, meeting the need for courses for new converts to learn on was their charge. Now there was a push for long and challenging courses—pushing the limits and engaging the better players. At the final USGA Green Section program of the 1950s, Robert Trent Jones noted, "The ideal course should demand alertness of mind as well as playing skill, for otherwise the players will not become absorbed in meeting the series of tests and challenges a course should offer. A course laid out with strategic soundness is bound to be interesting, no matter how many times it is played." Jones ushered in the era of increased length, and many other architects joined him, planning features that were not only more difficult to play, but also more difficult to maintain.

Three Hats

The years of 1945 to 1960 were filled with enormous change for the golf course superintendent, perhaps more than any other time in history. The job went from farming to management, from part-time to more than full-time, from getting by with materials mixed on-site to having choices between a multitude of commercial products and options. The amount of knowledge the successful superintendent needed to assimilate increased tenfold.

Hank Miller, superintendent at Briergate GC in Deerfield, Illinois, noted, "Greenkeeping 25 years ago was an art. Now it's an art and a science. It required just as much work 25 years ago as it does now, despite the extensive use of power equipment today."

Fred Grau agreed, writing, "The greenkeeper of yesteryear becomes today's superintendent by learning and applying modern techniques of business management. This means, first of all, organizing activities on the golf course in a business-like manner." Business manager, artist, and scientist—a rare combination in any person.

Chapter Five

Expansion

1961-1979

By Bob Labbance

A Method of Green Construction

In the earliest days of the twentieth century a discussion began in golf course design and maintenance circles regarding the proper construction of golf greens. Walter Travis was one of the first Americans who outlined his thoughts on the subject when he authored his 1901 book *Practical Golf*. Prior to Travis's thesis, greens were simply the point at which the hole terminated, with little thought to varying size, shape or construction. Starting in 1908, Travis modified his recommendations in several essays published in the *American Golfer* magazine, but the push-up green remained the most common putting surface in use in the country.

In the 1920s, Fred W. Taylor of Philadelphia advanced his own principles regarding the construction of greens. Taylor attempted to standardize materials and outlined two different methods of construction, both of which he began testing at Sunnybrook CC in Pennsylvania around 1914. When Drs. Piper and Oakley visited his experiments in 1920 they noted that both his slant and conglomerate methods of construction had problems, though the reliance on five layers of materials added significantly to the discussion. In a February 1921 article in *Golf Illustrated* the duo wrote, "On the slant greens the organic matter composed of fibrous peat and cow manure in the slant layer had shrunk causing a settling or collapsing, which in turn resulted in an irregular wavy surface. This interfered rather seriously with putting." But the scientists also found promise in Taylor's research, noting, "The germinating layer as he developed it constitutes a valuable addition to our methods of fine turf culture."

The issue lay dormant for much of the next several decades, with the construction of greens generally left to the architects' discretion in the post-World War II period. To the superintendents, this often meant customizing their cultural practices to whatever mysterious mixture lay beneath the course they maintained. While one could eventually determine a maintenance program for the club one was familiar with, this knowledge did not necessarily transfer to the greenkeeper's next assignment. As play increased in the 1950s, greenkeepers switched jobs with greater frequency.

At the USGA, Dr. Marvin Ferguson had been studying greens construction since 1947, incorporating the work of Dr. Raymond Kunze and Leon Howard at Texas A&M, agronomist W.L. Garman at Oklahoma State, Dr. Richard Davis at Purdue and Dr. Ray Lunt at UCLA. Ferguson also benefited from a timely study

USGA agronomist Marvin Ferguson was the driving force behind the USGA's specifications for putting green construction, first published in 1960.

by soil scientist Dr. Walter Gardner of Washington State University whose experiments on the movement of water through soils permitted a better understanding of how to layer sandy soils to retain moisture and support plant growth without becoming saturated. Gardner demonstrated that an underlying coarse layer would stop water movement at the interface until the finer soil above was saturated. This alleviated fears of greenkeepers that the new greens would require daily watering and constant fertilization. The Milwaukee Sewerage Commission presented the theories at many turfgrass conferences.

Although Ferguson credited the entire USGA Green Section with the work, he was truly the "Father of Modern Day Scientific Putting Green Construction." Citing ongoing research at Beltsville, Maryland and the universities, the USGA Green Section noted, "Many of the construction methods that were satisfactory in an earlier day will no longer produce greens which will withstand the wear that is now imposed upon them." Into this environment Ferguson released "Specifications for a Method of Putting Green Construction" in September 1960, and reaction was widespread, much of it critical. However, it was the scientific basis of his work that carried him through the initial phases of distrust and ridicule, and eventually installed the USGA method as the standard.

The USGA sought to establish a basis for specifications that clubs in all parts of the country could guide contractors with, but not to dictate precise detail. "Such specifications will place no limitations upon the individuality nor the artistry of any architect," the USGA held. "They will, however, provide a guide for the builder and for the club which wants to be assured that the greens they build will continue to provide good playing conditions for many years." The USGA believed that good drainage and resistance to compaction were the underlying goals, and although these goals at first appeared to be in conflict, it was quickly realized they could be simultaneously obtained with minimal compromise. This attempt at standardization was a comfort to superintendents who based their maintenance practices on the underlying composition of their putting surfaces.

The guidelines were quite specific and detailed, explaining the need for precision in the subgrade (14 inches below the finished grade); the layers of various materials and their placements; drainage tile recommendations; and the topsoil mixture.

"The subgrade should be compacted sufficiently to prevent

USGA Green Section specifications for green construction were published in 1960 and 1965 and revised in 1993.

future settling which might create water-holding depressions," the USGA report began. "Any suitable pattern of tile line arrangement may be used, but the herringbone or the gridiron arrangements will fit most situations," as long as the tile sloped uniformly with a minimum fall of .5 percent. Agricultural clay tile, concrete, plastic or perforated asphalt-paper composition were all deemed acceptable, but all were to be laid on a bed of gravel to reduce the possible wash of subgrade soil.

The tile and the subgrade were to be covered with pea gravel of one-quarter-inch particle size, followed by a coarse sand layer of two inches and then the topsoil layer of at least 18 inches. The soil mixture was to meet specific physical requirements of permeability, porosity, bulk density, moisture retention and mechanical analysis. The USGA realized, "Few natural soils meet the requirement stated above. It will be necessary to use mixtures of sand, soil and organic matter. Because of differences in behavior induced by such factors as sand particle size and gradation, the mineral derivation and degree of aggregation of the clay component, the degree of decomposition of the organic matter, and the silt content of the soil, it is impossible to make satisfactory recommendations for the soil mixtures without appropriate laboratory analysis."

Others believed they could add to this discussion. Based in Chattanooga, Tennessee, Alex McKay had been building greens throughout the South for nearly four decades when the USGA recommendations were released. In a March 1964 article in *Golfdom*, he detailed his findings which included reducing the topsoil layer from 12 to eight inches and adding peat to the topsoil. "My method is to spread ¼-inch of peat on the top of the green and rake it in with the fertilizer," McKay wrote. "This holds the water around the roots long enough for the roots to get the benefit of the water. The ¼-inch of peat helps cushion the green and keeps it from getting too hard on top."

McKay also believed that reducing the top layer from 12 to eight inches made a layer of stone under the green an unnecessary additional expense because the water could now get to the tile that much quicker. He also claimed that his greens could withstand temperatures in excess of 100 degrees for weeks on end without problems—a claim that had been proven true in the South over the many years of installation. One

The slant system of greens construction promoted by Fred Taylor in the 1920s resulted in an irregular wavy putting surface.

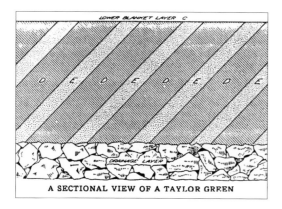

A SECTIONAL VIEW OF A TAYLOR GREEN

of the fallacies of McKay's specs became evident as greens settled and the eight inches needed to sink the cup interfered with soil layering.

From Downers Grove, Illinois, Stanley Wadsworth of the rapidly expanding Wadsworth Construction Company added his input to the greens discussion when he described the benefits of "off-site" mixing of soil components: "The important consideration here is uniform blending and screening of all materials." Previously, many mixes were made on the green site, a practice that no longer produced optimal results due to the precision now being suggested. "If sand, peat and top soil are not thoroughly mixed there is danger of layering with the resultant bad effects of poor water penetration. Also, the delivery of the mixture on the greens free of all stones, sticks, roots or refuse of any kind eliminates maintenance problems, provides a truer putting surface for the players and speeds up grading and seeding for the contractor," Wadsworth argued. The more precise the construction recommendations became, the more important the techniques to achieve them were as well.

In every category the recommendations for greens construction left room for the variances inherent in diverse conditions, but the USGA warned that shortcuts and elimination of steps could produce less than desirable results. "In short, do not attempt to incorporate some of these steps into green construction, unless they are all used in exact accordance with these recommendations," the article concluded. It was lack of adherence to this tenet that got most people in trouble when they attempted to take shortcuts to new greens.

In November 1965, the USGA revisited its standards when Ferguson, now director of the Green Section wrote: "After a period of five years, there are presently some 1,200 greens in existence that have been built by this method. There is no question that the method is both practical and successful. There are, however, some questions which continue to arise. There are some who failed to grasp the significance and the importance of each single step in the process. There are some who have experienced partial failure because they only partially followed the specifications." Ferguson addressed the most common problems with the specifications, a process that continued for most of the next two

Inspecting a field of Penncross in the early 1960s.

decades. In the interim the refinement of the suggestions brought many more situations under the ever-expanding umbrella, and helped many superintendents who were out of the highly populated regions build and maintain greens in a more efficient and standardized manner.

Penncross and *Poa*

In new course construction during this era, the architect or the green committee often made grassing choices, but in remodeling work the superintendent typically was included in the decision-making. The new grass of choice in the North for putting greens was Penncross, developed by professor H.B. Musser at Penn State University, and although it was released for use in 1954, the availability of the product was still very limited at the start of the 1960s. Initially distributed by Northrup, King & Co., of Minneapolis, Minnesota, the Penncross promotional literature noted: "It not only grows amazingly quick, but is strongly disease resistant, has unusual drought tolerance and fine uniform texture"—all qualities borne out by trial on the putting greens of America. An advertisement in September 1960 confirmed that the bentgrass, being produced in Oregon, was still "on the market in limited quantities," and so it would remain for several years.

Writing in *Golfdom* in March 1961, Dr. Fred Grau of the Hercules Chemical Company had these suggestions in response to a question about converting greens to Penncross. "Many old greens are being converted to Penncross by reseeding. This will be successful only if the thatch is removed, preferably by a machine that cultivates, aerates, and removes thatch all in one operation while leaving the green perfectly puttable. Seed Penncross at one-half pound per 1,000 square feet, no heavier! Top-dress lightly after seeding. The ureaform fertilizer can be used as a 'mixer' for the one-half pound of seed to make it easier to spread uniformly. Keep Penncross turf on the dry side—soak well when water is needed but let the surface dry as much as possible until golfers complain."

Penncross was accepted as a successfully seeded bentgrass right from the start, replacing Seaside as the most-widely planted grass for greens. But availability remained spotty well into the 1970s. When Tee-2-Green Corp., then of Kansas City, Missouri, took over distribution, Chairman Bill Rose wrote, "We ask for your patience while we expand our production to take care of the increased demand. We insist on giving you the highest quality seed available and we will not sacrifice quality for quantity. If your supplier is temporarily out of seed please be patient."

One problem that Penncross did not solve was encroachment into putting surfaces of *Poa annua*—hereafter referred to as *Poa*. Whereas some of the vegetatively planted bents could produce a dense enough mat of grass to resist *Poa* invasion, Penncross did not, and the resulting incursion resulted in more words being written about techniques and controls to counteract the threat than any other topic in the 1960s. It also resulted in some job losses for turf managers.

Poa, or annual bluegrass, has been a problem for superintendents for the entire second half of the twentieth century. It is found on six continents, and can be easily identified by its boat-shaped leaf, yellowish color and ability to produce seed heads even when cut to less than one-quarter inch in height. Although it produces a fine putting surface when conditions are right, it can quickly fade or die whenever the weather gets too hot or too cold. Hence, relying on it for a primary turfgrass is inherently risky as the slightest variance in its maintenance program can leave superintendents with brown grass, bare soil or both.

Nevertheless, it grows vigorously, can be cut close, germinates quickly, grows rapidly, heals well from injury, can grow in compacted soil and under other conditions in which perennial turfgrasses cannot survive. *Poa* will take over the grounds of a golf course when soil is compacted by machinery; when soils are poorly drained; when disease and insects have weakened grasses; when fertilizers, fungicides, insecticides or herbicides have been used improperly; or when turf is overfertilized or overwatered. Few courses in the 1960s were free of all these problems, hence the abundance of the grass. Even today, when several of these circumstances are combined, *Poa* will dominate bentgrasses or bluegrasses.

While we now know enough about the habits and management of *Poa* to combat its spread, in the 1950s and early-1960s superintendents were just beginning to educate themselves. Many products made promises or worked in specific situations, but the learning curve was long and fraught with danger for superintendents. Attempts to kill off *Poa*—both with preemergents and postemergents—often resulted in wholesale killing of other grass varieties, forcing those actions into the solution-was-worse-than-the-problem arena. Sodium arsenite was a common control method, but this "scorched earth policy" era often resulted in entire fairways being burned.

In 1959, Dudley Smith accepted a superintendent's position at Silver Lake GC in Orland Park, Illinois when the course was still covered with snow. When the snow melted he found 35 of 36 greens devoid of turf. His predecessor had applied calcium arsenate the previous fall, but when Smith reseeded, the seedlings emerged, turned red and died. Bent grasses could only be established when applications of phosphorus "neutralized" the soil. Smith went on to enjoy a 41-year tenure at Silver Lake, but many other superintendents were not as fortunate.

In the early 1960s, Henry Mitchell of the New England based Mitchell family (including course architect William Mitchell and a family of superintendents, golf professionals and turf farm operators) suggested combating *Poa* by reducing the organic content of the soil with nitrogen, lime, and water, thereby lowering the oxygen levels and retarding root growth. But he cautioned that "There is a narrow margin between too much and too little of this nitrogen-lime-water combination. When too much is applied *Poa* thrives on the resultant compaction." Also during this time period, Fred Grau suggested that the "best control is reduced irrigation and stepped-up fertilization when bluegrass is growing at its best. Arsenicals, used regularly, can reduce *Poa*."

In the south, Dan Hall, superintendent at Peachtree GC in Atlanta, found that a side effect of using sodium arsenite to step up the transition from overseeded ryegrass to bermuda was the destruction of *Poa*. At Charlotte CC, Palmer Maples Jr., studied the use of malic hydrazide on test plots located on the practice green. When applied at seeding time, Maples noted a substantial reduction in *Poa* on the green. In the fairways he found that application of four pounds per acre of sodium arsenite while the bermudagrass was still dormant curbed the *Poa* development.

The South had its own unique problems—comparable to *Poa*—in the control of crabgrass and goosegrass in warm season turfgrass. Dr. Glenn Burton began studying the control of these weeds in 1953, and by 1956 had MSMA and DSMA amounts determined. Professor B. J. Johnson at the University of Georgia, who refined the rates and time of application, continued his work. Experiments at the Griffin-Spalding CC in Griffin, Georgia, gave southern superintendents the tools they needed to combat these problems without threatening Tifdwarf and other cultivated bermudagrasses.

Back up north, writing in the *USGA Green Section Record* in March 1967, Eastern Region Director Alexander Radko suggested that shotgun mixtures of bentgrasses, Kentucky blues and creeping red fescues—grasses formerly found in abundance on fairways—adapted to various environmental conditions and kept *Poa* at bay. But as monostands of fairway grasses were planted, as grass was mowed lower and irrigation systems were employed, *Poa* infiltrated. Radko concluded that, "Those who began to mow closer than 1 ½ inches found that the creeping red fescue and the Kentucky bluegrass weakened badly; those who watered and fertilized heavily found that creeping red fescue died; those who watered and mowed high to keep the bluegrass and fescue found that the bentgrasses became too puffy and too soft to support a golf ball."

Radko laid part of the blame on the golfer. "Also involved are the desires of the playing members; they clamor for extending the golfing season by starting earlier in the spring and finishing later in winter. They also are looking for turf of summer quality the year round. Forcing permanent grasses only weakens it and encourages the *Poa annua* to take over."

In the Northeast, Sherwood Moore wrote several articles that impacted cultural practices and the maintenance, control or elimination of *Poa*. Moore knew the benefits of *Poa* as well as the disadvantages, noting "the disadvantages of *Poa annua*, however, outweigh its advantages. Annual bluegrass is very susceptible to many major turf diseases—the leaf spots, dollar spot, large brown patch and snow mold—and it requires continual spraying to maintain it. It is also very susceptible to winter injury. During winters of ice cover and desiccation, *Poa* suffers first."

TOP: *Irrigation testing began the long process of converting coupler systems and night watering to fully automatic coverage.*

BOTTOM: *Irrigation advances that began on the West Coast led to wall-to-wall coverage of golf course properties in the early 1960s.*

LEFT: *Early irrigation system installations—such as this one at North Shore CC, Glenview, Illinois—were often supplanted less than a decade later as the technology evolved rapidly.*

Moore believed that many factors were at work in the spread of *Poa*, citing mowing practices, too much fertilizer, overwatering and the pH of the soil. "I have been harping for years that superintendents do more damage to turf by overfertilization than by underfeeding," wrote Moore. "In the Northeast, two pounds of nitrogen per 1,000 square feet [per year] of established fairway turf is more than ample. It is also well known that annual bluegrass favors a liberal supply of available phosphate in the soil. If tests show an adequate supply of phosphorus, eliminate this nutrient from the fertilizer mix."

He also cited that: "Turf made strongly acidic by the use of sulfate of ammonia or other acid-forming fertilizers does not allow entry of annual bluegrass because of its low tolerance for high acidity." Moore admitted that even the smartest superintendents needed help from arsenicals, but he cautioned: "A fraction too much of an arsenical can destroy more *Poa* than a superintendent wants, leaving him with no turf and irate members." This was the danger that encouraged the status quo for as long as possible and prevented many from taking bold action. In later years some superintendents were also dissuaded by the state licensing required to purchase and apply pesticides. These burdensome regulations differed from state to state and the approvals to apply them were not reciprocal, adding red tape and frustration to the list of potential problems associated with *Poa*.

Changes in Irrigation

Many scientists, including James L. Holmes of the USGA Midwest section, laid much of the blame for *Poa* invasion on the new watering practices of superintendents. "Bluegrasses and fescues are deep-rooted, vigorous plants," he wrote. "The vast healthy root system will explore the soil to quite a depth. Therefore, frequent light waterings are not necessary. Rather, such watering practices will tend to reduce root systems and result in a tender, weak plant much more subject to attacks by pathogenic fungi. Thus, weedy growth is encouraged. *Poa annua* is the primary invader and it will gradually replace bluegrass and fescue under such environmental conditions."

Irrigation systems were undergoing the greatest transformation of any of the superintendents' tools during the time period of 1950 to 1980—and most of the impetus for change started in the western United States where water issues were of greatest concern. From fairway edge water valves, centerline quick couplers and night watering men to computer controlled automatic systems, the way a course was watered changed dramatically during this time span. Learning how best to utilize the new technology, when to replace an antiquated system, which of the new materials and products were right to install and maintain and where the technological march would end were questions that faced turf managers and club officials alike. The answers seem easy in retrospect, but the decision-making was complex and expensive in the early years of the 1960s and a large part of a club's maintenance budget was often at stake.

Concerns over water usage, water resources and water for recreational purposes began to build in the western United States in the 1950s. Dr. Robert Hagan at the University of California at Davis conducted much of the initial irrigation research, and many of the early irrigation companies—such as Rain Bird, Buckner and Skinner were born in the West to address the water concerns of the region. The combination of limited rainfall, a growing population, states' rights, and the vast expanse of federal lands translated into battles over allocation of available water. Issues that began with local farmers went to the state court systems before finding their way to the U.S. Supreme Court. In the Pelton Dam case, the Supreme Court decided that the federal government did not need to comply with California state laws regarding water rights when building on reserved federal lands.

This intervention by the court did not sit well with many independent thinking westerners. Subsequent conflicts over water arose not only between states and the federal government, but also between farmers, fishermen, boaters, and golfers. It is therefore not surprising that advances in delivery systems for irrigation were born in the West before being adopted throughout the country.

Prior to 1960, if a golf course had an irrigation system at all, it involved manual couplers and the infamous night watering man. Quick coupler valves were installed at various points on the course, sometimes only one at the green and one in the fairway. The worker would normally arrive at sunset and begin a watering ritual that would last throughout the night. Inserting a quick coupler key into the valve, he would either attach a sprinkler head or a hose and then water the area immediately adjacent to the sprinkler. When the area was soaked he would disconnect his equipment, load as much as 500 feet of hose back into his utility

Automatic irrigation systems with elaborate control centers became the norm by the 1970s.

truck and move to the next coupler. If he didn't get sidetracked by his friends to visit the local pub or fall asleep while water inundated a green site, by morning the golf course would be watered and play would resume.

There were other dangers as well, including vandalism in the urban environments, wild animals in the rural regions and the possibility of burglars anywhere. Every night watering man had a host of humorous stories and an occasional scare that made the job less than desirable for the weak-hearted. This complicated system was developed in the early 1930s; pop-up rotary sprinkler heads were added in 1935 and the method remained the most common irrigation system well past the end of World War II.

The problems with manual watering were essentially threefold: finding reliable people to operate the system, the lack of standardized water rates and the possibility of wasting valuable water resources. Naturally, the first improvement on the coupler system came in California—where resources were the thinnest—in the mid-1950s when a very few courses devised semiautomatic systems. Speaking at the International Turfgrass Conference in San Diego in 1963, Donald Hogan, a western irrigation specialist, noted, "The manual quick coupling system was the forerunner of today's permanent underground automatic sprinkler systems. Today fully automatic golf course irrigation systems are not a luxury, but rather a necessity."

Hogan advocated complete irrigation coverage of greens, tees and fairways, with some additional coverage in the roughs. "Best results are achieved by controlling relatively small areas independently," he maintained. Initially, turf managers viewed this total irrigation approach as wasteful, but as the case was made that labor would be lessened and that the tailoring of needs would result in less overall usage the trend toward automatic systems gathered steam rapidly.

Writing in the *USGA Green Section* in 1967, Clifford Wagoner of Del Rio Golf and Country Club in Modesto, California noted, "If your present watering schedule delays starting times and if you must water throughout the day, causing inconvenience to the golfer, you should seriously consider automation. If labor is not available for night watering, automation is a must. Unionization is steadily making its way into golf course maintenance and therefore every superintendent should closely check the restrictions and added costs it places upon management."

Wagoner wisely advised superintendents to hire competent

installers, cautioning against trying to do the job in-house. "Some very successful systems have been installed by golf course maintenance crews, but this should not be undertaken unless you are absolutely certain you have qualified help and have had experience in irrigation installations." Wagoner detailed some of the problems from inexperience, warning "no pipe should be laid until depths of ditches are checked; no wire or tubing laid until pipe is bedded in; no ditches filled until blueprints are checked making sure all fittings, wires and valves are correctly in place; and no sod laid until backfill is compacted to avoid settling. The success of the system very definitely depends upon exactness of installation."

The need for sophistication in watering systems, the development of the various components, the decisions regarding proper materials for construction, the need for a comprehensive design of the system, the studies that detailed the effects of watering patterns, and the advancements in the industry were driven by western needs—though the benefits slowly spread eastward throughout the late 1950s and early 1960s. The first course on the East Coast to install an automatic system was Sea Island in Georgia, a system installed by Mountain Lakes Corp., of Lake Wales, Florida. Harvey Linderman was the landscape architect who headed the project. "When I think back to 1964, it somewhat frightens me that I stuck my neck out so far in making statements on the advantages of automatic watering and the estimated years for amortization," he later said. But Linderman was sold on the benefits to golf courses, especially the ability of the superintendent to maintain uniform soil moisture, rather than the "feast or famine supply that existed under the manual watering system."

Within a few short years the movement to automatic systems was widespread. In the Northeast, the Colonial CC in Lynnfield, Massachusetts, led the way with a system designed by Larchmont Engineering of Lexington, Massachusetts. Superintendent Phil Mitchell had control panels in his pump house that activated any sprinkler on the course with the push of a button. He could also program a pattern of engagement or go to manual mode. "When I'm out on the course I can turn on any sprinkler manually without using any tools," added Mitchell. "I don't have to come back here to push a button."

In Cheltenham, Pennsylvania, Joe Tagnon, superintendent at Ashbourne CC, installed a system in 1962 that advanced his water delivery capabilities from 30 gallons per minute to 650 gallons per minute and eliminated the need for hoses snaking through the golf

The Environmental Protection Agency (EPA) and the Occupational Safety and Health Administration (OSHA), established by President Nixon in 1970, changed the way workers performed their tasks in every quarter of American society. Protection from pesticides was one of the most visible changes to operating procedures for turf managers.

course. The piping was designed with three separate zones and a single-line delivery.

By 1963, double-line systems were being installed, one of the first at PGA National GC in Palm Beach, Florida—a course deemed the "Course of the Future" for its advancing engineering. According to irrigation specialist John Singleton, "When it comes to questions of pump capacity, size of pipe, contour grade, wind velocity, soil, thatch and drainage, all of these factors can be related by a skilled programmer to arrive at optimum solutions that invariably stand the test of sound engineering. Operation of the water system is the superintendent's responsibility alone. His formula for constant prime conditions remain his property and adds to his value to the club."

Judging from the advertisements in the trade magazines, there was intense competition regarding the type of pipe used in systems being installed. Choices included polyvinyl chloride (PVC), plastic, transite and cast iron—each had its advantages and disadvantages under differing conditions and parts of the country. Each manufacturing company touted its products and contractors were forced to educate themselves and green committees if they wished to remain players in the irrigation installation scramble in the middle years of the 1960s.

Despite the belief it's a very recent phenomenon, it wasn't long after the modern irrigation system became the norm that some scientists looked to irrigation systems to carry more than water. In August 1970, agronomist Dr. James Watson of the Toro Company wrote, "An irrigation system is designed to function as a water dispensing system. Because of this, it should be capable also of distributing chemicals, including fertilizers. Using an irrigation system for these purposes could represent a substantial cost saving: First, it reduces labor costs; secondly, it saves equipment purchasing and maintenance. In addition, there is evidence to indicate, in the case of fertilizers, that small amounts of nutrients, applied regularly through irrigation water, produce plants of superior quality."

Watson cautioned that soil and climatic variations made the uniform application challenging, and that retrofitting a system not designed for such delivery was not simple—but nonetheless, in light of technological advances in controllers, valves, and sprinklers—fertigation, as the process became known, was a distinct possibility for turf managers. Salting out—or the crystallization of dissolved materials—could result in sludge buildup on components, but often this problem could be minimized by attention to temperature during delivery.

Some would say that 30 years later, all the problems associated with fertigation have yet to be conquered, but irrigation systems themselves have improved dramatically. By the end of the 1970s, water system capacities had increased from approximately 500 gallons per minute (gpm) to 1,500 gpm, reducing the overall time for completion of the job, and superintendents had moved from worrying whether or not the night watering crew would show up to worrying whether or not the computers that controlled precise delivery of measured amounts of water would crash. Advanced irrigation, when over-used by zealous applicators had led to the green grass syndrome, and courses once maintained lean and mean to promote the ground game now became lush retreats of wall-to-wall turf coverage. That would raise its own set of issues.

Silent Spring

While the limitation of water usage was one environmental concern that raised its head during the 1960s, it was by no means the most egregious. In the 1950s, most people enjoyed a certain ecological innocence and a complete lack of regulation in nearly every phase of their jobs. That was about to be eroded on all fronts during the 1960s. Between the impending environmental firestorm and the creation of the Environmental Protection Agency (EPA); the unprecedented regulation of the workplace through the Occupational Safety and Health Administration (OSHA); and the beginning of a societal shift toward litigation as a method of addressing grievances, superintendents felt they were expected to produce better and better courses with both hands tied behind their backs. Some of those who had enjoyed unbridled decision-making in the 1950s retired rather than be overwhelmed by the new regulations.

The first salvo was fired in May 1962, when Rachel Carson published her groundbreaking book, *Silent Spring*—a treatise on the dangers of pesticide use that made the world take pause and listen. "The crusade to create a chemically sterile, insect-free world seems to have engendered a fanatic zeal on the part of many specialists and most of the so-called control agencies," wrote Carson. "It is not my contention that chemical insecticides must never be used. I do contend that we have put poisonous and

TOP: *Ralph Nader's boring keynote speech at the 1972 conference in Cincinnati was an attempt to reach out to the opposition, but it won him few friends in the industry.*

BOTTOM: *Nader is peppered with questions following his keynote.*

biologically potent chemicals indiscriminately into the hands of persons largely or wholly ignorant of their potentials for harm. We have subjected enormous numbers of people to contact with these poisons, without their consent and often without their knowledge. I contend, furthermore, that we have allowed these chemicals to be used with little or no advance investigation of their effect on soil, water, wildlife and man himself. Future generations are unlikely to condone our lack of prudent concern for the integrity of the natural world that supports all life."

Carson cited DDT to illustrate her thesis. Though scientists poked holes in some of Carson's arguments, the book had a profound impact on the public and subsequently the chemical industry. Though it was nearly a decade before DDT was banned in parts of the world, the general public looked at golf course maintenance differently.

A bitter debate raged on many fronts, and overwhelming public opinion forced the establishment of national environmental oversight. In December 1970, President Richard Nixon established the EPA. The agency's effect on the profession of greenkeeping would be immediate and everlasting.

With the government now looking over a superintendent's shoulder out on the golf course, some felt the regulatory arm of Washington could not make life any more difficult for the profession—but they were wrong. At the same time he established the EPA, Nixon also inaugurated OSHA. The act that created this division of the Department of Labor was charged with assuring "safe and healthful working conditions for working men and women," by "assisting and encouraging the States in their efforts to assure safe and healthful working conditions; by providing for research, information, education and training in the field of occupational safety and health; and for other purposes."

Suddenly the government was also in the shop, monitoring everything from the workbench to the bathrooms to lighting to equipment storage. Eye, ear, mouth and nose protection were instituted, along with procedures for handling substances and worker's exposure to contamination. Storage of hazardous materials was also brought to the forefront. While all these concerns were valid and both OSHA and the EPA have brought needed safeguards, procedures, and improvements to the workplace, their inauguration was not always smooth, and their mandate to change existing methods was not always shared by all. The adherence to new regulations was slow to spread to all quarters of the green-keeping profession.

In an article for *Golfdom* in June 1969, Joe Doan wrote, "DDT is now a dirty word. But some supers think that after it has been banned for a few years and if an equally effective substitute has not been found, it will be reinstated—when the bugs and beetles once again infest the land." He noted that due to public pressure, DDT application at golf courses in the Chicago area was already down 60 percent, and superintendents who observed fish kills from drift of the product into Lake Michigan had discontinued its use completely. In a move certain to give greenkeepers pause, Paul Frankowski, superintendent of the Beverly CC in Chicago, was actually taken into police custody when drifting spray, aimed at his dying elm trees, coated cars at a nearby busy intersection. No charges were filed, but the Beverly staff was ordered to wash and wax the vehicles to satisfy motorists who were affected.

Positive reactions to the impending restrictions started where many of the radical American cultural ideas begin—in California. Fred Harris, superintendent at Los Coyotes CC in Buena Park, welcomed the new era, realizing that it would spur the chemical industry on. "Prior to the legislative restriction, if a manufacturer introduced a new chemical on the market, the superintendent was hesitant or unwilling to take a chance on it. After all, DDT and mercury were doing an effective job and were cheap, so why

By 1972 the conference and show were outgrowing smaller venues.

At Bob O' Link in Highland Park, Illinois, superintendent Bob Williams began his own program of training young people interested in turf management. Over the years he placed 70 protégés into the golf course maintenance profession.

switch from proven chemicals?" Harris noted that the bans would produce better control agents with less danger to the environment.

Ellis Geiger, superintendent at Doral CC in Miami, felt that the switch was already underway. "We have found many substitutes over a broad spectrum of chemicals which are effective, biodegradable and have very low toxicity," he noted in 1971.

In Leroy, Ohio, John Spodnik of the Westfield CC advocated a pesticide applicators' test and an effort to steer the conversation away from the term pesticides—preferring 'plant protectant' when talking about fungicides. Spodnik believed systemic chemicals would be found to control turfgrass pests just as effectively as the questioned compounds, with fewer problems.

By 1970, the drive was underway to embrace safer controls, adjust to the new world consciousness about chemical pollution and move forward in ways that would demonstrate that superintendents were responsible stewards of the land. To be at odds with the reasonable factions in the ecological arena was never in the interests of forward-thinking superintendents.

The Ecological Insect Service of Kerman, California, was advocating the praying mantis as a way of controlling beetles that bore into putting greens and destroyed the surface. In an article titled "Will the Insects Take Over," Dr. Fred Grau wrote, "Natural enemies offer hope in long-lived crops such as turfgrass where the predator population builds up without interruption. One excellent example of this approach is the milky spore disease of Japanese beetle grubs."

Grau also cited bacterial toxins, insect viruses, attractants and the possibility of sterilizing male insects as methods of control. "Considering the broad range of techniques that have been successful on certain insects, control of turfgrass insects by similar methods is foreseeable. If the female cutworm moth and the female sod webworm moth laid only unfertilized eggs there would be no larvae to eat the grass roots."

The environmental concerns that were raised during the 1960s and early 1970s went far beyond chemical usage. Oregon residents forced an end to open field burning of pastures used by grass seed growers in the Willamette Valley. The practice had been employed for decades to destroy field residues, control insects, dispose of straw before the next crop was planted, and to sanitize the ground by killing airborne diseases. But problems occurred when atmospheric inversions prevented the smoke from clearing the valleys and the resulting dense fog affected freeways, airports, and residents, prompting the action. Due to the ban on burning, a number of grass seed growers moved their operation across the border to Alberta.

In 1969, the Vermont legislature passed Act 250 — the country's first far-reaching environmental legislation — which imposed stiff water pollution fines in addition to requiring every project to pass hearings that took into account sewerage, air pollution, historical preservation, traffic patterns, loss of farmland, zoning, urban growth, and the concerns of adjacent landowners. It was a bill that brought golf course development in the state to a standstill for more than a decade.

When the GCSAA asked Ralph Nader to keynote the 43rd annual conference in Cincinnati in 1972, many of these issues were affecting not only golf courses, but also the general public. Nader left little room for debate. "It is not a question of can we afford to clean up our pollution," he noted, "but if can we afford *not* to. If we would spend one dollar on pollution prevention now, it would save spending $100 for cure later."

Though the threat of public consternation was motivation enough for change in the industry, it was the menace of legal action that drove many clubs to alter their activities. Suing a golf course was practically unheard of in the 1950s, but just a decade later, clubs and even superintendents lived in fear that disgruntled landowners, employees, suppliers, and members were potential litigants.

Suits were filed by those tripping on outdoor stairs; players who were allergic to control substances; passersby who were hit by golf balls; club bar patrons who were served too much alcohol and then caused automobile accidents; employees who were asked to apply hazardous substances; bettors who lost a wager due to the disruption of heavy equipment noise; cart drivers who careened off steep paths and were injured; players who claimed there were no posted warnings about lightning or evacuation plans during a thunderstorm; adjacent homeowners who were disturbed by lights that allowed ranges to operate after dark; and a host of other issues. If it wasn't enough for turf managers to

In 1964, David Moote became the youngest GCSAA president in the Association's history.

Turfgrass field days, such as this one at Michigan State University provided an opportunity to observe results in the field.

worry about the new spate of regulation, they now were reluctant to do anything that might result in a lawsuit.

As president of the GCSAA in 1976, Palmer Maples, Jr., wrote, "There was a time when the only form to fill out was the social security withholding form; that was our only contact with the government. Today a number of forms and lists have to be filled out and maintained as we go about the business of growing turf. Today regulations govern not only people and how they work, but machinery, chemicals, noise, pollution of air and water, and housekeeping of the maintenance area and building before we even get out to the turfgrass area itself."

Though Maples cited many extreme—and some may think ridiculous—examples of safety devices, protections, and regulation, he noted that the superintendent "must be aware of the law and how it affects his operation. He must maintain those necessary records, and if he doesn't, and the inspector finds cause to issue a citation, then upper management may wonder if it has the right man in charge."

Ben Chlevin (RIGHT), *assumed the role of GCSAA Executive Director from Dr. Gene Nutter* (LEFT) *in 1964 while President David Moote looks on. It was under his watch that a certification program was launched.*

Solutions in Education

It would be hard to find a profession that had changed any more than greenkeeping during the 30 years after the end of World War II. The industry reacted to the changes spurred on by the new regulations in the same manner it had to every other challenge it had faced—with education.

The annual Turf Conference and Show remained at the heart of the educational experience, but the focus changed from the science of growing grass to the new tools the superintendent needed. In 1971, one session at the national conference was devoted to pesticide regulation and another to how a superintendent can effectively conduct a public relations campaign—something few knew they needed prior to this era. Courses on irrigation and preparing a budget were also part of the program.

The show had seen steady growth in the 1960s. The 31st conference in Houston in 1960 drew 1,475 participants. More and more wives were accompanying their husbands to the shows and programs were being developed to interest them. The Houston show was dedicated to O.J. Noer of the Milwaukee Sewerage Commission, an agronomist who had spent 35 years helping superintendents nurse their turf. Noer had traveled far and wide during his career, meeting superintendents, discussing turf, taking photographs and passing on the accumulated wisdom. Now he had announced his retirement for 1960, and his friends planned a fitting testimonial.

"This is Your Life, O.J. Noer," featured a surprise appearance by his mother, daughter and granddaughter, in addition to images of him and his work over the decades. Combined with the Houston hospitality, it was a gathering to remember.

A new record for attendance was set in 1962 in Miami Beach when 2,141 attendees assembled, many drawn to the Sunshine State by warm temperatures and relaxing beaches and golf courses—especially after the previous year's weather in Toronto. In *Golfdom*, Herb Graffis wrote, "One of the most refreshing speakers of the entire education program turned out to be Ellen H. Gery, who finds time to be a leading Florida golfer in between making real estate deals. Miss Gery put such questions as these to the turf masters: 'Why do you invariably top-dress greens the day before women play a tournament? Why don't you recognize that Ladies Day is an established institution and save your heaviest maintenance work for some other day? Why don't men realize that if they bar women's play during certain hours on Saturdays and Sundays, the restricted periods are always the most desirable ones so far as the lady swingers are concerned?' These questions were submitted in good humor and in a bantering kind of way, but Ellen undoubtedly put across the point." It was years until the golf industry finally addressed these concerns properly.

Another attendance record was established in 1964 at Philadelphia with 2,250 on hand, as well as the election of David Moote to the presidency. Moote, superintendent at Rosedale GC in Toronto, was the third Canadian to hold the post, the group's youngest president ever and only the second president to hold an advanced degree in turf science (Marshall Farnham being the first). Moote received his bachelor's degree at Ontario Agricultural College in Guelph in 1951 and went on to graduate work at Rutgers. Moote represented a passing of the baton to a new generation of green masters.

By the 1970s, attendance at the GCSAA's annual gathering had topped 3,000, trade show floor space doubled, equipment demonstrations were a popular attraction, the conference assumed an international personality and the educational opportunities continued to expand. When asked the purpose of such cattle shows, Dr. Grau said, "One phase of a conference that merits recognition is the social aspect. For many this is the annual chance to visit with friends and exchange ideas. Closely associated are the bull sessions where informal discussions of turf management extend far into the night at GCSAA conventions."

Regional conferences were also growing rapidly. Programs at Texas A&M, as well as the Bob Dunning Turf Conference in Tulsa, Oklahoma; the Leon Short Turf Meeting in Keokuk, Iowa; the St. Louis Conference; the Midwest GCSA Clinic; the Florida Horticultural Association Convention; Reg Perry's Southern Turf Conference; Cliff Wagoner's Northern California Conference; Dr. Glenn Burton's Tifton gathering and the Illinois Turfgrass Conference all were drawing record crowds and expanding their offerings.

Some innovative superintendents also developed their own programs. At Bob O'Link in Highland Park, Illinois, superintendent Bob Williams trained as many as eight college students at a time; all were majoring in turf management at schools such as Penn State, Iowa State and the University of Illinois. "What it amounts to," said Williams, "is that everything these fellows learn in school suddenly makes sense when they see it demonstrated." Williams would eventually place more than 70 of his protégés in the profession thanks to these educational programs, as well as pioneer the position of assistant superintendent in the maintenance staff hierarchy. Trainees took turns serving as job supervisors, with their compatriots serving under them, and then the roles were reversed. Many lessons in leadership as well as what makes a good employee were learned. Similar programs existed at other Chicago-area clubs, including Olympia Fields, Gleneagles and Glen Oak.

University programs also expanded, accommodating interested students willing to spend two or four years studying turfgrass. In 1950 there were approximately five universities in the United States providing an education in turfgrass. Twenty years later the number was closer to 25. Higher education also began to fund more research by its instructors and scientists; at the same time scholarships were offered to promising students. The industry not only fed the interest but also created the demand for qualified people. Golf continued to boom in the 1960s and every new golf course that opened required a new staff. During the 1950s, there had been a 21.6 percent increase in the number of courses nationwide. In 1960 alone, 205 new courses were established—a record, but only until the next year had passed. The boom would continue until the energy crisis of the mid-1970s brought it to a screeching halt.

The Certified Superintendent

By the middle of the 1960s, the GCSAA felt that a yardstick to measure the performance of outstanding superintendents was needed. The prevailing opinion was that those who advanced their knowledge through the many educational opportunities should be rewarded and acknowledged. A committee was formed in 1968 that included past GCSAA presidents Walter Boysen and Cliff Wagoner. The committee spent many California nights hammering out a program that eventually agreed to the following principles: Any standards must be set by the superintendents themselves; the exam must be comprehensive, including a written test; and the program should be a professionally-administered long-term effort.

Under the primary direction of Dr. Paul M. Alexander—then GCSAA Director of Education—the program became a reality less than three years later. The written examination was quite extensive and centered on six areas of expertise:

1. Knowledge of the GCSAA, including history, purpose and ethics of the profession
2. Familiarity with the game of golf and its rules
3. Agronomic procedures
4. The selection, handling, usage, precautions, limitations, and legal issues regarding pesticides. Superintendents must also demonstrate an understanding of licensing and application of materials in their state
5. Record keeping, budgetary considerations and business administration
6. Personal relations, hiring, training, and supervising of personnel, public relations and staff management.

Applicants were given six hours to complete the exam, allowing them to budget their time to any area as required. A passing grade was required in all phases, but failure in one did not negate passing grades in the other. Applicants could be retested in the areas they failed as many times as they required before passing, as long as the entire test was completed within one year. If it was not completed in that time frame, applicants were required to repeat the entire exam.

Successful superintendents assumed the title of Certified Golf Course Superintendent (CGCS) and were allowed to place the designation on their business cards and letterhead, but the honor did not create another classification of GCSAA membership. The professional assessment was voluntary and could be sought only after three years of employment as a Class A member. A provision also allowed for some veteran superintendents to become certified without testing. Any member with Class A status for 20 years or more, who had been employed during that entire time, could apply in writing by September 1, 1973, under the "tenure and experience" provision.

The committee did not wish to embarrass or humiliate the superintendent in any way. No time frame from application to exam was set. Applicants were sent sample questions when they received their pre-exam packet. All materials and test results were handled confidentially. The test was an open book exam and applicants could refer to study materials sent to them in advance. In the event of failure, tutoring was available before a subsequent exam. The program was to be updated continuously to reflect new discoveries in research, new equipment and techniques.

The GCSAA saw many benefits to the designation. First, it established a type of job description for superintendents, defining what their areas of expertise was and what services they performed for their club. Secondly, it was hoped that the possibility of certification would bring new people to the profession through the promise of recognition and measurement of achievement.

The program also encouraged superintendents to remain current in their education, gave them a yardstick to measure their own development by, helped advance salary levels commensurate with their abilities, promoted greater career stability, and gave prospective employers something to measure an applicant's skills by, other than his local reputation. In formally announcing the program, Ben Chlevin, executive director of the GCSAA, said, "The process of examination and its content will alert club officials, golf course operators, club managers, golf professionals and golfers to the exact nature and extent of the superintendent's professional qualifications."

Writing in the *Green Section Bulletin*, Cliff Wagoner added that, "Certainly there is no guarantee that certification will improve the performance of the individual superintendent. On the other hand, it does unmistakably define the level above which any given super-intendent can be expected to perform."

The first year of the program brought more than 150 inquiries and eventually resulted in the first 32 certifications. In 1972, a similar size group of applicants resulted in 65 superintendents achieving the designation. By 1975, after five years of testing, 250 superintendents had earned the right to place CGCS after their names. The program has grown steadily ever since, with more than 1,750 active, certified superintendents today.

As the program was first instituted, pay scales for turf managers were not what they should have been, prompting GCSAA president Richard Blake to say, "Golf clubs, club officials, superintendents and everyone associated with the game of golf have played ostrich long enough. Superintendents have been shortchanged for their sincerity and dedication. They have been taken advantage of." Often, the chef or the caddie master at a private club was paid more than the superintendent, a situation that slowly began to change in the 1970s. The certification program was in part responsible for the change, by forever altering the image of the greenkeeper.

"It used to be that the golf course was built on a farm somewhere and a lot of people still picture the farmer in bib overalls out mowing on a tractor with steel wheels," noted Dave Harmon, superintendent at Golden Horseshoe in Williamsburg, Virginia. "Too many superintendents today still want to stay in their own little corners, they don't even want to go to the clubhouse. The way they dress and handle themselves, they still look like farmers."

But growing turf became less and less the focus of the job as the years went by. "Maybe 75 or 85 percent of the business today is not really growing grass, but learning how to coordinate people and how to convince them that you need to do this or that," said Don Clemans of the Columbus CC in Ohio. "Going out and actually doing the job—that's the least of my worries."

For many outside the green industry, the Certification program was the first realization that professional and management skills had become as much a part of the profession as pesticide application. As soon as the perception of professionalism infiltrated the job description, there was an increase in the wage scale. Superintendents such as Bob Williams in the Chicago area, Ted Horton in the New York metro and Bill Beresford in Los Angeles helped to expedite the move to higher salaries that were commensurate with the responsibilities and expertise needed in the position.

With the increase in salary came the need to trumpet one's accomplishments to both the members and the public at large, lest the Board might believe it wasn't getting all that it had paid for. "To be a successful superintendent, you have to deal with people, a lot more so than the average person thinks," noted Richie Valentine of Merion GC at the time. "There is a lot of public relations in our job today, and there's going to be more in the future."

Slowly, the education of the members, the advancement of the profession, the public relations work of the superintendent and the elevation of the importance of the job to the prestige of the club brought about a new era in salaries—and a new status to the superintendent. "If you can get hold of a club member or a green committee member who's a doctor you can learn to relate the phenomena of turf to the living processes within the human body," noted Clemans. "Once he understands you, he'll bring along five others who respect him because he's a doctor." By the mid-1970s the profession garnered a respect that should never disappear.

Equipment Advances

Throughout American society, the 1960s was a time of experimentation and the exploration of new frontiers. Conventional wisdom was questioned at every turn, and, often, something very new replaced something very old. Some ideas worked and were improved upon; others did not and were quickly forgotten, but society was moving faster than ever and there was little opportunity to look back and reflect.

One experiment that never gained much acceptance involved changing the look of courses and was unveiled in 1969 at the Bob Hope Desert Classic in Palm Springs, California. It was there that the 3M Company introduced Scotch-Rok—fractured rock granules that were infused with colored ceramic coatings and fired at high temperatures to produce bunker sand in kaleidoscopic colors. San Francisco scribe Art Spander said it best: "It's called Scotch-Rok, as it is not to be confused with scotch on the rocks, which will never be replaced. Scotch-Rok costs $15 a ton—people would drink to that if scotch sold at a comparable price. And it comes in 30 colors ranging from beige to turquoise." Fortunately for superintendents this was one 1960s fad that didn't last.

Other innovations that would eventually have an impact on golf did catch on. One was the power sand rake, first mass-marketed in 1971. Although several innovative superintendents had attached rakes to tractors in the past, the first real power sand bunker rake was invented by Stanley Clarke of LaGorce CC in Miami, Florida. USGA Agronomist William Buchanan observed his first exposure to the machine in a September 1971 article for the *USGA Green Section Record*. "Bunkers on many courses are costly to maintain, and until recently all the work was done by hand. Recently, power rakes have been developed that offer a tremendous saving in man-hours. While visiting one course this summer, we observed a power rake in use. The operation was timed in five minutes; according to the superintendent, it took one man 30 minutes to do the job manually. Therefore he saves 25 minutes in labor on that one bunker every time it is raked."

The power sand rake was first demonstrated at the International Turf Conference at Woodway CC in Darien, Connecticut in 1971.

The saving in time and money offered by power rakes could not be disputed, and many managers converted to their use as fast as the items could be added to the budget. Players saw the advantage in uniformity of the surface; increased depth of the raking, which eliminated weed growth; and the amount of time maintenance people influenced the flow of play on the layout. But over the span of several years the power rakes changed the shape of bunkers, and eventually the design integrity and vision of the architect.

Deep, flashed-up, small or irregularly shaped bunkers that gave a course its unique personality were never candidates for power rakes. Large, flat and oval bunkers were perfect for the devices. It was the bunker-types in between those two extremes that, over the course of several years, suffered from their usage. First, the operator needed an entry and exit point in every bunker. Accessing this ramp into the bunker over the course of several seasons meant that the shape of the bunker extremity at that point was altered. Instead of a lip that defined the sand, a compacted and often bare flat spot developed. In the event of a downpour, this was often the first point at which sand migrated from the bunker. Secondly, by spinning around a bunker in the most timesaving manner, slowly the shape of the bunker began to change. Corners were rounded and bunker shapes became less individualistic, eliminating the capes and bays, rough edges and unusual appendages that made bunkers visually appealing and unique. The bunker styles of great architects like Alister MacKenzie, Charles Blair Macdonald, George Thomas and A.W. Tillinghast were compromised.

The first commercially available triplex mowers were introduced in 1968, and radically changed greens mowing.

In the first year or two the euphoria over the time saved by the power rake blinded everyone to the drawbacks. After five or 10 years of such treatment the bunkers began to morph into less attractive hazards—if, in fact, anyone remembered their original outline. Twenty years of constant power rake use often resulted in such damage and loss of bunker character that restoration was needed. The observant turf manager realized where he could utilize the timesaving devices and where he needed to expend the money on hand-raking to preserve the integrity of the course design.

Another device with a similar history and effect was the triplex greens mower. For decades, superintendents mowed their greens by hand with walk-behind reel mowers. When the demands of the player were simple, greens were often cut just three times a week, and although the speed varied depending on how recently the green had been cut, the variance was not enough to alter the pleasure of the game. As the sophistication of the customer increased, greens needed to be mowed nearly every day, and the amount of time it took to mow all 18 greens then became a burden to a small staff. Hence the introduction of the riding greens mower was seen as a major advancement in course maintenance, cutting the time required to mow greens considerably. In the past where it might have taken four workers with walking mowers three to three-and-a-half hours to cut all 18 greens, now it took one person the same amount of time to cut all 18 with the triplex.

The first machines were introduced in 1968 and in a May 1971 roundtable discussion in the *USGA Green Section Record*, Eastern Region Director Alexander Radko estimated that, "By the end of 1971, I would guess 75 percent of our clubs will have one." Mid-Atlantic Director Holman Griffin noted that, "Most of the advantages—and there are several—are really tied into labor saving and money considerations. But the new units also make golfers happier because the maintenance crew isn't in the way as much."

USGA Green Section Western Regional Director G. Duane Orullian added, "Some superintendents have told me there is a savings on equipment parts as well. They believe it is less expensive to maintain one or two triplex mowers rather than six or eight conventional units."

Though the benefits revolved around less manpower to maintain the course, the disadvantages were agronomic. The new methods produced more compaction, additional grain, tracking or worn wheel paths, problems turning the machines around due to encroaching features in the surrounds, damage to the fringe and apron, difficulty mowing greens with severe contours and differences in the heights of the three cutting units. In addition, regardless of cost, it required a more sophisticated mechanic to keep the riding mowers working properly.

John Zoller, superintendent at Eugene CC in Oregon, summed up the problems succinctly: "Much has been said about the convenience and speed of the triplex putting green mower and these are important considerations in this day of high maintenance costs. I am not sure the story ends there however. In some ways it is a case of subordinating what is best for the golfer to what is best for the course superintendent. In our section of the country I have heard members of some clubs say that suddenly their greens don't seem to putt as good as they used to. They seem to be slower or not as smooth or they have more grain."

Zoller went on to detail many of the problems that would lead superintendents to eventually curtail or replace their triplex mowers. "By the very nature of triplex mowing, it is a must that all three cutting units be matched as to cutting height and balance. This must be checked every day. If a bearing or bushing on a roller shaft has some wear that means it will not cut at the same height as the other two. Another problem that we must guard against is damage to the putting green hole. The perimeter cut around the green presents another problem that demands attention. Because this cut can be made in only two different directions, a lot of swirling of the grass seems to develop. It can only be eliminated by vertical mowing and top-dressing."

Zoller summed up the feeling that infiltrated many of the better clubs that initially thought triplex mowers would help their efforts. "At our club, we are not sure that we want to sacrifice the quality that we feel we can get with single unit mowers for the quality we get with the triplex mower. The actual savings are not all that great. At no time have I heard any of our members favor lessening the quality of greens maintenance in order to reduce costs."

Lee Record, USGA Mid-Continent director, added, "Triplex units will improve when man realizes that the time element is not the key to successful putting green management. If the superintendent cannot economically cope with increased thatching, thinning and top-dressing, the triplex mower may have already reached its peak for use on greens."

As with many new devices in the golf superintendent's arsenal, the learning curve for proper operation of triplex mowers resulted in damage to turf and unhappy golfers at first. Slowly, superin tendents taught the techniques to the workers, monitored the results, and made improvements in technique. Some superintendents mowed by hand during the week and with the triplex mowers on the weekends. Others cut by hand during the height of the season but relied on the triplex in their off seasons when they operated with a reduced staff. Still others cut with the riding mowers for standard play, but hand-cut the greens before events and tournaments. Many of the turf managers who sold their hand mowers as soon as they bought the triplex came to regret that hastiness.

The problem they failed to see in the short term was the same problem that characterized the power sand rake. Greens with distinctive shapes slowly became rounded over the course of multiple seasons. And even those without distinctive shapes got smaller. The loss of about an inch a year from the size of a green may not seem dramatic, but over the course of two decades a considerable amount of the putting surface vanishes. When the crew stops cutting an arm of the green that extends beyond a right rear bunker and a similar section to the left front, before long two pin placements have been lost. If the staff changes, the new workers may not even know those areas were once there. Eventually the character of the course has been compromised without any intent to do so, and returning the greens to their original scale is a great deal harder than the loss. Some superintendents learned this lesson the hard way.

Other equipment advances of note during this time period included leaf raking machines, improved aerifiers, power greens rollers, groomers for putting green mowers, power sod cutters, spraying booms with computerized rate settings, spiking and slicing machines, more fuel efficient tractors, balloon tires for lessened impact on turfgrass, ditch diggers, greens squeegees, and vertical mowing machines. All these machines changed how a course was maintained, all required employee training, all led to further technological changes and all impacted the life of a superintendent.

High Stakes

Not all course maintenance challenges of this era resulted from advances in technology. Before World War II, hosting a major golf tournament was hardly a life-changing event. Put the course in good shape, prepare for a few thousand visitors, and stand aside so the professionals could play their game. In the 1950s, several factors conspired to change that.

As more and more events were added to the competitive calendar, pros like Arnold Palmer began to plan their schedules and chart the progress of their careers around the major championships. Just as Harry Vardon and Bobby Jones before him—and Tiger Woods today—Palmer elevated the stature of the majors with the intensity he brought to the tournaments. In fact, the British Open was on a popularity decline until Palmer convinced the other American pros to patronize the tournament, bringing attention to the courses and greenkeepers of the older courses of the United Kingdom in the process.

The popularization of color television also contributed. Previously fans could only access information about the event from the newspaper, and they might just read a single paragraph about course conditions. As the events began to appear in their homes in "living color" they were confronted with course conditioning for hours each day. Every inch of a golf course was on display for millions of people to see. The "Augusta National Syndrome" developed—where green committee members pressed their superintendents to put their course in the same condition they witnessed on television.

The increased attendance by both fans and the media also had a substantial effect. Accommodations for gallery access and player security had to be assured, and the devastation to the grounds could be substantial should the week be wet and the traffic areas muddy.

In a panel discussion at the annual conference in 1960, four superintendents who had recently hosted a U.S. Open shared their trials and tribulations with assembled superintendents. As if normal preparation were not enough, three of them faced a major crisis in the months leading up to the major tournament. Sherwood Moore had a February fire at Winged Foot that destroyed his maintenance building and most of his equipment; Elmer Border woke up one March morning to find out that his staff at the Olympic Club had gone out on strike; and Elmer Michael at Oak Hill suffered through 10 months of abnormally high rainfall prior to his event. Marshall Farnham, who had hosted the 1939 Open at the Philadelphia CC, admitted that he got off easy for his moment in the spotlight, saying, "Perhaps the course requirements weren't quite as stringent 20 years ago," and adding, "Yet, I'll say that one Open is enough for any superintendent."

The lessons that were learned at these post-World War II sites helped to standardize the practice of tournament preparation, and today there is constant oversight by golf's ruling bodies. This was not always the case. Border recalled that prior to his Open, a club official mandated that the rough should be grown as high as possible to prevent the pros from embarrassing the club with low scoring. "He wouldn't allow the rough to be cut. When Joe Dey, the USGA executive director, came to inspect the property a few days before the tournament, the rough looked like African bush. It was finally decided that the only thing that could be done was to cut a 6-foot swath adjoining the fairway to normal rough height. When the tournament was ended and the entire rough restored, 280 truckloads of grass were hauled away."

Even without misunderstandings between tournament planners and the course maintenance staff, one factor can always conspire against turf managers—the weather. At the Beverly CC in Chicago, superintendent Ted Woehrle hosted the 1963 Western Open when its status was just below that of the U.S. Open. Knowing that he would host the tournament during July, Woehrle's first thought was "I wonder how I will make out with the weather?" Foreseeing hot and dry conditions, high humidity and acres of wilted bentgrass, Woehrle set about to prepare for such conditions. "What I got was rain—oceans of it," said the superintendent afterward. "In the week preceding the tournament, Chicago's south side was flooded with nine inches of rain; on the Sunday evening before pros were to start practicing we had three inches of rain in about one hour."

Woehrle remained philosophical: "When it's all over, you're happy to know that you can handle a project as big and important as one of the year's outstanding tournaments." He also had some advice that has been heeded ever since. "Don't overlook the press and TV and radio men. On the morning the tournament started, I went into the press tent and described the condition of the course and explained how the heavy rains of the week previous had undone some our preparations for the tournament. Everyone was sympathetic and I'm happy to report that, as far as I know, not a single derogatory word was written about the course's condition." When he went on to host the 1972 PGA Championship at Oakland Hills, Woehrle drew on the lessons he had learned previously.

By the mid-1960s tournament sites were announced several years in advance, but the preparations were extended far beyond the setup of the fairways, greens and tees. Bridges were inspected and deemed satisfactory for maximum loads of spectators; shelters on the course were expanded and made available; proper space for tents to house media, tournament and pro shop sales operations were cleared; sanitary facilities were planned for; parking problems and entry points for shuttle buses were detailed; underground trenching to bury telephone and television cables was undertaken; service roads and the routes for vendors and emergency vehicles were carefully considered; fencing to delineate parking, boundaries and traffic areas were installed; spectator ropes to limit access were established; bleachers were erected and the problem of how to collect and remove trash was considered. Although not all of these problems fell to the superintendent, his coordination of the various factors was critical, and when something went wrong or was overlooked the superintendent was often the first to hear about the problem. This route was easier than finding a committee chairperson to address the issue. M.G. Miller, chair of the green committee for Baltusrol GC in New Jersey, summed up their preparations for the 1967 U.S. Open by saying, "Preparing for a championship entails more than providing a good golf course. The Open is played in four days; it took more than three years to get ready."

By the 1970s the job almost always involved a remodeling of the golf course as well. Superintendent Vance Price realized how involved this operation had become when he oversaw a Robert Trent Jones remodeling of the Tanglewood GC in Clemmons, North Carolina, in preparation for the 1974 PGA Championship. First the routing was altered to choose the best nine holes from the West course and the best nine holes from the East course. Then Price planted nearly 300 pine trees to block other tees from the selected holes, remodeled or downsized most of the huge greens and rebuilt each of the 110 sand bunkers—a process that entailed hauling in 10,000 tons of sand from 120 miles away. Such efforts became commonplace as equipment and the talent pool increased. The USGA and the PGA felt they needed to toughen up any course, even if it had hosted a major as recently as 10 years previously.

During this time period the USGA also appointed an agronomist to work with the host superintendent. The goals were "a uniformity of condition that inspires confidence in predicting the way the ball will act," according to an article in the July 1975 *USGA Green Section Record* authored by Bill Bengeyfield and Alexander Radko.

They went on to say, "Conditions must allow for the possibility of finesse throughout the prime target zone and provide a suitable penalty for all who stray from it. This is the role of agronomic preparation. This is where the golf course superintendent and consulting agronomists put their heads together to prescribe the best route to follow toward that end." A *USGA Golf Championship Manual* was assembled that detailed heights of every grass cut, nutrition programs, watering regimes, preventative disease and insect control programs, top-dressing and aeration guidelines, sand particle size specifications and even post-tournament procedures to return the course to the members for standard play.

Though the preparation for a major event consumed a substantial amount of a superintendent's time, energy and thoughts for the better part of a year, there were benefits as well. As Herb Graffis wrote in *Golfdom*, "There is no denying that a superintendent who grooms a course for a USGA extravaganza has his share of tribulations, but at least there are compensations. It often helps him salary-wise; he may be able to purchase equipment that the club has backlogged over the years; but probably most importantly, it vastly improves his stature in the eyes of the members." There may have even been an honorarium in it for him.

Eddie Stimpson

Over the centuries there have been many devices that have changed golf in ways that their inventors never envisioned. When Edwin Budding produced the first lawn mower he pictured it mowing home lawns, but gave little thought to how it would revolutionize golf. When Old Tom Morris accidentally dumped a load of sand on a green and watched the grass flourish he had invented top-dressing without even knowing it. Even the rubber-wound golf ball was an haphazard discovery, as Coburn Haskell sat around the Goodrich Rubber Company factory impatiently waiting for his playing partner to join him.

But practically no device has had a greater effect on the game than the Stimpmeter, despite the intent of the inventor. Even more amazing is the fact that this device sat on a shelf at the USGA for more than 30 years before it was put into use in 1975. In the quarter-century since, the device and its usage have become nearly universal throughout the world.

Edward Stimpson Sr., grew up in the Chestnut Hill section of

Newton, Massachusetts, just outside of Boston. He graduated from Harvard in 1927 and then the Harvard Business School in 1929. He soon joined his father's bank in Cambridge, before moving on to the trust department of a large Boston bank.

Stimpson was a member at Brae Burn CC in Newton in the early 1930s, playing to a five handicap and capturing the club championship on several occasions. In 1935, he won the Massachusetts State Amateur championship and also attended the U.S. Open at Oakmont CC as a spectator. The greens at Oakmont in 1935 were the fastest putting surfaces that the Open had yet contested on, and players were experiencing great difficulty with their putting. Stimpson noted that one or two greens out on the course, and the practice putting green, did not match the speeds of the majority of the surfaces, and this in particular gave the players fits. Not one player in the top 20 broke 75 on the final day at Oakmont and Stimpson felt something had to be done.

Back home, in the basement of a friend's house, Stimpson took a 30-inch piece of wood, carved a channel down the middle of it and a notch at the top. With a golf ball resting in the cradle at the top, Stimpson slowly raised the device until the ball rolled down the channel and on to a flat portion of a green surface. The distance the ball rolled on one green could be compared to the distance it rolled on another.

When he attempted to market his device the directions were simple: "Raise the stick until the ball rolls out of the niche, then measure the distance it rolls from the end of the stick." Armed with this device, Stimpson believed that superintendents could standardize the speed of their greens, allowing players to find the same speed on all 18 carpets.

As the device was perfected, Stimpson's friend said, "We'll make millions from this—everyone will have to have one." But Stimpson wanted nothing to do with profits from the device; he simply wanted to help players and superintendents. "Golf doesn't owe me a thing," Stimpson remarked. "I owe golf—I've had a marvelous life playing golf."

He sent the device on to the USGA, who shelved it, probably, as Stimpson observed, because "it didn't look like a sufficiently scientific thing." And there the device sat for nearly 30 years, until Frank Thomas arrived at the USGA in 1974. Al Radko, national director of the Green Section at the time was interested in developing a device to measure the speed and hardness of greens and had put Thomas in charge of the project. "I designed four different

Edward Stimpson had no way of knowing what he had started when he developed the innocent-looking Stimpmeter.

instruments," wrote Thomas, "each with an intricate ball release mechanism. These were all relatively complex designs with built-in potential for operator error," admitted Thomas.

Thomas went back to look at the Stimpson design and decided that some simple modifications could be made to bring the device closer to the desired mechanism. "The changes included a more precisely cut ball release notch, a V-shaped rather than round-bottomed chute and an increase in the length of the device to develop enough roll that significant differences in green speed were measurable."

After testing 15 wooden prototypes at six USGA championships, Thomas sought a company to manufacture the device. When he was informed that aluminum would be far less costly than wood, Thomas agreed to that final alteration and the Stimpmeter was made available only to superintendents. He cautioned, "Let's not misuse it! The Stimpmeter was not designed to be a speedometer." Despite his plea that the Stimp be used to judge the reaction to different cutting heights, the effect of top-dressing and other maintenance practices and the desire to produce uniformity on 18 different putting surfaces, the device had a life of its own.

Almost immediately, the USGA Speedstick, as it was briefly known before being renamed for its rightful inventor, was used as a way to increase green speed, rather than equalize speeds on differing greens at the same course, as Stimpson had intended. (Amazingly, despite the long incubation, Stimpson had an opportunity to see his stick gain favor, before passing away in 1985 at age 80.) In 1976, the USGA measured 750 greens in 35 states to establish criteria for tournament speed and daily member standards. Their findings illicit a chuckle from those who putt the mind-bendingly rapid greens of today.

At that time, the median green speed for member play was 6.5 on the Stimpmeter, the fastest greens were clocked at 8.5 and greens seen as slow crept along at 4.5 on the device. For tournament play, everything was advanced two feet—meaning the fastest greens for competition measured 10.5, but the median for important tournaments was still only 8.5 on the Stimp. In interpreting the results, Alexander Radko, national Green Section director wrote, "To consistently maintain a green in championship or tournament play conditions is an extremely time-consuming and costly project. One would therefore not expect to find greens on a particular course to be in tournament shape throughout the season."

Radko still hoped to perpetuate the notion that the device was released to assist the superintendent in standardizing the various greens under his care. "The by-products of having an instrument to measure a green condition may be very far-reaching. Seasonal changes may be observed and the effects of various management programs can be measured. This may also provide an early warning system as to a potential problem arising on a particular green."

Radko also foresaw the device's potential to avert mistaken pin placements. "A hole should be placed in such a position that no matter where the golfer is putting from it should be possible to stop the ball within approximately two feet of the hole. Thus a hole location which presented a fair challenge when the green speed was approximately six-and-one-half feet may quite possibly be a very bad position when the green speed is eight or nine feet."

Julius Albaugh, superintendent at Westmoreland CC in Illinois was one of the first to speak out regarding the dangers of judging greens based on Stimpmeter readings. "We alter our management practices to the turfgrass variety, soil and weather conditions," wrote Albaugh in 1979. "We top-dress, aerify, spike, verticut, comb and brush as needed to assure the best possible putting surface. These practices are not based on Stimpmeter readings, but, instead, on our agronomic background and on our ability to provide our membership with a uniform, true, healthy and green putting surface."

In an article entitled "How Fast is Fast?," Sherwood Moore noted, "The topic of conversation around locker and grill rooms of golf clubs these days is, 'How fast are the greens today?' It all boils down to the speed of the ball on the green. Lost is the art of stroking the ball—today a tap is all that is required. I think some golfers want the ball to roll into the cup just by looking at it. Are we becoming the victims of the Stimpmeter, fast greens and tournament play? Can we afford to maintain greens of this caliber— that require frequent top-dressing; frequent verticutting, daily cutting or double-cutting of greens; close, close mowing—even to the point of grinding the underside of already thin bed knives?"

With green speed the new religion, Moore was concerned for the future. "And in all my conversation and reading and listening, I have never heard anyone mention a thing about the little grass plant. How is it standing up under all this abuse? I was tutored under the late Professor Lawrence Dickinson of Massachusetts and one of his often quoted phrases was 'Give the grass plant half a chance. It wants to live.' Under these conditions of shaving the grass plant to ⅛-inch or less, are we giving it 'half a chance?' I do not think so. We are giving it very little chance. Sooner or later we are headed for trouble."

Moore's words were prophetic, as some championship venues have damaged or lost their greens while trying to increase their speed to new levels. Even as recently as the 1979 U.S. Open at Cherry Hills, superintendent Jim Young's putting surfaces were measured at only 9 for the early rounds and 9.5 for the weekend. By today's standards those greens would seem slow. Keeping greens healthy while they Stimp at 11 or 12 is a pursuit that has dogged modern superintendents in the past decade, no matter how many high-tech tools and genetically manipulated grasses they have in their arsenal.

Other Changes to the Game in the 1960s

It's hard to believe today, but as recently as 1960 there were very few golf courses tied to housing developments. Projects had been successfully developed at Pine Lake, Piping Rock, Hilton Head, Sea Island and Bald Peak Colony Club, but the concept was isolated to just a few outlets throughout the country. The idea of planning a community around a golf course took hold at places like Boca Raton, Florida, in the early 1960s, and by the end of the decade the National Golf Foundation (NGF) reported that 40 percent of new course construction involved real estate development. In 1969, the NGF reported, "A further refinement of this trend is developing in the clear, sunny climate communities of California, Florida and Arizona, where apartments, town houses and shopping centers have been built near recreational facilities." Although we take such things for granted today, they were unusual 40 years ago.

The impact of this housing on superintendents was substantial. Poorly planned subdivisions often spread the golf course out for miles, adding long travels between holes and a maintenance facility that was far from the center of activity. Instead of compact routings where multiuse roughs divided fairways, each hole now had its own buffer from buildings, and the amount of cultivated

Prior to the 1960s there were few golf course developments that involved housing adjacent to fairways. The pendulum swung entirely in the opposite direction in the 1970s, spreading out the maintenance of the course over a much larger area and bringing storm water runoff problems into play.

area to maintain grew. Eventually residents complained about early morning noise from machinery, forcing turf managers to adjust their schedules. Runoff from paved parking areas and roadways that intersected the fairways often caused washout and siltation problems. Before realistic setbacks were adhered to, superintendents might be forced to confront a host of issues resulting from the interaction of golfers and glass windows.

The continuous cart paths that were installed at golf communities, and later at nonhousing related courses, had an impact on the maintenance of the course also. As cart usage soared in the 1950s, the containment of the vehicles to paths became necessary—though in the early years paths were primitive, made from gravel, chat, stones, seashells or whatever material was readily available—and they never formed a tee to green roadway. In 1966, Texas pro/superintendent Odis Beck of the Ridgewood CC in Waco convinced his golf committee that a pathway was needed. The concrete path was built in stages for about $1 a running foot and the benefits included lower maintenance of areas where carts previously compacted soil, and the ability to put carts onto the course as soon as heavy rain was over. Los Colinas CC in Irving, Texas, was one of the first clubs to pour a complete 18-hole trail around the layout. The nearly five-mile-long ribbon was 10-feet wide and its favorable reception by members was a harbinger of things to come.

One 1950s trend that died out in the 1960s was night golf. Lighting courses for night play had begun as early as 1932 at the Ingleside Public Golf Course in California. But the trend died out during the Depression and World War II. In the 1950s, practice areas were first illuminated, then pitch and putts followed suit. Eventually course owners intent on improving the bottom line moved toward lighting short courses, and then in August 1963, Tall Pines GC in Sewell, New Jersey, became the first regulation length nine-hole course to turn on the towers.

"The technical and economic success of Tall Pines should encourage a nationwide string of illuminated courses which will make golf as much a nighttime endeavor as bowling, baseball, tennis, softball, football and all other spectator and participant sports," predicted Larry Dengler, marketing manager for General Electric's Outdoor Lighting Department.

But as electricity costs rose and, after the novelty wore off, participation fell, few courses followed suit. This was fortunate for the superintendent who had a hard time explaining that near round-the-clock use of the golf facility left little time for course maintenance or turf recovery, and that the glare of the big lights enhanced any surface imperfections on the greens.

Welcome to Kansas

In the early days of the GCSAA, when the organization was still named the National Association of Greenkeepers of America, headquarters were little more than an office in Cleveland from which the *National Greenkeeper* publication was assembled. In 1934, A.L. (Gus) Brandon of the St. Charles GC in Illinois took over as secretary and the office moved to the Chicago area. Relocation in 1957, still in St. Charles, tripled the office space—a space that the rapidly growing organization quickly filled. When Dr. Gene Nutter was hired as the first executive director in 1959, the office was moved to Jacksonville Beach, Florida, where the director lived. Nutter was an educator and outstanding speaker who brought credibility to the management staff and enhanced the GCSAA image during his tenure. The subsequent return to Chicagoland in 1965—this time to Des Plaines—was the result of the employment of Ben Chlevin as the second executive director.

As the membership ranks, the support staff and the role of the GCSAA continued to expand, the executive committee considered the need for a permanent and spacious home. In 1972 they voted to launch a nationwide search for the right location—a search that considered more than 130 cities around the country, but ended in Lawrence, Kansas.

Lawrence was never on the original list of possible sites, but the option arose during an inspection trip to Kansas City. Bob Billings, a real estate developer with the Alvamar Development Corporation, recalls, "They had tentatively come up with a site on a golf course in Kansas City. But for some reason, when they got down to the final negotiations, it didn't work out." Committee members were disappointed and decided to visit Mel Anderson, the well-known superintendent at the Alvamar Golf Course. "They worked really hard trying to find something suitable in Kansas City," Anderson recalls. "But they couldn't find anything zoned properly—and the prices were just astronomical."

Anderson had grown-in one of the first zoysiagrass golf courses in the country, opening Alvamar in 1968. The committee was

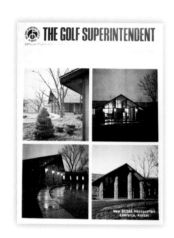

TOP: *The February 1974 issue of the* Golf Superintendent *announces the GCSAA move to Lawrence, Kansas.*

BOTTOM: *The first Association headquarters building in Lawrence. It was replaced by a new facility in 1991.*

impressed with the golf course and the area, and asked Anderson about adjoining land. "Mel called me," Billings continued, "and said, 'My Association is thinking about coming to the Kansas City area and they wondered if there was anything adjacent to the Alvamar golf course that might work for them.' I said, 'We'd be delighted to accommodate their needs,' so we looked at potential locations."

The committee was impressed with both the site and Billings's willingness to help in any way possible. "We have just been delighted to have the Association here in Lawrence," says Billings. "We've tried to be supportive in any way we could. But I would have to say that if the Kansas City situation had come together as it was originally anticipated, the Association would probably be located in Kansas City rather than Lawrence."

Using a cash reserve that was the result of careful spending and astute investment, the GCSAA was able to buy a one-and-a-half acre parcel of land at 1617 St. Andrews Drive adjacent to the highly regarded Alvamar Golf Course. The building that was erected was occupied on April 23, 1973, though it was not entirely finished until November, and a grand opening was scheduled for January 12, 1974. The entire property cost the GCSAA $195,279.00 — a sum that would have seemed unbelievable when the entire operation was housed in a single office just 40 years previous.

Though the spacious building was more than adequate to start, the unprecedented growth of the organization forced several redesigns, remodelings and expansions. Over the 15 years from the move to Kansas to the end of the 1980s, the GCSAA staff tripled, the membership of the organization went from 4,240 to nearly 11,000 and the annual budget ballooned from $750,000 to more than $7 million. In the fall of 1989, the Board of Directors approved plans for a new 44,000-square-foot facility and by spring 1990 ground was broken. Like the original site, the second headquarters location was on land purchased from Billings.

Energy Costs Rise

While the GCSAA was first settling into its Lawrence headquarters, international events were adding another challenge to the life of the superintendent. In 1973, the Arab oil embargo forced up the price and down the availability of gasoline. Though fuel costs accounted for less than five percent of a superintendent's budget, the wave of increases in petroleum-based products, including fertilizers, had a modest impact on future budgets.

Writing in the *USGA Green Section Record* in March 1974, Dr. James Watson noted, "Golf course superintendents, because of the very nature of their business, are excellent planners. They realize that one must utilize all of his managerial skills to analyze each maintenance operation. Even in instances where the cutback in fuel supplies was as high as one-fourth of precrisis deliveries, the superintendents foresaw few major problems on continuing a high level of maintenance for their courses."

To some resort courses the energy crisis did mean a small drop in business for a summer or two, as fewer people traveled to recreational destinations. But for other courses there was a rise in play. Local players stayed closer to home, utilizing their membership in a nearby club, rather than driving far and wide to enjoy a game.

The uncertainty about the future did influence course construction. For the first time in decades new course construction slowed, with the results appearing in 1975. The National Golf Foundation still reported that 256 new golf courses opened for play in 1975, though that number was down eight percent, or 21 courses, from the previous year. Though this drop was the first downward movement in a industry that had gone steadily up, the rise in course additions, prompted by increased play at local nine-hole venues, more than offset any overall drop in the expansion of facilities.

Most turf managers were ready to reduce the maintenance of their rough and out-of-play areas if need be, continuing normal operations on tees, greens and fairways. They made sure that the right piece of equipment was used for the job at hand, and realized, for example, that a riding greensmower, covering three times the area of a walking mower, made more efficient use of the fuel allotment.

They also revised mowing patterns to eliminate wasted travel, both on the fairways and between mowing locations. In some instances they raised the height of cut in the roughs, thereby adding one or two days additional to the interval between mowings. Superintendents noted that the increase in labor rates, attributed to the rampant inflationary pressures of the era, took a bigger bite out of their budgets than the rise in energy costs. Their conservative management of the budget brought them through the hard times, and Watson's advice was well heeded: "Superintendents must keep cool, remain objective and not become alarmists. The energy crisis provides turfgrass managers with their greatest challenge and their greatest opportunity in years. The production and maintenance of good turfgrass facilities can only grow in importance, for those facilities are a vital and necessary part of our way of life."

Half-Century Celebration

Two years after moving to Kansas, the organization's attention turned back to the north. The organization, and standing president Richard Malpass, felt that the proper celebration of the 50th anniversary of the GCSAA should take place at its origin—the Sylvania CC in Sylvania, Ohio.

On September 13, 1976, more than 600 people attended an emotional and noteworthy celebration of the founding of the Association. Members of Sylvania opened the doors of their clubhouse to the guests, including six charter members from that day long ago. Also on hand were 11 Outstanding Service Award recipients, 16 former Association presidents and keynote speaker Arnold Palmer. A letter of congratulation from United States President, and avid golfer, Gerald R. Ford was read. Citing the phenomenal growth in golf he said, "Much of the credit for this growth goes to you, whose dedication and concern for perfection have made our courses into beautiful and reliable playing areas. The imagination and energy you bring to your tasks assure our nation's golf enthusiasts of the world's finest golf courses."

Arnold Palmer, whose father Deke was a greenkeeper, spoke with emotion about what being raised on a golf course and learning from his father's work ethic had meant to his career. He encouraged everyone to aspire to greater professional heights and set a standard of excellence and involvement that would serve as an example to all those that would touch the profession in the next 50 years.

Displays of early greenkeeping equipment covered the lawn; demonstrations of horse-drawn mowers and numerous other early devices were offered; photos and minutes from early meetings were on display; a bronze plaque commemorating the birthplace of the organization was unveiled; the future of the GCSAA in the next 50 years was discussed; and a gala banquet concluded the day's events. Tears, laughter, reminiscences and heartfelt camaraderie characterized the gathering—the GCSAA had weathered

The 50th anniversary celebration on September 13, 1976 at Sylvania CC in Sylvania, Ohio, began with a bagpiper leading in the GCSAA officers.

some difficult times, but the idea from half a century previously had proved to be a good one—and not a single participant from those seminal meetings could have projected how grand the organization would become in such a short time.

Science Advances the Art

The increased research at the nation's universities, the burgeoning experience of so many qualified people in the business and the growing number of turf school scholarships and subsequent graduates advanced turfgrass science in many ways during the 1960s and 1970s.

Research into fusarium blight was conducted in Indiana at the Country Club of Indianapolis. Superintendents Terry Pfotenhauer, Dave Bolyard and Steve Frazier used fungicides on Kentucky bluegrass and bentgrass fairways to counteract the disease that thrived in the hot, humid summer weather. Pfotenhauer used the product as a preventative in June but also believed, "It's never too late to apply the fungicide for fusarium. If you've got it, you can apply the fungicide and stop the disease." The superintendents found Tersan by Dupont, applied at a rate of five ounces per 1,000-square-feet, produced the best results.

Turf breeding programs accelerated at the universities in this time frame. In a November 1967 article, Holman M. Griffin, USGA agronomist, wrote, "Until approximately five years ago, turfgrass breeding programs were either nonexistent or largely neglected in the general turf program. The money being spent on turfgrass research is insignificant when compared to the total expenditures. It amounts to something less than one percent." Griffin believed that geneticists who were improving field crops could develop turfgrass strains that would be disease and wear tolerant in any weather or conditions. Until this time most of the grasses in use were selections from nature that were observed in trials and singled out for their performance, but few had been improved through manipulation. Griffin wrote, "Next we should consider the use of radiation and mutagenic agents to create genetic variations. This method allows the plant breeder to work with the most outstanding varieties, and alter their genetic composition in hopes of producing an even better plant,

The surviving charter members at Sylvania included (LEFT TO RIGHT) *Willie Smith, Chester Mendenhall, Harry Hanson, Addison Hollander and Ralph Martin. Missing from photo is James Thompson.*

or of endowing the variant with a superior, transmittable characteristic."

The stumbling block was plants that reproduce sexually as compared with apomectically, and the number of variations possible when cross breeding was reliant on sexual reproduction. According to Griffin, Dr. Reed Funk at Rutgers "annually screens and evaluates some 50,000 individual plants of bluegrass, fescue, ryegrass and bent. Each year a large portion of these plants is discarded and replaced with new plants. Those with some superior characteristics will be retained for further evaluation." Infusing any one variety with all the desirable characteristics is a pursuit that has kept researchers busy for the ensuing decades.

Funk, along with Drs. Kenyon Payne, Richard Schmidt and R.W. Duell, spearheaded the research into fine fescues—noteworthy for their attractiveness, but also for their persistence in shade and acidic soils—environments where few grasses flourish. Summer heat, low mowing and heavy nitrogen fertilization resulted in deterioration of the fescues, but in combination with Kentucky bluegrass they formed a fine partnership. Banner, a chewings fescue developed at Rutgers by Funk, is typical of the variety. Composed of 45 clones from the Northeast, the grass is low-growing, fine-leafed, spreads slowly by basal tillering and can tolerate mowing heights down to two inches.

Another great advance in golf course grasses came in the South where Tifdwarf supplanted Tifgreen. Released to turf managers in April 1965, Tifdwarf had been studied and tested by Dr. Glenn Burton at the Georgia Coastal Plain Experiment Station in Tifton for three years. Burton found it to be superior to its predecessor in many ways. "For the modern golfer demanding fast greens, Tifdwarf will be a real improvement," wrote Burton in the January 1965 *USGA Green Section Record*. "Its tiny leaves hug the ground so closely that a number of them are never cut by the greens mower. This characteristic helps it to tolerate a $3/16$-inch cutting height much better than Tifgreen. Its softer leaves and fewer seedheads also contribute to its superior putting qualities." Burton went on to list its darker green color, increased winter hardiness, equal disease resistance, half as many clippings by weight and lower top-dressing requirements as benefits of Tifdwarf over Tifgreen. "These findings suggest that the amount of mowing could be less and, hence, labor costs might be reduced through the use of this variety."

Scientists postulated that Tifdwarf was a vegetative mutant that occurred in the first planting stock of Tifgreen released from the Georgia Experiment Station. Its superiority had allowed it to spread to an 18-inch diameter patch in two locations where it was selected by two groups unaware of the other's investigations. T.M. Baumgardner and Marion McKendree found the grass at Sea Island, Georgia, about the same time that USGA agronomist James Moncrief discovered a similar patch on a green at the Country Club of Florence in South Carolina. Genetically identical, the new grass was isolated, purified, studied and named before it was released to superintendents.

In the 1960s, few turf managers realized how their new irrigation systems affected the community of different grass species on their courses. In 1979, USGA agronomist Jim Snow wrote, "Although it is just one of many cultural factors which can influence competition between grasses in a turfgrass stand, irrigation is perhaps one of the most important." Snow went on to detail how fine fescues did best in droughty soils, Kentucky bluegrasses thrived in moist but well-drained environments and bentgrasses preferred moist but poorly-drained situations where occasional flooding occurred. Turf managers began to understand why some grasses would dominate and others would disappear due to the change in watering practices precipitated by wall-to-wall irrigation coverage.

Costs and the Crew

If there was one factor that characterized the 20 years between 1960 and 1980 it was the rising cost of maintaining a golf course. In a 1962 financial analysis by the accounting firm of Harris, Kerr, Forster and Company, published as *Clubs in Town and Country*, it was estimated that the cost of course maintenance averaged $3,307 per hole. That figure was up 45 percent from the previous decade, but the rise in the next decade would far outpace that percentage. (Of course golf course incomes rose in proportion to expenses as well.)

By 1972 the cost had doubled and with the energy crisis and rampant inflation in the 1970s it would increase even further. Every category of the budget showed a significant increase with fungicides, fertilizers and grass seed representing some of the biggest bumps. In addition to the daily maintenance, the cost of course improvements and investment in long-term projects and equipment—such as irrigation systems, cart paths, mowing equipment, and repairs—also skyrocketed.

The rise in educational opportunities for superintendents also produced a more sophisticated worker, one who expected a higher paycheck. Wages were one of the toughest line items to keep under control in any budget. The more advanced the machinery, the more highly paid the operator. The more regulation and procedure that needed to be adhered to, the more training and pay the worker required. At times, the inflationary spiral left managers seeking workers at pay levels below what they could obtain in the service industry. If flipping hamburgers paid more than physical labor in the hot sun, superintendents went begging.

In the July 1972 *Golfdom*, Norm Graft, superintendent at Stansbury Park GC in Toole, Utah wrote, "The most serious problem facing golf course superintendents is that of labor—not just finding employees, but locating competent, caring people." Graft solved the problem at the course he was opening by hiring women—a path that seems elementary, but at the time was out of the mainstream.

Graft started with one female worker and soon realized that her dedication to the job, competency and ability to make wise decisions led him to hire an entire female crew. "During my 14 assorted years in the grounds maintenance profession, I have never seen any crew handle sprinklers and care more about getting dry spots wet and take more pride in seeing the grass begin to germinate than the women on Stansbury's crew," Graft noted after watching the course grow in.

Furthermore, in an era when men doubted a woman's ability to perform difficult work, Graft observed, "Women can handle manual labor; women can operate equipment efficiently; women can work together; and women enjoy and care about maintaining golf courses." He went on to add, "They are personally neat, there is little absenteeism, women can handle foremen positions and their most outstanding quality is their pride in workmanship." Unfortunately, this integration of the golf course maintenance work force failed to catch on nationally, and today women account for fewer than one percent of the superintendents on the job—perhaps an underutilized source for the future of the profession.

Chapter Six

The Boom Years
1980-PRESENT

By Gordon Witteveen

Since the beginning of golf in North America during the latter part of the nineteenth century, participation in the game has increased at a steady pace. Likewise the number of golf facilities has kept pace with the needs of the golfers. The great depression of the 1930s brought golf's expansion to a temporary halt, but after World War II, golf's popularity once again ensured growth and expansion. Existing facilities expanded and new courses were added, not just private country clubs but also many public courses. Golf courses became part of housing projects and retirement communities. Resort complexes, hotels and skiing facilities added golf courses to their amenities. At first the impact of new golf courses on existing facilities was insignificant, since it was spread out over large areas. When, during the last quarter of the twentieth century, new golf courses opened at the rate of 400-500 per year, the new building boom affected everyone in golf.

Architects were in demand and became trained practitioners of the age-old art of golf course design. They combined the study of agronomy with landscape design. Some studied the old masters and paid visits to the famous courses in Scotland, Ireland and England. Well-known players on the PGA Tour began to take an interest in the design of new projects and lend their fame to the enterprise as a drawing card. Invariably, well-qualified assistants, who worked in the background, aided the PGA tour players. The resulting creations featured earthen mounds, rock formations, lakes, waterfalls, sand and grass in a mixture of at times breathtaking beauty and at other times resulted in ugly monstrosities. When these contemporary designs were showcased on television during competitions, they caught the eye of millions of golfers everywhere. These same golfers demanded that their home courses be improved and the spin-off effect was that many older facilities were upgraded, a process that is going on into the twenty-first century.

Many of the new golf courses featured improved varieties of grasses that tolerated lower cutting heights resulting in smoother, faster, and firmer turf on the playing areas. Multiple tees and consistent bunker sand became the order of the day. The pressure was on to meet the demands of the new breed of golfer, who expected perfection everywhere, every day of the week. The new breed of superintendents met the demand for improvements. College educated, schooled in the latest technologies, and equipped with

In the modern era golf grew in complexity and required the talents of several areas of expertise. At the Westchester CC in 1981, architect Geoffrey Cornish, second from left, discusses water conservation with superintendent Ted Horton and engineer Charles Eldreich. Westchester employee Rachel Therrien is looking on.

boundless energy and enthusiasm, the young tigers took charge and created showpieces of manicuring that have become the envy of the world. And if on a certain weekend, televised conditions were not up to snuff, there was always a new young tiger waiting in the wings to take up the challenge. Longevity and job security were no longer taken for granted as had been the norm in olden days.

The New Breed of Golf Superintendent

To meet the demand for new superintendents, colleges across all parts of North America instituted turfgrass management programs, varying in length from just a few weeks to several years. These programs graduated young men and women in prolific numbers, all with the ambition of becoming golf course superintendents. The number of new graduates far exceeded the demand to fill the need of new courses. The natural attrition rate in the profession took care of small numbers of new graduates but by no means dented the oversupply. The result was that many qualified people did not achieve their life's ambition. They worked for prolonged periods as assistants and for many that became the end of the road. Others gravitated to related fields in sales and service. Those who did persist, combined meaningful experience at name facilities with the best academic credentials and the cream came to the top as always.

Many young men and women who spent a summer on the golf course mowing greens or raking bunkers, developed a love for the job and for the out-of-doors. What had begun as a summer job became a vocation and eventually, a lifetime occupation. In the process, these young people funded their education with their earnings and received training at universities and colleges, but not always from programs that featured turfgrass management. Many obtained related degrees in physics, forestry, engineering, horticulture and even in the humanities before succumbing to the irresistible draw of the golf course. They found that their training in the sciences was an important asset and a solid base on which to build. Equipped with this foundation, the winter programs on golf course management became more meaningful. Participation in seminars dealing with specific turf related topics were icing on the cake for the trainee superintendent. A few ambitious individuals took yet another step and obtained their master's degree. Burton Anderson worked on the crew for famed superintendent Manny

Maintaining golf courses has become more complex. A disease diagnostic laboratory is an important part of the turf care center.

Foreign Member Count by Country May 8, 2001

Antilles 1
Argentina 13
Australia 42
Austria 13
Bahamas 6
Barbados 3
Belgium 7
Belize 1
Bermuda 7
Brazil 4
British West Indies 4
Canada 613
Cayman Islands 3
Chile 8
People's Republic
   of China 27
Colombia 2
Costa Rica 6
Curaçao 1
Cyprus 1
Czech Republic 2
Denmark 3
Ecuador 1
Egypt 5
England 69
France 10
Germany 38
Greece 2
Guatemala 1
India 2
Indonesia 3
Ireland 31
Israel 3
Italy 16

New superintendents attending a conference for the first time are often overwhelmed by the sheer size of the trade show, by the crowds of people at the opening session and with the wide range of topics available in the educational sessions. Suddenly these newcomers, young men and women, often from isolated locations, are made aware that they are part of a very large and important industry. They may be a small cog in a large wheel but at conferences they are exposed to grand ideas and they meet fellow superintendents from all over the world. Friendships are formed and relationships established. After a few days or perhaps a week of total immersion in everything pertaining to golf, everyone comes away on a high note with renewed enthusiasm for the profession. Forever after, these new superintendents will recall their very first conference and at future meetings they will speak glowingly about that first one, which often changed their destiny and kindled their desire to succeed.

Since the involvement of Drs. Piper, Oakley, and Monteith at the early conferences, the USGA Green Section agronomists have always been an important part of the proceedings. In recent years the educational portion of the conference contained an entire session presented by Green Section personnel. That portion of the conference became a drawing card for many delegates because it contains practical information about hands-on golf course maintenance. In addition, the USGA Green Section has a double booth on the convention floor where the agronomists meet with superintendents and exchange information. It is not surprising that the USGA's involvement with the GCSAA Conference has been so successful: Many of the agronomists in the field are onetime superintendents. That explains it all. There is a common bond that is cemented when superintendent and agronomist walk the grass together in the summer season.

Over the years some memorable keynote speakers have addressed the opening session of the conference to inspire the audience and to set the tone for the rest of the weeklong session. Best remembered are perhaps Terry Bradshaw, the quarterback of the Pittsburgh Steelers and Lou Holtz, the football coach at Notre Dame. From the political field we enjoyed James Rhodes, the Governor of Ohio; Earl Butz, the Secretary of Agriculture; President Gerald Ford; and a most charming lady, Barbara Bush. Air Force General Yeager, the man who was first to break the sound barrier, made a particularly inspiring speech and professional golfer Peter Jacobsen had the audience rolling in the aisles.

The same could not be said for consumer activist Ralph Nader whose tedious speech made no friends for his cause. A mountaineer from Michigan who was part of Sir Edmund Hillary's group to conquer Mount Everest, made us realize that in everyone's life there are mountains to climb and to conquer and goals to reach.

In 1981 the GCSAA instituted the Old Tom Morris Award to recognize individuals who have made outstanding contributions to golf. The awards were made at the annual banquet at the time of the conference and every year some well-known personality in golf highlighted the proceedings. From Arnold Palmer, the first recipient in 1983, to Patty Berg, from Robert Trent Jones Sr. to Tom Fazio, they all came to be honored at our annual banquet and in the process they gained an appreciation for the profession of golf superintendent.

Greenkeeping Advances

The impact of the riding triplex greens mower was far-reaching since its introduction in the late '60s and early '70s. At first the unit was used exclusively on greens, but gradually superintendents discovered that this lightweight machine had other useful applications as well. When superintendents replaced the old mowers with newer editions, the older mowers became available and were tried and proved successful on large tees. The next step was to use the triplex mowers for cutting aprons and from there it was only a small step for the decks or approaches on par-3 holes to be cut with triplexes.

There may have been others but Cal Gruber, longtime superintendent at the Coldstream CC in Cincinnati was one of the first to discover the versatility of the triplex mowers. Gruber observed that wear from the large mowing machines cutting fairways and turning in front of greens was causing stress to the turf. Soil compaction caused by the heavy machinery resulted in *Poa annua* becoming the dominant species. The heat and humidity of Ohio's hot summers proved to be the death knell for these stressed-out areas of *Poa annua* turf. For weeks and sometimes months in summer and fall these areas turned brown, became sparse and provided cuppy lies for golfers.

In 1978 Cal Gruber began cutting the approaches from the front edge of the green to the first fairway sprinkler of his center-line irrigation system on the fairways. He noticed an immediate

Foreign Member Count— *Continued*

Jamaica	7
Japan	53
Malaysia	17
Malta	1
Mexico	21
Morocco	1
Netherlands	2
New Zealand	3
Northern Ireland	1
Norway	4
Panama	2
Peru	1
Philippines	23
Portugal	19
Saudi Arabia	2
Scotland	16
Singapore	25
Slovenia	3
Republic of South Africa	13
South Korea	8
Spain	41
St. Lucia	1
Sweden	6
Switzerland	6
Taiwan	10
Thailand	10
Trinidad	4
Turkey	1
United Arab Emirates	7
Venezuela	7
West Indies	2
Total	**1,265**

improvement and the following year he continued the practice but in addition he cut two entire fairways which had been the most difficult to maintain. The results were startling. The turf remained healthy all summer long and it made for a fine quality playing surface. Gruber was and still is, an avid and competent golfer. He experienced the thrill of pinching the ball from his tightly mowed fairways so that it would almost dance on the green with backspin. He also noted that drives hit down the middle landed and rolled much further on the shorter cut fairways.

Gruber was elated and in 1980 he embraced the new program in its entirety and cut all 18 fairways with Toro 84 triplex mowers that came equipped with catchers. He used only three mowing units to get the job done, which was barely enough. His greens staff hauled away the clippings to a nearby field where they were scattered. From time to time the clippings in the field had to be shaken up so they would not turn to silage and generate a foul smell.

Word spread quickly about the superior fairways at Coldstream CC, a ranked golf course in America's top 100. On the advice of Dr. Joe Duich, Al Muhle, superintendent at the Country Club near Cleveland, flew down with two of his directors to check out the new method. They were impressed and became overnight converts of lightweight fairway mowing. Several others followed suit, including the Oakmont GC near Pittsburgh, Oakland Hills CC in Detroit and superintendent Bruce Sering, superintendent at Glen View in Chicago. When such highly regarded facilities adopted lightweight mowing, the movement quickly spread and attracted the attention of many superintendents at other courses.

When Ken Wright, superintendent at the National GC in Ontario, Canada, visited Bob O'Link in Chicago during the U.S. Open at Medinah, Superintendent Bob Williams was likewise experimenting with triplex mowers off the greens. Wright admired Bob's work on approaches and on the par-3 holes and was convinced by Williams that it was the wave of the future. Upon returning to Canada he instituted the program at his home course and the National became the number one ranked golf course in Canada largely because of Wright's sophisticated maintenance methods.

Many followed the example set by Gruber, Wright and Williams but acceptance of the new method was by no means universal. When Gruber did a presentation on his fairway program at the winter conference at Purdue, there was rumbling in the audience and many asked: "How can they do that, spoiling the golfers?" The advocates of lightweight mowing were not to be deterred, especially since it quickly became apparent that because of reduced compaction, bentgrass gained the upper hand at the expense of *Poa annua*. Thus was developed a totally painless way of converting *Poa annua* infested fairways to monocultures of bentgrass. Cal Gruber never applied one pound of seed to his fairways, yet within a few short years his fairway turf consisted almost exclusively of bentgrass. Others, who copied his methods, experienced similar results. The secret to success was to remove the clippings and scatter them elsewhere. It is noteworthy that superintendents solely developed this new method of mowing fairways. It proved of great benefit to the world of golf and it had been accomplished without the help of research on experimental plots. Even the manufacturers were taken by surprise but they gladly accepted increased sales. More triplex mowing units were produced and sold than any other piece of grass cutting equipment.

Clipping collection and removal became an area of concern. Some scattered the clippings in the adjacent rough, others hauled them away for composting. Still others made arrangements with disposal companies to have the clippings removed in large dumpsters.

Because of the large fairway areas, superintendents soon found that in order for the program to be more practical, fairway acreage had to be reduced. Architects were called to sculpt the primary playing areas with fancy curves, bringing the roughs in front of tees and shaping the outline of the fairway to meet the demands of the game. In the process fairway acreage was reduced by as much 50 percent from 50 acres to 25 acres. Target golf became the order of the day.

There was another spectacular by-product of the new practice: striping! Hitherto, striping had been limited to greens, where daily cutting in different directions resulted in eye-catching checkerboard patterns. The same could now be achieved on fairways. Superintendents using their imaginations, created spectacular landscapes on the golf course. Not everyone accepted the new fairway cut. The PGA Tour at first forbade striped fairways but later acquiesced. At Augusta National striping of the fairways was not a common practice. Superintendent Marsh Benson uses eight to ten riding mowers per fairway, all cutting in the same direction. The only striping at Augusta is done on the greens and tees, but since the grass is cut so short, the striping is hardly visible. Many superintendents at traditional golf courses have kept cutting their fairways the old-fashioned way and have continued to do so in contemporary times. For many others there was no choice. The new breed of young golfers wanted the best and the latest and virtually every golf course turned to striping at least some portions of their turf. The weekly menu of television golf accelerated the movement, and striping is no longer limited to tees, greens and fairways, it has also become common place in the roughs. In fact the word striping and striping mowers have become part of our new greenkeeping vocabulary. As part of tournament preparation many superintendents now "burn the lines" by going back and forth several times in the same direction over the same swath to emphasize the contrast between light- and dark-colored turf. The striping of fairways by whatever means is mostly cosmetic and does not really improve playing conditions. Just the same it is yet another fine example of the extra efforts that superintendents often make to please the golfers.

Thus if you see a particularly attractive mowing pattern on a golf course, a baseball diamond or a football field, think of the man who started it all, Cal Gruber, a true pioneer in the world of greenkeeping. Gruber has long since retired to Florida, where he still cuts fairways occasionally for golfing privileges and to keep himself occupied.

The Switch to Larger Fairway Mowers

The process of cutting fairways with riding greens mowers had one major drawback: it was tedious and slow because of the narrow five-foot swath that could be cut. Only high-budget golf courses could afford this new method. One enterprising superintendent, Oscar Miles at Butler National near Chicago, in collaboration with his mechanic, decided to do something about it. To a Toro triplex greens mower they added an extra unit to each side. That certainly made the job easier and quicker. Lesco and Jacobsen quickly took note and began manufacturing five-gang units as well.

Fairways are now mown with three-, five-, and even seven-gang units. All are lightweight and reduce compaction. Fairways are being cut shorter than ever before and step by step our contemporary fairways are beginning to look like the greens of just a few years ago. Some have even applied the Stimpmeter to fairways, and readings in excess of six feet are not uncommon. Fairways are aerated, top-dressed, verticut, sprayed, and fertilized just like greens and the quality of the turf has improved magnificently.

No story on cutting fairways would be complete without mention of the use of walk-behind greensmowers to cut fairways. Richard Bator at Pine Valley first tried it in 1985 during the Walker Cup Matches. In preparation for the 1997 U.S. Open at the Congressional CC in Washington D.C., superintendent Paul Latshaw likewise cut all fairways with walkers. U.S. Open venues are notorious for the long rough. Latshaw was concerned that riding mowers would press down the long grass on the turns in the roughs. To solve the problem he decided to cut all fairways with walking mowers. It took 28 operators, many of them area superintendents, to get the job done. The expense must have been horrendous but the results were breathtaking. Latshaw was well known long before he hosted the Open, but his fame spread rapidly within the world of golf because of his novel methods.

On the Greens

The riding greens mowers were originally meant as a laborsaving device. One riding triplex operator easily replaced four men with walkers. The same had happened when power bunker rakes were introduced and for a while the number of greens workers on many courses was reduced. This resulted in substantial savings and lower golf course maintenance budgets. Then problems developed on greens that were continuously cut with the triplexes. Damage first showed up along the perimeter. Repeated tracking of the mower over the same area during the cleanup pass resulted in the typical triplex ring syndrome: three concentric wheel marks that were often stressed out and frequently void of grass. The damage was worst on small greens of less than 5,000 sq. ft. and greens with tight turns.

There was another problem. Mechanics had difficulty adjusting the mowers to perfection and making all three units cut the same. When golfers demanded faster greens, the bed knives had to be filed thinner so the mowers could be adjusted to a lower height. Eventually manufacturers caught on and produced thinner bed knives.

As a result of these problems with riding

During the 1997 U.S. Open at the Congressional CC the fairways were cut with walking greens mowers. It took almost 30 operators to get the job done.

Waste areas became common on North American golf courses in the latter part of the twentieth century as shown at the Tournament Players Club in Ponte Verda, Florida.

greens mowers many superintendents returned to walk-behind or pedestrian units. The initial enthusiasm of cutting greens faster and more economically was reassessed. Quality of cut became a major concern and many realized that the walkers provided a more gentle method of cutting the turf that resulted in a faster putting surface. When dwarf varieties of both bentgrass and bermudagrass were introduced, the shorter grasses required a tighter cut and walking greens mowers once again became the machine of choice. Riders are still used on large greens by golf courses operated for profit. Country clubs with large budgets use walkers almost exclusively; when staff is not available on weekends they switch back to riders.

The concern for quality had the same effect on the riding bunker rake. Again, the machine had been introduced with great fanfare and promised to save labor and cut budgets. The often boring and time-consuming job of hand-raking bunkers seemed destined for obsolescence. But it did not happen that way. The mechanical trap rake was at its best in large, level bunkers. It did not climb very well on the steep flashes that many architects prescribed. Repeated usage of the mechanical rake often resulted in rippling, and uneven distribution of the sand. Thus, while the bunker rake is doing a more than adequate job in many operations, many superintendents have discarded it. Hand-raking of bunkers, like cutting greens with walkers, had once again become the preferred practice at high-end golf courses.

There was another dimension that led to increased staffing and higher budgets. Golfers demanded that work on the golf course be done before they came to play. This meant an earlier start for workers in the morning and a greater number of workers to accomplish more in a shorter time span. Superintendents have always gone the extra mile to satisfy the golfers. In the years leading up to the twenty-first century, maintaining a golf course took on a new meaning. It meant having the golf course in tournament condition every day of the week. Colonel Morley many years ago had admonished his colleagues to "look after the little things and the big things will take care of themselves." In the parlance of the contemporary superintendents there was no end of looking after little things. Bunkers were edged as often as once a week, and cart paths were regularly trimmed. Tee boxes and surrounds were decorated with flowers and shrubs. Hazards were marked with paint at least every week and marking ground under repair was no longer reserved for special events but became a daily chore. Not surprisingly, budgets soared. It was not uncommon for 18-hole courses to employ more than 20 workers, sometimes in excess of 30 and have operating budgets of more than one million dollars, all of this dictated by the demands of the golfers.

A Major Disaster

Since 1920 when Dr. Piper first introduced the stolonizing of putting greens with Washington bent, the practice had become widely accepted by superintendents and proliferated to include many other bentgrass varieties. One such was C-15 or Toronto bent. The grass was reported to have been found alongside a creek on the Scarborough GC, a suburb to the east of Toronto. Others claim that it originated at the Toronto GC in the western part of the city. The grass had many fine qualities that made it suitable for putting greens. It was a popular turf among superintendents for many years until the tide turned and Penncross became the grass of choice for greens.

The office secretary became an important part of the turf management team. Rich Bator and Joanne Santone at the Oak Hill CC in Rochester, NY.

During the late '70s Toronto bent experienced a brief revival. For botanical reasons the name of the turf had been changed to C-15. Many new golf courses were being built at that time and there was a renewed demand for C-15. Once more greens were stolonized instead of seeded. Warren Turf Nurseries in Chicago and Godwin Turf near Detroit both produced the C-15 stolons by the bushel and shipped truckloads of the grass to wherever needed. Many of the finest new courses in the Great Lakes region planted C-15. And at first everything was fine, but after just a few years the turf began to thin out for no good reason. The grass took on a wilted look, then withered and died. The process took only a few days but the results were devastating. Superintendents tried every possible concoction of fungicides under the sun but with no success. They tried liquid feeding with trace elements but it did not help. In desperation turfgrass researchers were called in to help solve the problem. The GCSAA and the USGA Green Section jointly funded a massive research project at several institutions. Samples of sick greens were collected and examined in laboratories under the scrutinous eyes of professors. They found no cause nor cure for the disease. Nearly a year later Dr. Vargas and his lab technician David Roberts at Michigan State University discovered that the conducting tissues of the grass were clogged with bacteria-like organisms. They used an electron microscope to find the bacteria in the conductive tissues. Hence the name bacterial wilt of Toronto bent. True science had prevailed.

Many superintendents could not wait for a cure and proceeded by taking action in various means. Some killed the turf completely, sterilized the soil with methyl bromide and overseeded new bentgrass varieties. Others simply overseeded into the existing turf and overcame their problems in that manner. Probably the most important result of the disaster was that the GCSAA and the USGA were on a path together to jointly fund turfgrass research. Both organizations contributed generously from their ample resources and funded many more projects in years to come.

When the Western Open was played at Butler National in 1980, the greens were referred to as "the brownies." C-15 had claimed another victim. Dr. Duich was called in to investigate. He explained to the members and Paul Butler, the owner of the club, that the turf was at fault and not the superintendent. When the course had to be closed to replace the turf, the members rebelled and forced the owner into firing the superintendent. Paul Butler finally did so with tears in his eyes. Oscar Miles was hired as superintendent to carry out Duich's recommendations. The greens were fumigated with methyl bromide and overseeded with Penneagle bentgrass. One year later when the Western Open was again played at Butler, the course was fine and met with approval from both the players and officials. Many superintendents struggled with C-15 decline disease for several years. More than 20 golf courses followed the "Duich Program" as done at Butler National including Medinah and Butterfield in Chicago. Others by means of persistent overseeding converted to more desirable grasses.

A problem with vegetative propagation of bentgrasses was that "off-types" occurred. Such was the case with Toronto C-15 bent. Sod and stolon producer Ben Warren in Chicago extracted a plug of turf from the ninth green at the Westmoreland CC with the assistance of superintendent Julius Albaugh. Subsequently all stolons and sod were found to have been infected with bacterial wilt. Fortunately for Warren and Albaugh no one sued for financial losses. Such would not be the case today.

In Canada

An interesting situation took place at the Glen Abbey golf course near Toronto, a spectacular Nicklaus design that hosted the Canadian Open for many years in succession. The greens at the new Glen Abbey Course were to be established with C-15 Toronto bent. At the time, it seemed appropriate to use this Canadian variety for Canada's Open Championship. It turned out to be a case of false nationalistic pride. Jack Nicklaus himself approved the selection, since it was also used at his home course, Muirfield Village in Ohio.

Dennis Pellrene was the grow-in superintendent and it was his responsibility to make sure that the stolons were planted properly and nursed along to make a perfect putting surface for the touring professionals that were soon to come. Pellrene's position was like working in a fishbowl with every authority watching his moves. There was the Royal Canadian Golf Association who footed the bill and were anxious to get quality for their money and have the project completed in time. Then there was the Nicklaus organization, just as anxious to create a masterpiece, a monument to Jack Nicklaus and an acclaimed course on the PGA tour. Pellrene also came under the watchful eyes of his peers in the Toronto area, many of whom were ambivalent about an American architect creating what was meant to be the cathedral of golf in Canada. Pellrene completed the job on time. The greens were quickly established and for the first few years both the greens and the golf course were praised by the players. Skeptics became converts to the cause and all earlier misgivings were forgotten. But all was not well. Gradually the turf on the greens developed stress symptoms and started to thin out. Conventional fungicides did not help and experts called in to help, offered no solutions.

When the Canadian Open once again came to Glen Abbey in the summer of 1981 the course was in less than perfect condition. The greens in particular were suffering. Jack Nicklaus, who played a practice round, was not pleased. Nor did he hide his displeasure. "The greens and the fairways? They both stink!" said Nicklaus in the sports pages of the *Toronto Star*. He was no less complimentary in the *Globe and Mail*. Even the *New York Times* reported the plight of the greens and its keeper. It was intimated and suggested widely in all newspapers that the "greenkeeper" should be fired. Such undue criticism did not inspire the hardworking greens staff at Glen Abbey. According to Pellrene the workers were really upset and "ready to walk." Such action would have been disastrous and detrimental to the conclusion of the tournament.

Nicklaus got wind of the rumblings and became concerned that perhaps he had gone too far with his criticism. He decided to make amends and he paid a visit to the old white, former horse barn near the 17th hole at Glen Abbey. Nicklaus spoke softly, according to Michael Van Beek who was the number one assistant at the time. He alleged that he had been misquoted and that he really appreciated the hard work of the greens workers. That pacified the situation somewhat but the damage had been done.

After the tournament Pellrene worked hard at restoring the greens by overseeding repeatedly with Penncross bentgrass. The course was never closed during the repairs but all the hard work was not enough to save Pellrene's neck. The Nicklaus group maintained that "their C-15 at Muirfield showed no signs of stress," implying that not the grass, but the management was at fault. Pellrene became the scapegoat and was fired. Within a short time the greens at Muirfield also gave up the ghost to the bacterial wilt. Muirfield was closed for much of the season, the greens gassed and replanted with a new grass.

Pellrene fared much better than his greens had at Glen Abbey. He was snapped up by the Scarborough GC, the very same course that had given birth to C-15 many years ago. In his new position he put the course in order and made a reputation for himself. The fiasco at Glen Abbey never hurt Pellrene one bit. Some years later he moved to Vancouver and became superintendent at the Capilano GC, a highly regarded Stanley Thompson layout.

The End of Stolonizing Creeping Bentgrass

The disastrous ramifications of the C-15 decline spelled the end of stolonizing greens in the northern climatic zone but in New England stolonizing with velvet bentgrass continued. Of course in the bermuda belt, the practice of sprigging greens continued with excellent results but northern superintendents turned to seeding and/or sodding.

Sod farmers quickly developed not only nursery sod but also bentgrass sod for putting greens and fairways. Sod was shipped over great distances and often in refrigerated trucks. From hand-lifted squares in the early days, sod production had advanced and become mechanized with time. The mechanical sod cutter was introduced by Ryan Companies after World War II, soon to be followed by the Brouwer sod harvester which made it possible to cut, roll and place sod on pallets, all in one operation. Next came large rolls of sod that reduced the number of seams and speeded the sod laying operation. The introduction of washed sod, a grass mat without soil, made shipping much easier. Washed bentgrass sod, enough for nine regulation-sized greens has been shipped by air in a single load. Thus it became possible for a golf course to become established quickly. The grow-in time was reduced and a return on investment obtained much sooner than had been the case in the past. There are now many cultivars of bentgrass seed and sod to choose from and the list has grown longer as plant breeders intensified their efforts to create a miracle grass for greens.

Bentgrass had always been considered a cool-season grass. Many also believed that bentgrass provided a superior putting surface. Superintendents on the Northwest coast have claimed that *Poa annua*, when properly maintained, is as good as bentgrass. In the Northeast superintendents have learned to live with a mixture of bentgrass and *Poa annua* that provided smooth putting. In the South the new bermuda cultivars were considered equal to or as good to putt on. In the end, the customer, the golfer, as always, had the final say and the golfers embraced bentgrass not only in the Northern zone but in the sunbelt areas as well. Greens overseeded with ryegrass or *Poa trivialis* were often found to be sluggish and golfers demanded faster greens. With the encouragement of the PGA Tour players and low handicap golfers, many Southern courses began to switch to bentgrass on their greens. It happened from Miami to Hawaii and south into Mexico.

One of the first superintendents who introduced bentgrass to the Southwest was Art Snyder at the Paradise Valley CC in Phoenix, Arizona. It was discovered that some varieties of bent were more suitable for Southern locations, but if bent could survive in the hothouse climate of the Arizona desert, then there seemed to be no limit to its adaptability. Architects with doubtful agronomic qualifications began to prescribe bentgrass where its survival was uncertain. Superintendents were challenged to keep bentgrass alive under climatic conditions that were very difficult. Plant breeders came to the rescue. They introduced Tifdwarf bermudagrasses with the help of James Moncrief and the USGA Green Section. The pendulum swung once again toward native grasses for Southern courses. In southern Florida Tim Hiers at

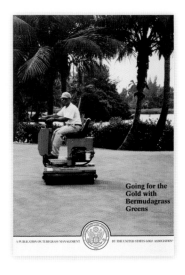

In the quest to increase green speed, rollers imported from Australia made their appearance on American golf courses

Collier's Reserve maintained bermuda greens throughout the year. So did many other south Florida courses.

Southern fairways are routinely overseeded with ryegrass, bluegrass and fescues. For a time the Tuscon National golf course painted its dormant bermuda fairways with a green dye to accommodate television producers during an annual PGA Tour event.

Up north meanwhile plant breeders developed a whole new array of dwarf bentgrasses that could be cut and survive at less than an eighth of an inch. There came the A, G, and L varieties. Most of the new bentgrasses resulted from Green Section sponsored research in the late 1980s. Drs. Duich, Engelke, Skogley, Kneebone, and others all had Green Section support. All new grasses required special care but under optimum management practices, these new cultivars also resulted in faster greens, something that the majority of golfers seemed to long for.

Wall-to-Wall Irrigation

Prefabricated pumping stations as modular units made their appearance on the golf course. Pictured is superintendent Ed Walsh at the Ridgewood CC, New Jersey.

For many years and for most golf courses a single centerline irrigation system was deemed satisfactory. However, when a dry year came around the roughs burned out and the perimeters of the fairways became stressed, golfers demanded perfection and brown or dormant turf was not acceptable. The irrigation companies answered with sophisticated, computer controlled systems that made it possible for superintendents to water almost every square inch of a property. Sprinklers could be operated remotely and weather stations helped determine the need for water. The new systems worked so perfectly that they were used not just to deliver water but also fertilizers mixed with the water and wetting agents. One of the first superintendents to install a fertigation sytem was Scott Sincerbeau in 1976 at the Royal Palm CC in Boca Raton, Florida. Others were quick to follow and added injection systems at the pump house for wetting agents and even to add acid to control the pH of the root zone. This was high-tech greenkeeping and the new generation of college educated superintendents embraced the new methodology unabashedly. Many of the old guard superintendents question the value and accuracy of fertigation and weather stations. They maintain their courses much like they had done for many years before to the satisfaction of their golfers.

For some the irrigation computer was the first exposure for superintendents to a keyboard and a computer, soon to be followed by introductions to the Internet, digital cameras and PowerPoint® presentations. The new technology gave a new meaning to the phrase "to promote the exchange of information," one of the reasons that had led to the formation of the greenkeeping association in 1926.

Fountains not only keep the ponds healthy by recycling water, they also add beauty to the landscape.

In 1993 Duane Patton, superintendent at the Lawrence CC, Kansas, introduced Turf-Byte to the world of golf course maintenance. It was a bulletin board dial-up type system. Everyone had to phone long distance to connect to a computer in Duane's home. He received help and encouragement from his colleagues and also some technical assistance from the GCSAA. Eventually Patton's Turf Byte ceased to exist at about the same time that GCSAA initiated its web site. The next step was interactive online conversations by subscribers. GCSAA encouraged its members to become connected and to participate in the exchange of information. Turfnet from New Jersey was another network much favored by many superintendents as a medium for information about golf course maintenance. No longer was it necessary to wait for the annual conference to find out about the latest, the newest, and the best. Answers were often immediately available simply by keying in on the Internet. If a manufacturer produced a lemon, word spread instantly across the continent and indeed across the world. The spread of a fungus disease or an insect problem could be followed on the Internet. Superintendents in the most remote areas no longer felt isolated. No matter where one lived or worked, information on just about any topic was instantly available. Ironically, some superintendents with the fanciest watering systems available, still hand-hosed the greens. It should never be forgotten that all the technology in the world does not replace sound judgment and in that regard, greenkeeping has not changed since its earliest days.

Women in the Workforce

Men had for many years dominated the world of greenkeeping. At times female workers were used when men were not available. That happened during both World War I and World War II but after the wars the women returned happily to whatever they had been doing before. Except for one Mildred Corrie who graduated from tractor driving at the Wilmington CC in Delaware to virtually any job on the course. Mildred had a mechanical bent and she quickly took charge of the maintenance shop and issued work orders to the men. For a time, during World War II, she played the role of active superintendent. But when her boss returned, Mildred resumed her former responsibilities. With her deep knowledge and love for grass she could have become a superintendent in her own right, but instead, she chose to remain at Wilmington from where she retired at a mature age.

If Rachel Carson influenced superintendents to use fewer pesticides, then maybe Gloria Steinem can be held accountable for encouraging more women to enter the workforce. They did, and many found work on the nation's golf courses. Years before the feminist movement of the 1960s, a very small number of women had been employed at golf courses at various levels of responsibility, but it was a rarity to see women cutting grass.

At the Coal Creek CC, Illinois, Laura Knudson took over as greenkeeper when her husband passed away in 1941. In 1956 Bonnie Stanley took over as superintendent at the De Anza CC in Borrego Springs, California, when her husband became too ill to carry out this duties. Zelda Baxter who became a full status superintendent at the Keokuk CC in Iowa in 1959 closely followed her. She was encouraged by her husband who was president of another golf club in the same town. Chester Mendenhall at Mission Hills CC in Kansas City had a female assistant and two other women as crew members in 1959. Thus, some women were successful in our industry before the advent of the feminist movement.

Female workers on the greens crew became commonplace at many golf courses. So did the deep tyne aerator, a Dutch invention and contribution to the turfgrass industry.

By 1960s and '70s female workers on the greens were commonplace. The Woodlands CC in Fort Lauderdale, Florida employed as many as 25 young women. Woodlands superintendent Joe Yuzzi commented "that the mere presence of female help on the golf course changes the total working environment. Everything is cleaner and neater. The language is civil and a happier atmosphere prevails." Joe was so pleased with the women that he promoted Debbie Winters to an assistant position. Debbie, who had trained to be a physical education teacher now found herself driving tractors, cutting grass, and spraying for diseases. Debbie probably never knew about Zelda Baxter and Bonnie Stanley but she too wanted to become a superintendent. We don't know if she ever succeeded.

According to the late Tom Mascaro: "the mechanization of the golf course operation had eliminated much of the backbreaking hard work and the walking behind machinery. Dragging and lifting heavy hoses had given way to automatic sprinklers. Brains rather than brawn were in demand, hence the evolution to female workers."

Dudley Smith, longtime superintendent at the Silver Lakes GC near Orland Park, Illinois, armed with a degree in agronomy from Penn State, was highly regarded by his colleagues. He gave a talk about females in the workplace, first at Purdue and then at the Minneapolis Conference in 1976. Dudley Smith's fame had spread before him. There was standing room only when he made his presentation. He did not mince words either and he did not disappoint. He recited case after case of female workers being superior to their counterparts, but often for the wrong reasons. By today's standards the talk would show bias and some women who read the contents of his presentation called Smith "a chauvinist." Dudley Smith survived the uproar, a tempest in a teapot. He retired from Silver Lakes in 2001 after 40 years of faithful service.

In the '80s and '90s female superintendents had become commonplace, not in great numbers but they no longer drew attention to themselves by being the exception. Vergie Ross from Ames, Iowa, was a frequent attendee at the GCSAA conferences and a respected superintendent. Jean Esposito was the first female to become certified. She was a superintendent at Hinkley Hills GC, Ohio. Jean served as president of her chapter. Nancy Pierce graduated from the University of Guelph with a degree in agronomy and became superintendent at the Links of Crow Bush GC on Prince Edward Island. Like Jean Esposito, Nancy became president of the Atlantic GCSA. In 2001 GCSAA had almost 500 female members and of that number at least 75 were acting superintendents.

There are many women who have excelled in our ranks and it is only a matter of time before a bright woman will become director of the GCSAA and ultimately its first president. No one will even blink an eye.

Beetles on the Warpath

During the mid-seventies, several golf courses in the Midwest discovered a hitherto unknown pest: a tiny black beetle that chewed at the roots of green or fairway turf. The quarter-inch grub made no distinction between bent and *Poa* and devoured the roots of both species. Dr. Harry Niemczyk, professor at Ohio State University, researched the pest and baptized the critter as "the black turfgrass ataenius." Easterners dubbed the insect "the dung beetle" because it belonged to the dung beetle family. The scientific name of the rascal is *Ataenius spretulus*. By whatever name, damage from this root feeding insect was severe and many golf courses lost greens and acres of fairway turf. Niemczyk discovered that resistance to the insecticide Chlordane® had much to do with the insects becoming a serious pest. Control was achieved with treatment of Dursban® or Diazinon® applied in early May to kill adults before they laid eggs. Naturally occurring *Ataenius sp.* milky disease often reduced reoccurrence of the problem. Insecticide applications for cutworm control on greens minimized damage on greens, and development of new effective insecticides has generally resulted in only occasional damage to golf courses.

A similar case involved another beetle, the European chafer. First reported in eastern New York and the northeastern seaboard, the insect quickly spread to the west and in short order was reported in the Great Lakes area. The chafer beetle itself does little damage but the larvae actively feed on turf roots. Further damage occurs when skunks, raccoons, seagulls, and crows fed on the fleshy grubs and in the process tore the turf to shreds. It was a sorry sight to see roughs and bunker faces demolished in the morning after an all-night feeding frenzy by animals.

When properly applied, insecticides were effective in controlling the grubs, but, when areas were missed or left untreated, superintendents often had to contend with damage from animals. Some responded by trapping the animals and exporting them to another locations. Others simply repaired the damaged turf by seeding and sodding. Insecticides and natural controls have reduced the *Ataenius sp.* beetle to only an occasional pest. The European chafer has persisted and is now not only a serious pest of golf courses, but home lawns as well.

In addition to the *Ataenius sp.* beetle and the European chafer, the *Hyperodes sp.* (annual bluegrass) weevil caused considerable damage on some golf courses. But like the other pests, damage seems to run in cycles. It was severe in some seasons and at other times there was only minimal damage.

Fungus Diseases Continue to Baffle Superintendents

Ever since the early days when small brown patch scorched the greens during hot and humid summers, superintendents have been confronted with fungus diseases that attack golf course turf. Certainly, small brown patch or dollar spot was the most persistent and the most costly disease to control. There were many other fungi that have tested superintendents to keep their turf alive. Among these was Anthracnose, a leaf spot disease that attacked mostly *Poa annua* grass in late spring or early summer. It has remained a threat to the survival of turf even in contemporary times. Pink and gray snow mold flare up on northern courses with almost predictable regularity. Patch diseases are more recent threats that were first identified by Dr. Dick Smiley from Cornell University, New York. Spring dead spot on bermuda turf was something to worry about for southern superintendents after the snowbirds left for the north.

In the transition zone, pythium continued to wipe out grass at a prodigious rate. During hot days and languid nights, pythium also struck turf on more northern locales. Its sister disease, cold temperature pythium, became a definite threat early in the spring-time over large areas of the U.S.A. and Canada.

The 1980s spelled the near end of Kentucky bluegrass fairways in many areas where the cutting height had been lowered to near half an inch and watering increased. Most high-end courses converted to bentgrass; others chose ryegrasses. Ryegrass was relatively easy to establish by overseeding. Bentgrass establishment was more difficult since the existing *Poa annua* turf had to be killed by glyphosate. This latter method became known as the "scorched earth technique."

During the last decade of the twentieth century, a most devastating disease on ryegrass wiped out large areas of fairways and roughs in the transition zone during late summer and early fall. It has become known as gray leaf spot (GLS) and proven very difficult to control, often requiring weekly pesticide applications. The disease perplexed golfers and in some cases the poor conditions were blamed on superintendents. Before GLS was brought under control, some superintendents lost their jobs or moved voluntarily to other positions. GLS became a nightmare for superintendents at a time of year when the end of the active growing season was in sight.

Workers were required to become licensed pesticide applicators and this involved wearing proper protective clothing.

Pesticides *that have been banned on golf courses in the U.S. and other countries during the last quarter century:*

PMAS *(phenyl mercuric acetate solution)*

Calo-Chlor

Dyrene

Benomyl *(Tersan 1991)*

Chlordane®

Dursban®

Diazinon®

2, 4-5T

During the period between 1965 and 1985 the actual number of pesticides to combat and control these problems was sharply reduced for environmental reasons. The family of chlorinated hydrocarbon insecticides were taken off the shelf. So were the mercury-containing fungicides. In addition, severe environmental restrictions were placed on many other products. The drive to remove or eliminate pesticides received unexpected publicity when a golfer who had been exposed to Daconil® during golf on the Army Navy Club in Virginia, became ill and died. His widow sued the manufacturer of Daconil® and the case dragged on for several years. Daconil® was eventually and totally exonerated but the public relations damage had been done.

Then there was the mistaken belief on the part of the public that pesticides applied to golf courses leached through the soil and contaminated the groundwater. Golf courses were under the gun to reduce or eliminate pesticide applications. Some municipalities forbid lawn spraying altogether. Golf courses were seen as the playgrounds for the rich and the privileged and the media and the masses cried for controls. Because of this erroneous conception, golf saw its image tarnished. Something had to be done.

The Cape Cod groundwater study proved to be at least a partial answer. Spearheaded by Ed Nash, superintendent at the Bass River GC and with great assistance from Dr. Stuart Cohen, formerly with the EPA, the study confirmed irrefutably that groundwater runoff contained only negligible amounts of pesticide residues. In addition, the GCSAA and the USGA spent millions of dollars to prove that turf was an effective filter that

Wall-to-wall green grass was augmented by naturalized areas left undisturbed as at the National GC on Long Island. The club's windmill is a landmark in the area.

prevented the passage of pesticide residues. Both organizations were committed to be proactive in the battle over pesticides.

A hard to cure and persistent problem during the '90s has been the appearance of moss on putting greens. It was not an isolated phenomenon but prevalent in many areas. Moss appears to become established on the highest and driest parts of putting greens. It has been suggested that the quest for speed and lower cutting heights are contributing factors.

No cure has been found for the elimination of moss but applications of the dishwashing liquid "Dawn" have been somewhat effective. This method of control was discovered by a group of superintendents spearheaded by Frank Dobie at the Sharon GC in Ohio.

Longtime superintendent Paul Voykin at the Briarwood CC near Chicago smells the flowers. Voykin was one of the first to let grass grow in nonuse areas and to establish wildflowers.

The Audubon Movement

Golf courses have always been havens for wildlife. The combination of streams, forests, and open spaces was ideal for animals of many species. It was only natural that superintendents with an instinctive love for the out-of-doors, should encourage the proliferation of the many species of plant and animal life that occur on golf courses.

There may have been a time when grass was mown from fence to fence, when trees were trimmed and brush cleaned out. It was a time when some courses looked like parks and the animals, the birds, the deer, and the foxes disappeared for lack of shelter.

Overgrooming became an affliction to which many superintendents succumbed, sometimes with the active encouragement of the various golf and green committees. But there were a few far-sighted individuals who saw the errors of our ways. They initiated the process of letting the roughs grow in undisturbed out-of-play areas. They planted wildflowers and native species of plants and trees. Their golf courses adopted a natural look and, lo and behold, the animals returned. Butterflies darted among the wildflowers, foxes once again hunted rabbits, hawks circled overhead to look for little critters hiding in the long grass and even an occasional deer leaped across a fairway.

When longtime superintendent Paul Voykin from the Briarwood GC near Chicago addressed the USGA Green Section meeting in New York, the year was 1976, and his topic was: Overgrooming Is Overspending. Voykin stated that the desire to

improve and excel had been carried to a ridiculous and expensive
extreme. His contention was that if there was less grooming of
the roughs, the clubs could save money. Paul Voykin practiced
what he preached and let 10 acres of remote rough grow to its natural height and in the process saved substantially on the club's
budget. His presentation had a catchy title and an interesting mes-
sage. He repeated the talk at numerous conferences and in that
manner he became the forerunner and the advocate of the back- to-
nature movement.

Bill Bengeyfield, a USGA agronomist and editor of the *Green
Section Record* at the time, shared Voykin's feelings. He stated that
the word "grooming" was overworked and in need of redefining. A
well-groomed course did not mean that every blade of grass had
been perfectly clipped. It meant that the course played well from
tee to green, according to Bengeyfield.

In Florida an owner/superintendent was caught by the natural-
ist bug. Paul Frank and his father converted swampland near
Naples into a golf course surrounded by quality cluster homes.
The course was suitably baptized as the Wilderness GC, because
Paul Frank had a love for flora and fauna that existed on his
course near the edge of the Everglades. He planted trees to provide shelter for the wildlife and rarely removed the skeletons of
dead trees because the snags served an important link in the lives
of birds. In time mature trees, draped with Spanish moss, surrounded Frank's course. Swamps were left undisturbed and to play
the Wilderness GC was to take a journey through a reserve,
observing the different species while trying to concentrate on
one's golf game. Paul Frank's dedication to nature was made easier
because he owned the course and did not have to deal with interference by committees.

Thus, with the role of the superintendent as an environmentalist well established in the golfing community, it remained for
the general public to be awakened to the realization that golf
courses were not just playgrounds for the rich but served as an
oasis for wildlife and the preservation of nature in the urban landscape. That's where Ron Dodson and the Audubon International
entered the picture. Dodson, an avid golfer, recognized at an early
stage that golf courses offered potential for nature and golfers to
live and play in harmony. Dodson developed a program that led to
sustainable resource management and development and the creation of wildlife habitats. Participating golf courses were asked to
achieve standards of excellence in several categories that included

water and waste management, energy efficiency, and integrated pest management. In practice the program led to a reduction in pesticide usage and the establishment of a wildlife oasis. Birdhouses became an important part of the golf landscape. At first there were only a few courses that participated in the Audubon Cooperative Sanctuary Program. The first course to achieve the coveted recognition was the Bayhill GC, part of the Kapalua complex on the island of Maui in Hawaii. A plaque near the first tee commemorates the achievement and a tour of the golf course confirms that the lands overlooking the blue Pacific Ocean are special. Dodson and the Audubon movement were also encouraged by Bill Bengeyfield and Chuck Smith, administrative director of the USGA. Both men arranged for Dodson to speak at the USGA session during the Orlando conference in 1990 where he preached the gospel of conservation.

Tim Hiers at Collier's Reserve in Naples, Florida was in the forefront of the Audubon movement. Not only did he practice the Audubon creed on the golf course but also in his maintenance facility and in the yards of the homes surrounding the golf course. There were others like Peter Leuzinger at Ivanhoe and Tim Kelly at the Village Links GC, both near Chicago. David Stone at the Honors Course in Tennessee and Paul Dermott at the Oakdale GC near Toronto were also in the vanguard of the new movement and lived and preached the gospel of conservation and the return to nature. They were featured speakers at conferences and by their example, encouraged others to follow.

The stringent certification program made it difficult for many golf courses to achieve certified status, but those who did proudly advertised their achievement on scorecards or near the first tee on the golf course. By the time of the GCSAA 75th anniversary more than 300 golf courses had become certified sanctuaries.

The marriage of the Audubon International and the world of golf was mutually beneficial. Audubon gained a multitude of sanctuaries all over the continent and the world of golf improved its environmental image with the public. Just as our forefathers laid the stones of the superintendents' movement, our contemporary leaders in the Audubon movement helped advance our cause.

In 1995 GCSAA partnered with 20 other golf associations and environmental organizations to conduct an Environmental Summit in Monterey, California. Through subsequent meetings GCSAA assumed a leadership role in the drafting of guidelines for developing and maintaining golf courses. This initiative was

David Stone was one of the early leaders of the Audubon movement. At the Honors Course in Tennessee he practiced respect for the environment and was recognized by the USGA in 1995 with their Green Section Award.

Superintendents utilized ingenious methods to deal with the profusion of trees on golf courses.

hailed as a first step in bridging the gaps between groups that had been adversaries.

Golf Courses and Trees

Golf, as we know it, had its beginnings on the windblown open spaces of Scotland's treeless coastal plains. When golf came to North America trees became part of the golf course setting. Those courses that did not have natural growth of trees embarked on ambitious programs to plant trees. Fairways became separated by rows of trees. Trees were planted behind greens to achieve depth perception and near tees to provide shade for golfers. When Dutch elm disease attacked and killed American elms there was a period when skeletal remains dotted the landscape. The elms were removed at great expense and replaced by maples, ashes, and oaks. In the process many golf courses became overplanted. What had been spacious layouts became confined playing areas that lacked views and vistas. Overplanting spoiled some great designs.

A side effect of the tree planting frenzy was that the trees grew at the expenses of grass and the areas near trees became sparse and unfit for play. Near greens and tees, trees competed for plant food and water. Trees restricted air movement and increased humidity and disease activity. Superintendents realized that they had been all too eager to join the tree planting spree and that they were as guilty as the committees of planting too many trees. They also knew that once a tree becomes established it achieved the status of a sacred cow that could not be tampered with.

What to do? Advice was sought from architects. They studied the problem of too many trees very carefully and designated specific trees that had to be eliminated. Their advice was not always popular with all golfers but being impartial in the politics of golf club governance, the architects were at least listened to with a degree of respect.

Some superintendents did not wait for architects and took the initiative to remove trees. During the off-season trees were felled and the evidence of there having been a tree was covered with soil and sod. Some superintendents used a novel approach for tree removal. They carried in their runabouts two chainsaws, one named "thunder" and the other "lightning." When golfers asked what had happened to the maple on the fourth hole, they could honestly reply that lightning struck it and thunder claimed the oaks on the eighth.

Arborist Scott Robinson from Ontario invented a novel means of determining which trees surrounding greens needed to be removed or trimmed. During an on-site visit, with the help of sun angles and hours of shade and sunshine, Robinson was able to specifically identify the trees that contributed to the problem of shading and air movement. Some superintendents installed high capacity fans to increase air movement and lower temperatures.

If too many trees and too much shade was a problem the annual fall of the leaves presented superintendents with a horrendous cleanup job. In the early days, when the roughs were burned the leaves were burned as well. On heavily treed courses, the leaves were raked and swept into piles and the piles transported to dump sites. One of the first leaf sweepers was the Parker Lawn Sweeper, a walking unit. Blowers worked off the PTO on a tractor or were self-propelled. As time progressed, both blowers and sweepers increased in size and were assisted by vacuum cleaners. Leaves were still hauled away, until some superintendents modified their rotary cutting units and began mulching leaves. It was faster, cleaner and the golfers liked it. Mulching leaves has become the accepted method at many courses.

Superintendents as Writers

One of the first greenkeepers to write about the profession was Rocky Rockefeller at the Inverness Club in Toledo, Ohio during the beginning of the twentieth century. He was a frequent contributor to the early *USGA Green Section Bulletins*. His style was explicit and descriptive. Much of what we know about greenkeeping in early times was through Rocky's vivid portrayal of the work. He shared his successes and his failures with his colleagues of the time. He was highly regarded at his club as well as by the readers of the Green Section publication. Rocky was a leader in our industry and fully supported the aims of the NAGA when it was formed in 1926. Because of his writing skills, he was appointed as the association's first secretary.

John Morley, who was a gifted speaker as well as a writer, followed Rockefeller. Both qualities guaranteed the success of the fledgling greenkeeping association. Morley chronicled his travels, of which he took many, across the Northeast, and one of his stock phrases was that he found the courses that he visited "in the pink of condition." When Morley became president of the NAGA he

Clinton Kent Bradley at his typewriter in New Jersey. He was a greenkeeper/ superintendent but is best remembered as a writer for various periodicals including the Greenkeepers Reporter. *In later years he became an inveterate letter writer and was at times a thorn in the side of the Board of Directors.*

wrote monthly messages that were inspirational and which encouraged other greenkeepers to write as well. One of the best was William Chinery from the York Downs GC near Toronto. In his recitals of work on the golf course he exhibited a subtle sense of humor. His tale of how he combated skunks that tore up his greens is hilarious and has been written about in Chapter Three.

Then along came Leo Feser, a humble greenkeeper from Minnesota, who almost single-handedly filled the pages of the *Greenkeeper Reporter* for several years in the 1930s. He was a gifted and philosophical writer, perhaps even a frustrated journalist. Month after month, year after year, Leo Feser wrote thought-provoking articles about the profession of greenkeeping. He helped educate his colleagues when very little education was available elsewhere.

Gus Brandon was superintendent at the St. Charles CC in Illinois during the late 1930s. He became acting secretary of the NAGA as an employee. In that capacity he wrote many articles for the *Greenkeepers Reporter*. He served the Association till 1949.

Clinton Kent Bradley, a superintendent the Passaic CC, New Jersey who taught the rudiments of greenkeeping to a youthful Sherwood Moore (1936-38), besides being a good teacher was also a prolific writer. Bradley served on the board of directors of the National Association for a time and in his latter days much of his correspondence was directed to the Association and its president. He remained a valuable source of historical information. Because Bradley wrote so much and on so many different topics, he often used a pseudonym to protect his identity.

During the 1950s and '60s many chapters began to distribute their own newsletters. The New England Association produced one of the first newsletters, but one of the best known of these often primitive publications, was the *Hudson Valley Foreground*. For two dollars one could get an annual subscription to this publication and the list of subscribers included readers from coast to coast and beyond the borders of the U.S.A. How could such a relatively obscure organization produce a newsworthy publication that caught and retained the attention of all who read it?

Bill Smart, son of a Scottish greenkeeper produced, wrote and edited the *Hudson Valley Foreground* for 20 consecutive years. Its Gestetner-duplicated pages were stapled at the top but its modest appearance belied its contents. Smart philosophized about greenkeeping the way Leo Feser had done before him, except that Smart was much more direct and outspoken. He did not worry about his image as a superintendent but he did worry about his grass all summer long and shared his worries with his readers. During his lifetime he served at three golf clubs and he survived most seasons because he babied his turf during "one hundred days of hell" when the summer became hot and humid and grass needed special care. Smart related in the pages of the *Foreground* his trials that were typical of greenkeeping in his time. His readers sympathized with him and related to his problems. Bill's subtle sense of humor added levity to his writing. Often he included poetry on the pages of the *Foreground* much like the doggerel that Gertrude Farley had produced many years ago, except that Smart rhymed from on-the-job experience and from the bottom of his generous heart. One of his best pieces is the following:

When the Frost is on the Penncross

When the frost is on the Penncross and the water-line is drained,
And ever Southward go the golfers; Cads and Jags so aimed,
Hear the rustle of the leaves as they cover rough and green...
And traps and fairways...and most everywhere in between;
Oh, it's then the time a feller is a feelin' at his best
With the risin' Sun to greet him from a nite of peaceful rest,
As he wears a sweater mornins' and the clocks have all been changed,
When the frost is on the Penncross and the water-line is drained.

When the heat of Summer's over and the coolin' fall is here...
Of course we miss the foursomes and the markers on the tees
And the rumble of the mowers and the buzzin' of the bees;
But the air's so appetizin'; and the landscape thru the haze
Is the crisp and sunny wonderland of early Autumn days
And you can count up on your fingers all the times it's rained
When the frost is on the Penncross and the water-line is drained.

The husky, rustle of seed heads on the Poa.
The clank and bang of units as in the shed they go;
The flags in greens...kinda lonesome, but still
There's a few die-hard golfers whose needs we have to fill;
The ballwashers are in the workshop; the sprayers in the shed;
The hose is coiled up neatly on the rafters overhead!
Oh, it sets my heart a-beating...with a fury never tamed
When the frost is on the Penncross and the water-line is drained.

William Silver Smart retired in 1987 and he died in March of 1993. His obituary acknowledges Smart as the "Golf Course Chief." That was his style, right to the end.

The Midwest *Bull Sheet* provided opportunity for a number of superintendents in the Chicago area to demonstrate their writing ability. Foremost among them was Paul Voykin who was a frequent contributor. Paul wrote opinion pieces about the profession of greenkeeper, a term that he seemed to prefer to the more common name of golf course superintendent. His readers did not always share his thought provoking views. Paul's writing skills were good enough for his articles to be included in *Golf Digest* and the Rand McNally Company published two of Paul Voykin's garden books: *A Better Lawn the Easy Way* and *Ask the Turf Doctor*. Both books were widely read and helped promote the image of the professional superintendent in the garden world.

On the California coast superintendent Richard Viergever wrote a book entitled: *The Modern Golf Course Superintendent*. The book was issued in 1979 and for a while it was used as a text in turf management programs at several institutions.

In Colorado, a young superintendent with a degree in journalism made a mark for himself and started his chapter's newsletter in 1965, and before long he was writing editorials and articles about our profession. Stan Metsker initiated a certification program for the Rocky Mountain GCSA. The Colorado program became the inspiration on which Cliff Wagoner and Walter Boysen built the GCSAA Certification Program. Stanley Metsker remained a superintendent all his working life and in 1996 he wrote a book entitled *On the Course*, which relates the life and times of a superintendent and captures the spirit of the era.

In Florida, Dan Jones, a golf course superintendent at the Banyan CC near West Palm Beach brought new life to his chapter newsletter: *The Florida Green*. Jones and his wife Irene wrote and published the magazine for 14 years. They turned their home into a print shop. Another well-known editor and writer for the Florida Green was Joel Jackson who became a regular contributor to the recently revived *Golfdom* magazine.

Terry Buchen, a peripatetic superintendent/writer, now works as a consultant to golf courses but has maintained his certified status. Terry wrote for *Golf Course Management*, for *Golf Course News* and more recently for the bimonthly *Superintendents News*. He is a member of the prestigious Golf Writers Association of America.

The Wisconsin GCSA has been renowned for its quality annual

conference that is hosted in conjunction with the Milwaukee Sewerage Commision, the manufacturers of the world famous Milorganite fertilizer. It is not surprising that the Wisconsin chapter has also produced two fine superintendent/writers. Both Dan Quast and Monroe Miller are frequent contributors to several publications and their articles have always been widely read and quoted.

The Impact of the Superintendent Writers

Every superintendent who regularly wrote in either their chapter's newsletter or contributed to *Golf Course Management* or any other publication influenced their readers far beyond their immediate vicinity. Turf publications have always been passed on from one person to another and are widely read not only by superintendents but also by golfers and by the supply industry. Thus the influence of the writing superintendent is much greater than one may think at first. These men have contributed greatly to the advancement of the profession over the years.

Families of Superintendents

Does greenkeeping run in the blood? For some families it definitely does. Take the Snyder family as an example. Arthur Jack Snyder was born in Pennsylvania in 1898. After stints as greenkeeper at the Alcoma CC and the Longue Vue Club near Pittsburgh, he moved his family to Arizona after World War II. He became superintendent at the Paradise Valley GC and raised a family of three sons, all of whom were destined to become superintendents in their own right. Meanwhile Art's younger brother, Carl Matthew Snyder also became a greenkeeper, first in Pennsylvania and then he followed his older brother to Arizona. Again, Carl Matthew Snyder` had a son who followed in his father's footsteps. The third generation included three superintendents, two of whom were Art's grandsons and the third was the grandson of his brother. Altogether there were nine superintendents. The number of golf courses that these men looked after at one time or another added up to the astounding total of 34! Included in this number were such highly regarded courses as Oakmont, The Boulders Golf Resort, Royal Kaanapali, Yorba

The Monroe Doctrine

At a time when golf courses and superintendents came under attack by the environmentalist movement, Monroe Miller defended his colleagues both in Wisconsin and at the national level. In the *USGA Green Section Record* of March 1987, Miller stated that:

By the very nature of our profession, all superintendents are environmentalists and have been since the beginning of golf in America.

He identified the enemies of golf, the fanatic and militant forces that preached gloom and doom and wanted to ban and restrict the use of pesticides.

He emphasized that superintendents must recognize their responsibility to apply pesticides safely and only when necessary.

He urged his fellow superintendents to unite with other organizations in the green industry and to combat jointly the foes of grass and golf.

Monroe's doctrine was embraced by many superintendents, and with the combined assistance of the GCSAA and the USGA, the industry fought back to win the battle of public opinion.

Linda CC, the Tuscon CC and of course Paradise Valley. Among Art Snyder's offspring are a golf course architect who served as president of American Society of Golf Course Architects (ASGCA), a turf farm operator and a regional superintendent for American Golf Corporation.

Art Snyder was a close friend of John Pressler, one of the first greenkeepers in North America. Both men worked in the Pittsburgh area. Art Snyder was an avid golfer with a fine swing and he played in the Association's first golf tournament. During his lifetime (1898-1997) he personally knew all GCSAA's presidents. Besides looking after his family, he also looked after his friends. When Harold Stodola, GCSAA President 1941-1945 fell on hard times in Minnesota, Art Snyder invited him to Arizona and gave him a job as a greensman at the Paradise Valley CC. A few years later Stodola became superintendent at the Tucson CC, no doubt with a recommendation from his friend. During his lifetime Arthur Armstrong Snyder received many distinctions and awards but his greatest legacy is most certainly the sons and grandsons that he prepared to look after and design golf courses.

If you ask the Snyder clan about the Maples family in Georgia, they refer to them as the Snyders of the East and of course any Maples family member will refer to the Snyder family as the Maples of the West. Whatever the case may be, the descendants of James Maples Jr. 1856-1909 also made an impressive contribution to golf. In three generations there are eight superintendents, two golf course architects and three PGA professionals. Best known in the early days was Frank Maples who was the greenkeeper at Pinehurst in the days of sand greens and worked in close liaison with architect Donald Ross. Henson Maples succeeded his father at Pinehurst and his brother Ellis became an architect. Palmer Maples Jr., who served as GCSAA President and later as the Director of Education, represents the third generation. Ellis Maples and son Dan both served as president of the ASGCA.

Other Families of Superintendents

A father and son team attended the NAGA inaugural meeting at the Sylvania CC in 1926: John McNamara senior and junior. Father and son combinations are quite common in the industry and there has even been a father and son who both served as GCSAA presidents: Bob (1958) and Bruce Williams (1996). Three generations of superintendents in the same family are much rarer, but there are several. Four generations of greenkeepers/superintendents are almost unheard-of. Neither the Snyders nor the Maples can lay claim to that distinction. The Smart family in New York State and the Smith family in Ohio can.

Great-grandfather Silver Smart was the greenkeeper/starter on the Barrie Links course at Carnoustie, Scotland in the late 1800s. His son Jimmy immigrated to America and became greenkeeper at the Dutchess GC in New York. In addition to being an excellent greenkeeper, Jimmy was a fine golfer and the members at Dutchess often asked him to play. However, Jimmy never played unless invited and never accepted invitations during normal working hours and for years, after a round of golf with members he went directly home from the eighteenth green to his house on the golf course. Jimmy died prematurely in 1947 after a long illness. By today's standards he was not a successful man. He was not above laboring with the men on the course when necessary; he spent no winters in Florida, and his salary never reached $90.00 a week.

His son Bill Smart, who besides being an excellent greenkeeper, made a name for himself as a writer/editor of the *Hudson Valley Foreground*, succeeded Jimmy. Bill Smart's son Jim, named after his grandfather, is the fourth generation of his family to be involved in the golf course industry.

William Smith from Cleveland, Ohio was a charter member of the NAGA in 1927. During the Great Depression the club where Bill Smith was employed, went under and like so many other greenkeepers, he found himself without a job. His son Colin Smith subsequently became greenkeeper/superintendent at the prestigious Shaker Heights CC in Cleveland. Colin was mentor to several budding young superintendents including John Spodnik, GCSAA President in 1969. Colin's son Timothy became superintendent at Beechmont CC in Ohio from where he retired. His son Ken, the fourth generation, after an education at Ohio State University and a superintendent's position at the Acacia CC, returned to Beechmont and now lives in the same house where he was brought up as a youngster.

The Creed family from Winnipeg in Manitoba can likewise lay claim to four generations of superintendents. Mike Creed is the superintendent at the Wyldewood GC near Toronto. His father is superintendent at the Cutten Club near Guelph, Ontario. His grandfather was superintendent in the U.S.A. and his great-grandfather was the greenkeeper at the St. Charles CC in Winnipeg, Canada during the depression in the 1930s.

Three Generations Are More Common

Peter Lund is superintendent at the Rhode Island CC in Barrington, Rhode Island. His dad was superintendent at the Western Hills CC in Connecticut. The grandfather built the East Mountain GC in Waterbury and became its first greenkeeper.

In 1928, in Crestview Hills, Kentucky, James Cahill converted a dairy farm into a golf course. He served as its greenkeeper/superintendent for the next 35 years. His son Pete Cahill, who was superintendent until 1995, in turn succeeded him. Nephew John Cahill then took over the management of the course. John was a graduate in agronomy from the University of Kentucky. All three generations of Cahills were lifelong members of GCSAA.

A Revolution Underfoot

In the 1950s the Green Section's Dr. Marvin Ferguson initiated a study at Texas A&M of golf shoe spikes and their effect on putting green turf. Ferguson proved conclusively that metal spiked shoes not only reduced putting quality but also damaged grass crowns and blades. In addition, Ferguson also proved that metal spikes caused long-lasting soil compaction and resulted in shallow-rooted turf. The golf shoe industry and the golf professionals, both having financial interests in shoe sales, paid no attention and neither did golfers.

An attempt was made in the early 1980s to promote rubber-studded shoes for use on golf courses in place of common metal spiked shoes. The rubber shoes were at first used by golf professionals as teaching shoes and also by some farsighted superintendents. Golfers generally were ambivalent about trying the new shoes. The USGA and Bill Bengeyfield at Industry Hills GC in California undertook a second "Golf Shoe Study." This second study attracted widespread attention and interest. The results were undeniable: metal spikes were bad for putting greens. The resulting push to do away with metal spikes was not immediately successful.

In 1991 a pair of golfers, Ernie Deacon and Faris McMullin from Boise, Idaho, developed a plastic cleat as a means to protect putting green turf during cold weather in the winter. It worked! Not only did the greens suffer less metal spike scuffing, golfers discovered that the plastic cleats provided secure and comfortable footing on frozen ground. It was not long after that that the new plastic cleats were worn all season long.

The rights for the new spikes were sold to the Softspikes, Inc. and with some ingenious marketing, the revolution was on! One of the first superintendents to convince his committee to try Softspikes, was John Malloy, at the Wyndstone GC in North Barrington, Illinois. After just a few holes of golf, wearing the new footwear, the Wyndstone directors enthusiastically endorsed the new cleats. Wyndstone was a new course, just a year old and with tender greens. The plastic spikes were gentle on the grass and Softspikes became mandatory almost overnight. Other clubs followed quickly including the Inverness Club near Toledo, Ohio, always a leader. The switch to Softspikes received unanimous support from the USGA Green Section and its agronomists. The agronomists spoke with authority about the damage being caused by metal spikes and the alternative method of smooth footwear that left no mark on the greens. Of course there were other benefits that made the switch to plastic spikes more palatable, such as reduced wear and tear on clubhouse rugs, bridges on the golf course and even golf carts. Superintendents enthusiastically embraced the move and when GCSAA was reluctant to take a stand on the matter, there was a groundswell from the members to endorse the new spikes. GCSAA quickly acquiesced and at the golf superintendents' golf tournament of 1995, nonmetal spikes became compulsory.

Metal spikes disappeared from the golf scene during the past decade. They were replaced by all manner of grass friendly footwear. Suddenly it even became acceptable to wear sneakers or sandals on the golf course.

Few changes in the world of golf have been as dramatic and as beneficial as the change from metal spikes to nonmetal or soft spikes. Virtually all superintendents endorsed and applauded the new spikes. They recognized the great improvement in smoother putting surfaces. They also observed that grass under stress in the heat of summer survived much better with the gentler footwear. Initially it was thought that bentgrass greens would benefit the most from nonmetal spikes but George Manual at the Pine Forest CC near Houston, Texas found that plastic spikes provided relief for bermuda greens as well. Many superintendents were able to convince their committees, as John Malloy had done in Illinois, to ban metal spikes. The number of courses with exclusively soft spikes grew quickly. At first it was mostly private clubs that mandated Softspikes but public facilities were soon to follow. Dennis

Lyon, director of golf for the city of Aurora in Colorado, made the switch on the five public courses that he managed in 1995.

Not surprisingly, golf professionals were reluctant in the beginning to accept the new footwear but the advantages of plastic spikes became so obvious and the movement spread so quickly, that the pros would have been left behind had they not seen the light. The same could not be said for many of the touring professionals. Davis Love III won the 1997 PGA Championship wearing Softspikes. Several other professionals repeated that feat. But among the touring pros there are still a goodly number that wear the metal crunchers. On weekends, television viewers may still observe the havoc being wreaked on greens subjected to metal spikes when the touring professionals come to play.

By the year 2000 virtually all golf courses, both public and private, had banned metal spikes. It seems only a matter of time that the ban on metal spikes will become universal. Superintendents will applaud that day.

Education and Technology in the Twenty-First Century

The GCSAA education program has been one of the most successful initiatives ever undertaken by the Association. The seminar program is the cornerstone of that endeavor. Almost 200 different seminars on any topic relating to golf course management are available to superintendents at any time of year, most of them at conference time. Not only certified superintendents who need seminar attendance to keep their certification status current, but thousands of noncertified superintendents, representatives from industry, and golf course operators participate as well. Attendance is not limited just to North Americans, delegates from other countries and other continents flock to the seminars hungry for information.

Most of the seminar teachers are university professors, architects and consultants, but superintendents also share their knowledge willingly. Superintendents Bruce Williams and Roger Stewart have addressed the topic of training assistants. Cleve Cleveland, an owner/operator from New York and an accountant, deals with "Financial Essentials." John Miller, a superintendent from Little Rock, Arkansas, deals with "Strategic Planning."

Mention must also be made of Geoffrey Cornish who, in conjunction with his colleague Robert Graves, for years has taught the rudiments of golf course architecture to countless superintendents and golfers. Golf course architect Dr. Michael Hurdzan also has presented a popular seminar on golf course architecture and construction. Dr. Norman Hummell from Cornell assisted Hurdzan. Hurdzan's book this same subject is widely read. Likewise Geoffrey Cornish's book on the same topic can be found on most superintendents' bookshelves.

What came first, the chicken or the egg? We don't know and so it is with turf texts and seminars. One thing is for certain: there are now more turf and golf course related books available than ever before. When Burt Musser first wrote his book on golf course management in 1950, it was virtually the only text around. Fifty years later there are as many books on the subject as the number of years that have passed. Dr. James Beard's *Turf Management for Golf Courses* became the bible of the industry. Written in conjunction with the USGA, the book was revised and reissued in 2001. Annually, at conference time, in the bookstore located in the registration area, the GCSAA sells hundreds if not thousands of books to avid readers from every field of life in the industry. In addition, a mail order service for books is available for those who do not attend the conference. Ann Arbor Press in Michigan became publishers of golf and golf course related books. They encouraged budding authors at colleges and in the practical field to put pen to paper and the result has been a multitude of turf and golf course texts on any conceivable subject.

The GCSAA serves as a clearinghouse for information. Students still graduate from universities and colleges, but then they turn to the GCSAA for more knowledge. The GCSAA faculties of educators, the people who teach the seminars, represent the best brains in the industry and what can't be found at a seminar can always be learned from a book at the GCSAA bookstore.

While there are still superintendents who have come up through the ranks, the majority of young men and women entering the golf course maintenance field are college educated, either with diplomas or more often with degrees. The sophisticated new technology of greenkeeping necessitates academic knowledge as a requisite to success. Laboratory testing for nutrient levels and the identification of disease organisms are commonplace. Computer controlled sprayers have become standard on many golf courses. Cell phones have made superintendents easier to find and more accessible than ever before.

When regular greens needed repairs, temporary greens were installed. The quality of temporary greens improved greatly as the twentieth century progressed. Superintendent Ray Davies at the Candlewood CC in California.

The pace of greenkeeping advances has accelerated tremendously during the last 100 years but especially during the last few decades. All greens on an 18-hole golf course may now be aerated and top-dressed in less than a day and the topdressing material can often be purchased ready-made from a supplier. An entire golf course, tees, greens and fairways can be aerated in less than a week. The modern maintenance complex resembles an equipment warehouse with several mechanics looking after the machinery for just one golf course.

The superintendent's office features the latest in computer technology. Often a secretary is on hand to perform administrative work and the course assistant spends as much time crunching out numbers for the budget as supervising the greens personnel. Pesticides are stored in specially constructed buildings or containers and the wash pad for cleaning equipment often has its water recycled. Fuel for machinery is stored in aboveground tanks. There are utility vehicles for nearly every crew member. The modern superintendent must keep track of every operation and carries a heavy administrative burden. The superintendent of today is expected to produce conditions comparable to Augusta National in April every day of the week, every week of the season. Not in their wildest dreams could John Pressler, Rocky Rockefeller, Frank Maples and Colonel Morley have imagined what greenkeeping would be like in the twenty-first century.

The business of golf course and club management has become so complex that many golf clubs no longer wish to be involved in the day-to-day operation of their facilities. Club management companies have taken over entire operations of golf clubs, for a fee of course. Then there are multiple course operations and companies that own and operate more than one golf course. How has this new type of management approach affected the superintendent? Large corporations tend to provide better benefit packages than can be obtained at small golf clubs. Committee interference is reduced since the superintendent only has to deal with a regional superintendent instead of a green and golf committee. Some management companies have replaced veteran superintendents who enjoyed generous salaries with young and inexperienced novices as a cost-cutting measure. In the scheme of things, a position is as good as the person who holds that position. Good people will always fit in and rise to the top no matter what type of management they must work under.

The World of Greenkeeping Revolves around Lawrence

From the days of John Morley and Gertrude Farley, the green-keepers movement has grown and grown under the guidance of a GCSAA Board of Directors but with salaried administrators in charge of the daily operations. A variety of capable people put their stamp on the NAGA, the GSA, the NGSA, and the GCSAA and have left their mark. Our membership has grown from a few dozen to more than 21,000. We started with just one part-time employee and now there are more than 120 dedicated staff personnel that look after the needs of the members. Our Association has moved from Ohio to Illinois, then to Florida, back to Illinois and finally to Kansas.

When GCSAA found a home in Lawrence, it was a small prairie town and many questioned the wisdom of such a move to the heart of America. But as our Association grew, so did Lawrence and it is now a virtual suburb of Kansas City. Once hard to get to, it has become easily accessible from all parts of North America. Hundreds of committee members, delegates and visitors trek to Lawrence annually. Those who visit headquarters for the first time are always struck by the sheer size of the building, the many offices and the impressive setting in suburban America.

Inside the building are the people who write our magazine, maintain our web site, people who schedule and prepare our conferences and do a myriad of other duties that keep the members informed and proud of our profession, not just in the United States but all over the world. That is our building and its people and on our own land. Stately and proudly it stands; it is our "Church in Turf."

In the Footsteps of a Giant

The patron saint of all greenkeepers and superintendents is Old Tom Morris from St. Andrews in Scotland. His humble personality, his dedication to the game of golf, and his constant search for greenkeeping perfection have influenced generations of green-keepers that followed. A hundred years after his death this influence is still felt by contemporary superintendents. His statue in front of our headquarters stands as a beacon and a symbol of our dedication to the perfecting of our courses.

A bronze statue of Old Tom Morris graces the front of the GCSAA headquarters in Lawrence, Kansas. It was sculpted by golf course superintendent and artist Brad Pearson, on the occasion of the Association's 75th anniversary.

Chapter Seven

The Presidents

By Gordon Witteveen

Although many of our past presidents are no longer with us, they should not be forgotten. Others are still active and continue to contribute. All these men had their year of glory during their term in office. For some it was less glorious than others, particularly for those who served during the Great Depression when the Association was virtually broke and struggling to survive. At the times of their presidency they were in the limelight at conferences, meetings and even at tournaments to make presentations. They wrote messages in magazines and made speeches at USGA Green Section meetings. In their own way they were all leaders in our industry, some of greater stature than others but they all contributed unselfishly to the profession and the Association.

When their term was completed they blended back into the general membership. Some remained greenkeepers or superintendents. Others left the profession and pursued other ends. On the following pages we have related some background material on these men and as much as we know about what happened to them after their term as president. The information is by no means complete and it may not even be entirely accurate. We relied on interviews with next of kin or other superintendents who had known a particular past president. In many cases obituaries in past issues of our chronicles proved to be helpful. What follows is an interesting story about the lives of past presidents and how they fared in our industry. Being leaders in their own right, it is not surprising that many did remarkably well even after they reached the pinnacle of their profession. Most presidents served only one year at the helm of the Association, with the exception of John Morley, Harold Stodola, and Marshall Farnham who were president for multiple terms.

1. John Morley 1926-1932. Morley was born in England in 1867 and came to America as a humble immigrant during the latter part of the nineteenth century. A talented man, he started both the Cleveland District Greenkeepers Association in 1923 and the National Association of Greenkeepers of America in 1926. He was a longtime greenkeeper at the Youngstown CC in Ohio. Morley died in 1946. *See also Chapter Three.*

2. John MacGregor 1933. Born in 1886 in Scotland, he came to America and in 1921 became the greenkeeper at the Chicago GC, one of the oldest and most prestigious clubs in the Midwest. MacGregor was twice president of the Midwest

Association, a group which he helped start. During his time on the NAGA board, he was a frequent traveling companion of Colonel Morley. MacGregor died in 1963 at age 77. Among the pallbearers at his funeral were his fellow superintendents Robert Williams and Ray Gerber.

3. William Sansom 1934. He was an English gardener who immigrated to Canada at the turn of the twentieth century. He was employed as greenkeeper at the Toronto GC, the oldest golf course in Ontario. Sansom worked under the yoke of a stern club secretary and a domineering golf professional. He found time to start the Ontario Greenkeepers Association in 1924. At the end of his term as president of the NAGA in early 1935, he changed jobs in midseason and was replaced by a college-trained superintendent. One of the Toronto GC members hired Sansom to look after his estate, which included a small golf course. He died in 1973 at the age of 95.

4. Fred Burkhardt 1935. He helped start the Cleveland District Greenkeepers Association in 1923 and served as the group's first secretary. Later he became president of that group. He was the greenkeeper at the Westwood GC near Cleveland. He died in 1957 at age 81.

5. John Anderson 1936. He was a founder of the Greenkeepers Association of New Jersey in 1926 and served as their president and held various other offices. John Anderson was the longtime greenkeeper/superintendent at the Essex County GC, in West Orange, New Jersey, where he managed 36 holes. He was previously greenkeeper at the Crestmount CC in New Jersey.

6. John Quaill 1937. From the Bellvue GC near Pittsburgh, Pennsylvania, he was a charter member of the NAGA. Quaill served as secretary-treasurer of NAGA during the difficult times of the Great Depression. Not much is known about John Quaill.

7. Joseph Ryan 1938. He was greenkeeper at the Rolling Green GC near Philadelphia. He served with the Philadelphia group as secretary and held various other offices. He also helped start the South Florida association while he was vacationing in Miami in 1938.

8. Frank Ermer 1939. He mowed the fairways by horsepower at the Dover Bay CC in Ohio. For a while he was assistant to Fred Burkhardt and in 1925 he became greenkeeper at Ridgewood CC in Cleveland, Ohio.

9. John Gray 1940. He was born in Scotland in 1885 and came to Canada in the early part of the twentieth century. He found work at the Essex GC near Windsor, Ontario, which he helped build and maintain for more than 40 years. Gray was active in the Michigan Border Cities Greenkeepers Association and served as its president in 1937. He was a charter member of the NAGA. He died in 1958.

10. Harold Stodola 1941-1945. He was one of the first college-educated greenkeepers in America, born in Hopkins, Minnesota. He was an avid golfer and won a number of events. He became greenkeeper at the Kellar Park GC in Minnesota. At the 1941 conference in Detroit he succeeded John Gray as a result of an unusual election for the office. When World War II broke out, meetings and conferences were suspended and Stodola remained president and guided the Association through the difficult war years.

11. Marshall Farnham 1946-47. He was superintendent at the Philadelphia CC, Pennsylvania. Like his predecessor, he was also one of the early college-educated. Often called on to speak at functions, he became an outstanding speaker, frequently being mistaken for a college professor. At his club he was quiet and soft-spoken but in association politics he was a tiger that few dared to tangle with.

12. Chester Mendenhall 1948. He was a charter member of the NAGA and employed at the Mission Hills CC, Shawnee, Kansas when he served as president. He was at that club from 1934 to 1965. After retiring, he did some construction and design work. In 1982 he moved to Salt Lake City for health reasons and shortly after that to Green Valley, Arizona. He continued to attend conferences, often in the company of his wife Sue. His last farewell was at the dedication of GCSAA headquarters on September 6, 1991. He died shortly after the dedication at age 96.

13. Carl Bretzlaff 1949. A veteran of World War I, he became greenkeeper at the Meridian Hills CC, Indianapolis, Indiana, in 1923. He stayed there until his retirement in 1965. He remained active after his retirement, both building and consulting on golf courses. He died in January 1971 at age 75.

14. Ray Gerber 1950. He was a cowboy in his younger days, driving cattle across the Missouri River near the South Dakota badlands. In 1916 he helped construct the Woodhill CC in Wayzata, Minnesota. For a while he assisted the Toro Company with his knowledge of reel type mowers. Later he worked on the construction of the Medinah CC in Illinois and various other golf courses around Chicago. He retired from the Glen Oak CC in Chicago in 1971 at age 72. He served as editor for many years of the *Bull Sheet* publication until his death in 1983 at age 83.

15. William Johnson 1951. He worked on golf courses since 1924 in Southern California. At the time of his presidency he was employed at the Griffith Park Municipal GC, Los Angeles, California, from which he retired in 1958. He then became involved in golf course architecture and was a member of the American Society of Golf Course Architects. He died in 1979 at age 80.

16. Malcolm McLaren 1952. He was a charter member of the NAGA, and a longtime greenkeeper at the Canterbury CC in Ohio where he hosted the 1940 and 1946 U.S. Opens. In 1947 he moved to the Oakwood CC near Cleveland Heights in Ohio and stayed there until his retirement in 1965. He then worked with the Lesco Company in their irrigation division. He died in 1982.

17. Leonard Strong 1953. He was born in England and came to the U.S. with his famous brother Herbert Strong who was a golf professional and later a well-known golf course architect. He designed the Saucon Valley "Old Course" in Bethlehem, Pennsylvania in 1920. Leonard Strong was superintendent at the Saucon Valley CC, Bethlehem, Pennsylvania from 1940 to 1959 when he retired. He passed away in 1977. His son, William Strong, still works at Saucon Valley on the greens crew.

18. Norman Johnson 1954. He was a navy veteran of World War I and again joined the forces during World War II. He was superintendent at Medinah CC, Arlington CC and the LaGrange CC, all in Illinois. After World War II he moved to Florida where he became superintendent at the San Jose CC, in Jacksonville, LaGorce CC in Miami and the Delray Beach CC in Florida. He was the first editor of the *Bull Sheet*, which was the newsletter of the Midwest Association. He died on March 19, 1969 at age 68.

19. William Beresford 1955. He started his career in 1927 at the LA CC. He landscaped the golf course by planting over 40,000 trees and shrubs. He became golf course superintendent in 1941 and remained in that position until his retirement in 1971. During that period, besides tending his golf course, he served on the boards of local and national associations including the USGA Advisory Committee. After his retirement he traveled to New Zealand and assisted that country's Turfgrass Advisory Council. He died in 1980 at age 78.

20. Ward Cornwell 1956. He was superintendent at the Lochmoor GC in Michigan and then moved to the Detroit GC. Six years later in 1962 he moved to the Evanston GC in Illinois, where he stayed till his death. He encouraged young people to obtain a degree in turf management as a requisite to advance their careers.

21. Paul Weiss 1957 He lived and worked at the Lehigh CC in Allentown, Pennsylvania, for 43 years. After his presidency in 1957, he remained very active in Association affairs. He often attended the annual meetings of the GCSAA and asked questions that kept the board of directors on their toes. Paul Weiss retired at age 68 and died 12 years later. His son, Paul Weiss Jr. also became a superintendent.

22. Bob Williams 1958. He was superintendent at the Beverly CC on the south side of Chicago, Illinois, at the time of his presidency. He later moved to the Bob O'Link GC. Bob Williams is probably best known for the dozens of young men that he brought along into the golf course management field. Always an avid golfer, he became a lifelong student of the golf swing. Bob and his wife Bobbie live in Lindenhurst, Illinois.

23. Elmer Border 1959. He entered the golf business in 1922, constructing golf courses in California. He served as manager/ park superintendent at Rancho Santa Fe. From 1954 to 1958 he was superintendent at the Olympic Club in San Francisco, California. He also worked and consulted on golf courses in Mexico. He died in 1984 while working at the El Caballero CC in Tarzana, California.

24. Jimmy Thomas 1960. He was a former golf professional who late in life became superintendent at the Farmington CC in Charlottesville, Virginia. Later he moved to the Army Navy Club. He was active at the local level and a three-time president of the Mid-Atlantic Association. In 1960 at the GCSAA annual meeting he was nominated from the floor and became president. He stayed at the Army Navy Club until retirement.

25. L.E. "Red" Lambert 1961. He was superintendent at the Prairie Dunes GC in Kansas at the time of his presidency. A few years later he moved to the Oakwood CC in Kansas City. He had been appointed Chairman of the Host Committee for the 1966 Conference in Kansas City, but died suddenly at his home in late 1965 at age 64.

26. Sherwood Moore 1962. He was superintendent at the Winged Foot GC during his presidency in 1962. In 1967 he moved to the Woodway CC in Connecticut but returned to Winged Foot 12 years later, just in time to prepare the course for the inaugural U.S. Senior Open Championship in 1980. In 1984 he hosted the U.S. Open. The following year he helped Cornish and Silva with the grow-in for the Captains Golf Course on Cape Cod. He then joined the USGA Green Section as a consulting agronomist, followed by a stint with the International Executive Service Corporation. He worked in Egypt, Morocco, Kenya, and Mauritius. Sherwood Moore is the only superintendent to have received the Old Tom Morris Award. He lives with his wife Marie in Brewster, Massachusetts.

27. Roy Nelson 1963. He joined the army during World War II as a private and rose to the rank of lieutenant. He was wounded by a sniper but recovered and his disability checks were used to support children in Third World countries. He became

superintendent at the Ravisloe CC near Chicago and reached the peak of his profession in 1963 when he became GCSAA president. Together with David Moote and Ted Roberts they became known to their colleagues as "the bright boys in the industry." Nelson was independently wealthy and always paid for conference expenses from his own funds. He trained many young college students in the art of greenkeeping. After suffering a near fatal stroke, he retired to Florida.

28. David Moote 1964. He was superintendent at the Rosedale GC in Toronto at the time of his election. Later he moved to the Essex GC near Windsor, Ontario. He quickly advanced to become General Manager and very successfully hosted the Canadian Open in 1976. Later he returned as superintendent at the Scarborough GC near Toronto and then continued his career in Florida. He worked briefly on a project with Gene Sarazen on Marco Island before retiring. He spends the winters in Florida and summers in Ontario.

29. Bob Shields 1965. He was a World War II veteran who became superintendent at the Woodmont CC in Rockville, Maryland. During his presidency he advocated an open approach to keeping the members informed and he was universally liked. Flying was his hobby and he once had to make an emergency landing on a public highway when his plane ran out of gas. He died at age 70 and a commemorative plaque on the first tee of the Woodmont CC remains as a legacy to this much-loved superintendent and president.

30. Ted Roberts 1966. He was a third generation superintendent. He remembers his grandfather and father talking about horse-drawn mowers. Ted worked for his father at Lulu Temple GC in Pennsylvania. At the time of his presidency he was superintendent at the Fairmont CC in New Jersey. He later moved to Canoe Brook CC and the last 14 years of his professional life were spent at the Kings Mill GC in Virginia. He is now retired and plays golf at least twice a week at Kings Mill.

31. Walter Boysen 1967. He was superintendent at the Sequoyah CC in California where he stayed for 38 years until his retirement. He then joined the Oakmont CC in Northern California as a playing member and served as green chairman

for that club. According Oakmont superintendent Mike Clark, Mr. Boysen was the best greens chairman he ever had. Walter Boysen died in May 2001 at age 93. He was a 53-year member of the GCSAA.

32. James Brandt 1968. He was superintendent/general manager at the Danville CC, Illinois, when he ran for vice president of GCSAA in 1965. Many thought that he was defeated because he was a general manager. He ran again and won to become president in 1968. He remained at the Danville CC in the dual capacity until his retirement in 1988. He is a regular golfer at his old club and also enjoys fishing and gardening.

33. John Spodnik 1969. He was the longtime superintendent at the Westfield CC where he trained more than 20 young men to follow in his footsteps. John worked for GCSAA past president Malcolm McLaren. He was active in the Northern Ohio GCSA and served as secretary of that group for 35 years. In 1964 he was elected to the board of the GCSAA and became president in 1969. He stayed at Westfield CC till 1999 but remains active as the secretary of the Musser Turf Foundation. John has recruited more than 100 members for the GCSAA.

34. Norman Kramer 1970 was superintendent at the Point-O-Woods CC in Benton Harbor, Michigan. It was during the summer of his immediate past presidency that he suffered a heart attack on the golf course and died in 1971.

35. Dick Blake 1971. He was superintendent at the Mount Pleasant CC near Boylston, Massachusetts. After his presidency he went to work for Lawrence Rockefeller at the Woodstock CC in Vermont. From there he went to the Florida Keys where he maintained a golf course. He has since retired and lives in Florida.

36. Bob Mitchell 1972. He was superintendent at the Portage GC in Ohio. After his presidency he moved to The Greenbrier in West Virgina. Twenty-five years later he retired, bought a home in Florida for the winter and with the help of a motor home has toured the United States from coast to coast. Mitchell is the only president to have won the GCSAA Golf Tournament and continues to be an avid golfer.

37. Cliff Wagoner 1973. He worked all his professional life (1954-1985) at the Del Rio CC in Northern California. At the conclusion of his presidency in 1974 he was promoted to Executive Manager, responsible for all departments with the exception of the pro shop. After his retirement he made a coast to coast trip in a Model A Ford that he had restored in his spare time. Later he joined the International Executive Service Corporation and consulted on golf courses in Morocco, Tunisia, and Egypt. The Wagoners were avid skiers until advancing age took its toll. He has recently recovered from heart surgery. Cliff remains active with the Northern California GCSA.

38. Charles Baskin 1974. He was superintendent at the Waterbury CC in Connecticut during his time on the board. He remained there till 1996 when he retired to Cape Cod. Always a leader in the community, Charlie has remained active in civic and church affairs.

39. Palmer Maples Jr. 1975. He was superintendent at the Standard Club in Atlanta when he was elected to the board. Palmer became GCSAA's Director of Education in 1976. For a while he was also interim Executive Director. In 1981 he became superintendent at the Summit Shade GC and remained there until retirement in 1997. He received the USGA Green Section Award, and in 2001 he was inducted into the Georgia Golf Hall of Fame.

40. Dick Malpass 1976. He worked for many years at the Riverside CC in Portland, OR. After his GCSAA presidency he became Executive Secretary of his local chapter. He was very active in the Oregon Rose Society. He has since passed away.

41. Ted Woehrle 1977. He was superintendent at the Oakland Hills CC in Birmingham, Michigan. In 1991 he joined the Orchards GC, a Robert Trent Jones Jr. design, during construction and grow-in. Ted has remained there as superintendent and is finishing his 45th year as a GCSAA member and continues his work as a superintendent.

42. George Cleaver 1978. He was employed at the Newark CC in Delaware. Four years later he left the golf business and

became involved full-time in his lifetime hobby of antiques.

43. Charles Tadge 1979. He was superintendent at the Mayfield
CC in South Euclid, Ohio until 1988 when he moved to
Cincinnati to become a District Superintendent for the
Hamilton County Park District. Among the three golf courses
under his responsibility is the Vineyard GC, the county's pre-
mier course. Charlie has remained active in association affairs,
serving as secretary-treasurer and voting delegate of the
Cincinnati Chapter.

44. Mel Lucas Jr. 1980. He was superintendent at Garden City GC
and later at the nearby Piping Rock Club on Long Island, New
York. He has since branched out to central Europe where he
has consulted on construction and grow-in of golf courses.
Mel has had a lifelong interest in the history of golf and has an
extensive golf book collection with an emphasis on early
course maintenance. He served for two years as president of
the Golf Collectors Society, is a life member of Golf Writers
Association of America, and is the only American member of
the Slovenian Greenkeepers Association.

45. Michael Bavier 1981. He came from a small country town in
Minnesota, studied at Penn State College and since 1969 has
been superintendent at the Inverness GC in Palatine, Illinois.
Bavier went through the chairs in the Midwest Chapter. He
remains active in his chapter, on the Musser Foundation, and
on the Turf Advisory Board of the Chicago District Golf
Association.

46. Jim Wyllie 1982. He was superintendent at the Bayview GC in
Thornhill, Ontario. He finished his career at the York Downs
GC in Unionville from which he retired in 1988. In 1987
Wyllie started his own golf course maintenance company and
did extensive consulting with new projects. In 2001 he
received "The John Steel Award" from the Canadian Golf
Superintendents Association for his contributions to the
industry.

47. Robert Osterman 1983. He was superintendent/general manager of the Connecticut GC. In 1988 he moved to the Redding
CC in Connecticut as general manager. In 1986 he bought a

picnic and banquet catering company in Bethel, Connecticut, which he still operates. He joined the Newtown CC and is currently the house chairman on the board of directors.

48. Jim Timmerman 1984. He was superintendent at the Orchard Lake CC, Michigan from which he retired in the fall of 2000. He is now a consulting agronomist for the Torre Golf Management Company.

49. Gene Baston 1985. He was superintendent at the Birmingham CC, Alabama. He then moved to Ridgewood CC in Waco, Texas. He has since moved to the Far East, where he does grow-in and maintenance work in Korea and China.

50. Riley Stottern 1986. He has built and maintained many courses in the Western Region and is presently the superintendent at the Southern Highlands GC in Las Vegas, Nevada.

51. Don Hearn 1987. He was for many years superintendent at the Weston GC, Massachusetts. In the fall of 2000 he left Weston and is currently the superintendent at the Vesper CC in Tyngsboro, Massachusetts. He remains an active member of his local association, the GCSA of New England, and the GCSAA. He is also currently serving as a board member of the Massachusetts Department of Food and Agriculture.

52. John Segui 1988. He was superintendent at the Waynesborough CC in Pennsylvania from which he retired in 1995. Segui belongs to three regional associations and plays golf as often as possible. When he is not golfing, he looks after his grandchildren.

53. Dennis Lyon 1989. He continues as the Manager of Golf for the City of Aurora, Colorado, a position he has held since 1976. After his presidency he has served as project manager for the construction of two new championship city courses, Saddle Rock and Murphy Creek, and was also involved in the acquisition of a military course. Aurora Golf currently operates seven courses. Dennis Lyon has remained active and is currently a vice president of the Colorado Golf Association.

54. Gerald Faubel 1990. He has remained at the Saginaw CC, Michigan, after his presidency. He has been at the club since 1969. Besides being a full-time superintendent, he is also a partner with Bruce Williams in Executive Golf Search, Inc., a company that assists in the placement of superintendents. Jerry has remained a leader in the scholarship and research foundation. As chairman of the Book Subcommittee Faubel has shepherded this book through its various stages to completion.

55. Steve Cadenelli 1991. He was the golf course manager at Metedeconk National GC in Jackson, New Jersey. During his 30 years in the business he has been active in promoting the role of education and professionalism in the golf course management profession. He continues to be active in the profession, having recently served for three years on the Membership Standards Resource Group. Cadenelli moved to the Cape Cod National GC where he coordinated construction and grow-in.

56. Bill Roberts 1992. He was the golf course superintendent at Lochmoor Club in Grosse Pointe Woods, Michigan. He left Lochmoor in 1994 and formed a small management company with Lochmoor's club manager, which continues to operate a public golf facility in Michigan's Upper Peninsula. He entered law school in September 1997, graduated in January 2001, and passed the Michigan bar examination. He and his family have since relocated back to the Chicago area.

57. Randy Nichols 1993. He led GCSAA during a very difficult period at headquarters in Lawrence, Kansas. At the time of his presidency he was superintendent at the Cherokee Town CC in Dunwoody, Georgia where he served for 24 years. He is now working in the commercial turf industry.

58. Joe Baidy 1994. He was superintendent at the Acacia CC in Lyndhurst, Ohio. Four years later he accepted a position as director of golf courses with the Turning Stone Casino Resort in Verona, New York. In that capacity he is responsible for three golf course, as well as the grounds at the resort. He remains an active and dedicated superintendent.

59. Gary Grigg 1995. He was superintendent at the Royal Poinciana GC in Naples, Florida. He spent 34 years in golf course construction, grow-in and maintenance and was responsible for building some of the finest golf courses in America. He was certified in both GCSAA and BIGGA. He retired from greenkeeping in 2000 to become a principal and cofounder of Grigg Brothers Fertilizer.

60. Bruce R. Williams 1996. He was the superintendent at the Bob O'Link GC in Highland Park, Illinois. In 1997 he moved to The Los Angeles CC. From 1997 to 2001 Williams was the Chairman of the Membership Standards Resource Group. This group focused on elevating membership standards and formulating the Professional Development Initiative (PDI) for GCSAA. He was the driving force behind the PDI movement. He and his father Bob Williams are the only father-son past presidents in the history of GCSAA.

61. Paul McGinnis 1997. He was superintendent at the Alta Mesa CC in Mesa, Arizona. He has since moved to the Pebblecreek Golf Resort in Goodyear, Arizona. Pebblecreek is a 36-hole layout to which Paul will be adding 18 holes.

62. George Renault 1998. He was superintendent at the Burning Tree CC in Washington, DC. He is presently superintendent at the Eagle Creek GC in Naples, Florida.

63. David Fearis 1999. He was superintendent at the Blue Hills CC in Kansas City, Missouri. He left Blue Hills in the fall of 2001 and started his own consulting business in golf course management. He has remained active in Association affairs.

64. Scott Woodhead 2000. He was superintendent at the Valley View GC in Bozeman, Montana and is currently director of golf at the Heart River Municipal Golf Course in Dickinson, North Dakota.

65. Tommy Witt, 2001. He has been superintendent at the Austin CC and Bent Tree CC in his native state of Texas prior to accepting the position of director of golf course management and special projects at the Kiawah Island Club in Charleston,

South Carolina, where he remains serving while president of the Association.

Our past presidents have left an interesting legacy in the annals of golf course maintenance and turfgrass management. What is even more remarkable is that many have lived long lives. The oldest at the time of his death was Chester Mendenhall who lived for 43 more years after his term in office. William Sansom, unceremoniously fired from his position as greenkeeper at the Toronto GC in 1935, nonetheless lived and worked for another 38 years till he died in 1973. Many others lived well into their 80s. Both Bob Williams and Sherwood Moore, approaching their 90th year, are living examples that the great outdoors is a healthy environment that contributes to longevity.

The record of our past presidents deserves to be as accurate as humanly possible, but time was of the essence, and deadlines had to be met. There is much more information stashed away in dusty journals and dark attics that would add to interesting stories about these great men who led us. We invite and encourage our readers to inform headquarters of any errors and omissions they may have spotted while reading these pages. Perhaps, at the time of our centennial celebration in 2026, the record will be precise and complete.

Epilogue

During the summer of 2001 the GCSAA geared up for a large celebration. The 75th anniversary was to be a momentous occasion highlighted by the unveiling of a larger-than-life statue of Old Tom Morris at the entrance to the headquarters building. Dignitaries from allied associations and leaders in the golf course industry were invited. Many of GCSAA's past presidents were slated to return. Several hundred committee members as well as many other members were planning to be present in Lawrence on September 13th.

As the anniversary drew near, anticipation heightened and the GCSAA staff prepared for the arrival of approximately 500 guests. Then the unthinkable happened.

Almost immediately after the terrorist attacks of September 11, 2001 it became evident that the planned festivities could not take place. Airlines were grounded. The world was stunned.

GCSAA President Tommy D. Witt, after consultation with GCSAA CEO Stephen F. Mona and headquarters staff, issued a statement that began: "Now is not the time to celebrate." A subdued GCSAA membership agreed and joined the rest of the population in mourning. The festivities were postponed for another day.

Charter Members

Stanley M. Aldrich
A.J. Allen
John Anderson
Paul Anderson
Walter Anderson
Paul Andress
C. Bain
O.S. Baker
William Ball
C.G. Barton
George Bauer
David M. Bell
Alex Binnie
James W. Bolton
Carl Bretzloff
Mack Burke
Fred Burkhardt
Frank Burns
H. Cartwright
James J. Connaughton
Emil J. Corlett
John M. Coutre Sr.
Edward B. Dearie
Leonard DeBruyn
Perry Del Vecchio
Lewis W. Dobson
J. Dolsen
Thomas E. Dougherty

Robert Duguid
Leroy Dustin
Lawrence Eats
W. Elphick
Charles Erickson
Frank Ermer
Marshall Farnham
Leo J. Feser
Arthur G. Fovargue
Albert Franz
Peter Gamier
Victor George
Ford Goodrich
John Gray
Louis J. Gregory
William Guthrie
Harry Hanson
Neal D. Harrison
Robert Henderson
L.B. Henry
Addison Hollander
Lawrence Huber
Fred Ingerson
John R. Inglis
G.F. Jacob
Charles Jarman
W.E. Knowles
S.B. Kuns

James M. Laing
M. D. LaMoreaux
Edward M. Lang
Arthur Lavin
A.E. Lindstrom
George Livingston
James Livingston
Emil Loeffler
John H. Lord
Hugh Luke
James Lyons
John MacGregor
Ralph C. Martin
Eugene B. Marzolf
Frank Maslen
Frank Mastroleo
Joe P. Mayo
J. McCrammer
James McElroy
John McGlynn
Alex G. McKay
John McNamara Sr.
John McNamara Jr.
Alex McPherson
George J. Megown
William F. Mellon
Chester Mendenhall
Gordon A. Meyer

Charles Meyers
Henry A. Miller
R.J. Miller
C.A. Mills
Hugh C. Moore
John Morley
James Muirden
C.W. Newbon
Charles M. Nutall
Michael J. O'Grady
M.M. Parsons
Jack T. Patterson
William Philipson
Emil H. Picha
John Pressler
Robert D. Pryde
John Quaill
Emil F. Radden
Walter C. Reed
Cloyd Reichelderfer
Frank Richardson
George Robb
W.J. Rockefeller
Ralph Rodgers
William J. Rueck
Jacob Sands
Alfred A. Schardt
Jake Schnapp

W.H. Schrader
Frank Schubie
Harry Scott
Herbert E. Shave
Burdette G. Sheldin
J. Sheridan
Fred W. Sherwood
Vernon A. Sincerbeau
William Slack
Robert Smith
William Smith
Willie Smith
Peter Stewart
Clarence W. Strouse
Frank Svehla
William H. Sweisberger
Joseph W. Tagnon
James Thomson
D.R. Valentin
Joseph Valentine
Jack Welseh
O. Woodhouse
Ben W. Zink
Bob Zink

Index

P

Pahl, Erich, 99
Palmer, Arnold, 126, 127, 173, 185, 197
Palmer, Milfred J. ("Deke"), 126, 127, 185
Paradise Valley CC (AZ), 207, 223, 224
Park, Willie, 39
Parker Lawn Sweeper, 219
Parsons, M. M., 99
paspalum, 120-121
Passaic CC (NJ), 220
Patton, Duane, 209
Paul, Erich, 60
Payne, Kenyon, 187
Peachtree GC (GA), 150
Pearson, Brad, 231
Pebble Beach (CA), 52, 60
Pebblecreek Golf Resort (AZ), 246
Pellrene, Dennis, 205-206
Penncross, 137-138, 147, 148-152
Pennsylvania Lawn Mower Co., 34, 36
Pennsylvania State College, 66, 84, 115, 133, 137, 194
Pentagon building site, 62
Pfotenhauer, Terry, 186
PGA, 40, 121
PGA National GC (FL), 156
Philadelphia Association of Golf Course Superintendents, 68, 71
Philadelphia CC (PA), 173, 236
Philmont CC (PA), 67
Phoenix Foundry, 21, 22
Picha, Emil, 99
Pickering, F. G., 99
Pierce, Nancy, 211
Pine Forest CC (TX), 227
Pinehurst Resort (NC), 41, 89, 112, 224
Pine Valley GC (NJ), 91, 135-136, 201
Piper, Charles Vancouver
  co-author of *Turf for Golf Courses*, 55
  death, 81-82
  legendary status, 53, 56, 120
  selects Washington bent (C-50), 137

on slant system green construction, 144
speaking engagements, 65, 69, 71
work with greenkeepers, 62, 63, 74, 196
Piping Rock Club (NY), 243
plant tissue testing, 110
Playfair, Sir Hugh, 23, 24
Poa annua
  and bentgrass mixtures, 148-152, 207
  early greens, 53
  M. Francis incident, 118
  practices favoring growth, 53, 197
  and reduced soil compaction, 199
Pocono Golf Turf Association Newsletter, 129
Point-O-Woods CC (MI), 241
Ponkapoag GC (MA), 123-124
Portage GC (OH), 241
Power, Robert
  green chairman, 41, 69
  publisher/editor, 76, 85
  supports local greenkeepers, 70, 79-80
power sand rake, 169-170, 172, 201, 202
Practical Golf (Travis), 144
Prairie Dunes GC (KS), 239
Pressler, John ("The Squire"), 42-43, 86, 99, 224
Price, Vance, 175
Progress CC (NY), 77
Provan, Jim, 96
Pryke, Harry, 97
public golfing, 60-61, 102, 123
Purdue University, 114
Put-in-Bay GC (OH), 87

Q

Quaill, John, 79-80, 235
Quast, Dan, 223

R

Radko, Alexander
  Green Section events, 130, 132-133
  on *Poa*, 151
  predicts success for triplex mowers, 170
  White House green, 125-126
  work on the Stimpmeter, 177-179
  work on *USGA Golf Championship Manual*, 175-176
Rain Bird Co., 153
rakes, 82, 112, 169-170, 172, 201, 202
Rand McNally Co., 222
Rasmussen, Martin, 97
Ravisloe CC (IL), 40, 240
Ray, Ted, 74
Record, Lee, 171
record keeping, 103-104
Redding CC (CT), 243
Rees, David, 77, 99
Rees, Mrs. David, 69, 77
Reid, John, 34, 35, 41
Renault, George, 246
Rhode Island bentgrass, 52
Rhode Island CC (RI), 77, 226
Rhode Island Greenkeepers Association, 71
Rhodes, James, 196
Richardson, R. A., 131
Richardson, William, 80
Ridgewood CC (NJ), 208
Ridgewood CC (OH), 236
Ridgewood CC (TX), 181, 244
Rieke, P., 194
Riverside CC (OR), 242
Roach, Sgt. Edward, 88
Roaring Twenties, 60
Robb, George, 99
Roberts, Bill, 245
Roberts, David, 204
Roberts, E., 194
Roberts, Ted, 240
Robertson, Allan, 17, 23, 24
Robertson, Peter, 17
Robertson, Thomas, 17
Robinson, Scott, 219
Rockefeller, John D., 47
Rockefeller, Lawrence, 241

Photo Credits

The majority of the photographs in this book are from the GCSAA Archives and the GCSAA magazines—*The National Greenkeeper* (1927-1933); *The Greenkeepers Reporter* (1933-1951); *The Golf Course Reporter* (1951-1966); *Golf Course Superintendent* (1966-1978); and *Golf Course Management* (1979-). The Publisher would like to thank the following photo agencies, photographers and institutions that have also supplied photographs for this book. Mr. Jim Snow and Dr. Kimberly Erusha of the USGA Green Section were especially helpful. The photographs are credited by page number and position on the page as follows: (T) TOP; (B) BOTTOM; (L) LEFT; (R) RIGHT, etc.

USGA Green Section: 49, 50, 63, 64, 65, 193, 195, 201, 202, 203, 207, 208, 210, 216, 217, 218, 227, 230

USGA Collection: 62, 65 (T); 107 (T); 114 (T); 116 (T); 117; 121 (T)

Joseph M. Duich, Ph.D.: 66, 67 (B), 84

David Halford: 20 (T)

Melvin B. Lucas Jr.: 15

Bruce Mathews: 231

Northern Ohio Golf Course Superintendents Association: 40

Notown Communications Archives: 17, 18, 19, 24; 177

Arnold Palmer Golf Management: 127

St. Andrews Golf Course, NY: 34

The South Carolina Historical Society: 31

Victoria Golf Club: 37, 47

The publisher has endeavored to ensure that all the photographs in this book are correctly credited. Should any illustration in this book be incorrectly attributed, the publisher apologizes.

Acknowledgments

When GCSAA neared its Diamond Jubilee, the importance of its history was thrust to the forefront and a variety of actions resulted. President Joe Baidy (1994) and his board established a Historical Preservation Committee under the chairmanship of the immediate past president. Committee members represented a wide-ranging perspective from the golf course industry, but all had one thing in common: an appreciation of history!

The committee decided that one of its first priorities was to collect artifacts of historical significance. Next they recommended to the Board of Directors that a curator be hired to catalogue our old books, documents, and magazines and, as a result, Susanne Clement came aboard. In just a few years she established an emporium in the basement of headquarters that included old mowers, machinery, photographs, books, and magazines. These reconditioned artifacts are now on display at the headquarters museum and at our annual conferences.

At some time during the many meetings of the Historical Preservation Committee, it was decided that a book needed to be written detailing the birth and growth of our profession and our Association. That idea grew to encompass not only the history of the greenkeeping association but also the development of the greenkeeping profession from its earliest days in Scotland to its establishment on North American shores to the recognition that professional golf course superintendents have achieved today.

A book committee, under the chairmanship of Gerald Faubel, selected two men to coauthor the book and they began their arduous task in the spring of the year 2000. Bob Labbance and Gordon Witteveen originally intended to blend their writing styles and to work jointly, but it quickly became apparent to the authors and to the committee that to write jointly was well-nigh impossible. Instead the authors decided, and the committee approved, to divide the proposed book into six chapters each detailing a specific time period, and that each author would write three chapters.

So it came about that Bob Labbance wrote the first chapter, and Gordon Witteveen wrote the second chapter, and so on. Once the writing began, the work of the authors was scrutinized on a regular basis by the Book Review Committee. This committee quickly became the final arbiter of the book and what it was to be about. The authors learned to accept what was to be included and excluded from the story. Faubel's book committee had no mercy for fiction or fancy. It wanted an accurate account of the history of greenkeeping and individual members of the committee crossed every "t" and dotted every "i." They were tenacious and at times frustrating, but the process resulted in the book that lies before you.

Our research into the beginnings of greenkeeping led us to many books and publications. Horace Hutchinson's *Golf Greens and Greenkeeping* was a valuable source as was *Turf for Golf Courses* by Drs. Piper and Oakley. We learned from the pages of *Golf Illustrated* and the *American Golfer*, two early American publications that contained information on the establishments of golf courses on the continent that could be found nowhere else. Similarly, the *Canadian Golfer*, first published in 1917, included pertinent facts about golf courses in the beginning. Other great sources of information were *Golfdom*, the *USGA Green Section Bulletin*, and our own magazine the *National Greenkeeper*. The early issues of these magazines are full of first-hand accounts and early gems of wisdom about greenkeeping and greenkeepers.

We need to thank the Book Review Committee under Chairman Faubel. Committee member Bill Bengeyfield has a wealth of knowledge about individual superintendents, greenkeeping practices and about the USGA Green Section. Mel Lucas Jr. has been a historian since the days he worked for his father at the Piping Rock Club on Long Island. We tapped his wealth of historical knowledge for the benefit of this book. Palmer Maples Jr., scion of a long clan in Georgia, reflected the southern points of view. Dr. Joseph Duich made sure that we got the grasses right and also contributed information about Joe Valentine. Bob Williams, still spry at a ripe age, prefers to stay home with his wife in Lindenhurst, Illinois, so we took the meetings to him and he was extremely helpful. Dr. Jim Watson was a guiding light in the history of mowing and other cultural practices. Dr. Watson personally knew many of the players in this book. Sherwood Moore is an icon in our industry, an inspiration not just for students and new superintendents but for professionals everywhere. Sherwood inspires all his friends and colleagues to keep going and to remain active.

Besides the committee, there were many other superintendents who deserve to be mentioned for information that they provided. Charlie Tadge and Michael Bavier were often called on and always helped with advice and information. Eb Steiniger, long since retired from the Pine Valley GC in New Jersey, has a retentive memory and patiently explained how, why, and when things happened so many years ago. Similarly, Arthur Jack Snyder, son of the famous Art Snyder, told us all about the Snyder clan. Christina Valentine-Owsik and her uncle Ritchie Valentine were very helpful in providing information about the legendary Joe Valentine. Lee Dieter from Virginia was quick to respond to e-mails and share with us his knowledge of the olden days. Dennis Pellrene, superintendent at the Capilano GC in Vancouver, unabashedly related how he was fired because his greens were infected by C-15 decline, a disease for which there was no cure at the time. Leon St. Pierre, longtime superintendent at the Longmeadow CC in Massachusetts proved a great help with information about the New England region. Doug Vogel in New Jersey and Steve Humphries in New York were a valuable source of information. Joel Jackson in Orlando filled us in on the Florida scene. Garold Murphy supplied much information about the early days in Minnesota, and there are dozens more on every hill and in every dale of the country who shared stories and information. We thank them all.

We came into contact with almost all the living past presidents, and they proved a valuable source of information. The interesting trivia that we uncovered about our past presidents led us to add an extra chapter to the book about the experiences of these men after the completion of their term in office. At some time during our work, we decided to omit the title "CGCS" from all the names for the sake of brevity and readability. The past presidents were no exception.

We thank many members of the Golf Collectors Society who have preserved antique greenkeeping materials and shared them with the co-authors; Patrick White of Notown Communications for research and editing and David Cassidy, editor of *Turf* magazine for the inspiration to go forth and talk to the people in the maintenance trenches who make it happen every day. Also a special thanks to Joe O'Brien who kept the process moving with expert guidance when it was most needed.

Finally, we must thank Susanne Clement and the GCSAA Historical Preservation staff who helped us from start to finish and made sure that we met our deadlines. We sincerely hope that you will enjoy reading the book as much as we did writing it.

— Gordon Witteveen and Bob Labbance

75th Anniversary Sponsors

Special Event and Diamond Level Patron

Diamond Level Patrons

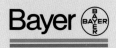

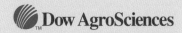

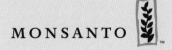

M O N S A N T O

Ruby Level Patrons Griffin L.L.C.

Milorganite

Sapphire Level Patrons Eagle One Golf Products

LESCO

Turfco Manufacturing

A Special Relationship

Thoughts on an Association milestone from Syngenta Professional Products—Special Event and Diamond Level Patron of GCSAA's 75th Anniversary Initiative

A proud profession and a rich heritage—GCSAA and its golf course superintendent members have both. From 1926, when Col. John Morley and 60 greenkeepers gathered at Sylvania Country Club in Toledo, Ohio, to form the National Association of Greenkeepers of America, to today's GCSAA with more than 21,000 members, superintendents have constantly striven for a higher level of achievement and professionalism.

Syngenta Professional Products shares with GCSAA members that proud profession, rich heritage and a passion for its mission—creating and maintaining golf's playing fields to the highest possible standards. Syngenta, like GCSAA itself, has evolved from its "legacy" entities, and looks back at its heritage with pride and gazes toward the next 75 years with confidence.

The corresponding goals of GCSAA and Syngenta have, over the years, created a unique bond—a special relationship—between the company and golf course superintendents. The company's continuing support of GCSAA, demonstrated by its status as a long-time advertiser in Golf Course Management magazine and its annual exhibit area at the International Golf Course Conference and Show, is but an example of that ongoing connection. It is because of that special relationship that Syngenta also is the proud Special Event and Diamond Level patron of GCSAA's yearlong 75th Anniversary celebration.

Syngenta was born in 2000 by the merger of Novartis Agribusiness and Zeneca Agrochemicals. Novartis began with the creation of an insecticide by one of its "legacy" companies—Geigy Chemical in Basle, Switzerland. That product helped protect Allied troops during World War II. The development of this and other well-known products such as atrazine and diazinon were instrumental in what eventually became Ciba-Geigy, and later Novartis.

John Stauffer launched Zeneca in 1885 as a small plant for grinding cliff stone in North Beach, California. The Canadian arm of the company started in 1862 as Hamilton Powder. Acquisitions and mergers brought Stauffer and Hamilton together.

The coming together of these two firms was significant internationally because the new company focused solely on agribusiness and instantly became one of the largest suppliers of pesticides to the turf industry.

Syngenta is based in Basel, Switzerland. The Syngenta U.S. Professional Products Group—headquartered in Greensboro, North Carolina—is an organization dedicated exclusively to professional products, including turf and ornamental. Uniquely, the Professional Products Group has a voice in decisions made at the global level concerning its core competency—the development and manufacture of fungicides, insecticides and herbicides.

Because Syngenta plays a key role in global decisions on marketing strategy, resource allocation and research, its experience with and input from golf course superintendents is critical—another reason for the close ties between the firm and GCSAA. The result is greater focus than ever before on the needs of the turf and ornamental industries, including, among other things, earlier screening of promising molecules for possible use by GCSAA members.

Syngenta and its legacy companies have partnered with superintendents over the years to be more than just a supplier of chemicals. From the beginning, the organization has asked GCSAA members to help it explore innovative ways—such as the Internet—to provide new technologies and services to help superintendents do their jobs better.

GCSAA and its members also have provided input that has helped Syngenta's dedicated turf and ornamental field representatives and scientific experts provide golf course superintendents with the close attention they need.

Finally, like their superintendent customers, the people of Syngenta Professional Products have been committed to the goal of environmental stewardship, an area where the two groups have been able to make great strides together.

Proud profession, rich heritage. No wonder GCSAA members and Syngenta have formed a very special relationship.